Pelican Books
Essays in English History

A J P Taylor was born at Birkdale in Lancashire in 1906. He
was educated at Bootham School, York, and at Oriel College,
Oxford. He was a lecturer in Modern History at Manchester
University from 1930 to 1938; since then he has been a Fellow
of Magdalen College. A Fellow of the British Academy, he was
Ford's Lecturer in English History at Oxford (1955–6) and
Leslie Stephen Lecturer at Cambridge (1960–61). Recently he
has given the Creighton Lecture at London University and the
Andrew Lang Lecture at St Andrews. He is an honorary DCL
of the University of New Brunswick and D. Univ. of York
University.

He has given six series of history lectures on television and is
the only lecturer to face the cameras for half an hour without
notes or visual aids. He contributes regularly to the *Sunday
Express* and the *Observer*.

His books include The Course of German History, The Struggle
for Mastery in Europe, 1848–1918, Bismarck, The Troublemakers
and From Sarajevo to Potsdam. A number of his books have
been published in Penguins: The Origins of the Second World
War, The Habsburg Monarchy, The First World War: an
Illustrated History, English History 1914–1945, Europe:
Grandeur and Decline, and Beaverbrook. He has also
contributed a long introduction to the Penguin edition of The
Communist Manifesto. His most recent works are The Second
World War: an Illustrated History and My Darling Pussy:
the correspondence of Lloyd George and Frances Stevenson.

Essays in English History

A J P TAYLOR

PENGUIN BOOKS
in association with Hamish Hamilton

Penguin Books Ltd,
Harmondsworth, Middlesex, England
Penguin Books,
625 Madison Avenue, New York, New York 10022, U.S.A.
Penguin Books Australia Ltd,
Ringwood, Victoria, Australia
Penguin Books Canada Ltd,
41 Steelcase Road West, Markham, Ontario, Canada
Penguin Books (NZ) Ltd,
182–190 Wairau Road, Auckland 10, New Zealand

Most of these essays were first published in book form by
Hamish Hamilton in the four volumes:
From Napoleon to Stalin, 1950
Rumours of Wars, 1952
Englishmen and Others, 1956
Politics in Wartime, 1964
This selection first published simultaneously with
Hamish Hamilton in Pelican Books 1976

Made and printed in Great Britain by
Hazell Watson & Viney Ltd,
Aylesbury, Bucks
Set in Linotype Juliana

Contents

Contents

Preface

This volume assembles the essays on English political
personages and events that I have written over some
thirty years – a counterpart to those on European
history which appeared under the title, Europe :
Grandeur and Decline (Penguin Books, 1970). I am
aware that Keir Hardie was Scotch, Casement Irish,
and Lloyd George and perhaps Cromwell Welsh. But
historians in their old-fashioned way divide their
subject into English and European, or nowadays
world, history, and I am too old to change. At any
rate the essays are written in the English language.

Some of the essays started as book reviews. Some
were written to mark an occasion – a fiftieth or a
hundredth anniversary. Some were given as lectures
for some foundation or other. Essentially they are
about men – prime ministers, monarchs and radicals
– together with one woman, Queen Victoria. The
events I recall are also political – mostly on foreign
affairs in my earlier days, later on domestic affairs,
as my interest shifted from Europe to England. Most
of the essays have appeared in four volumes
published by Hamish Hamilton : From Napoleon to
Stalin (1950); Rumours of Wars (1952); Englishmen
and Others (1956); and Politics in Wartime (1964).
Four (1, 25, 30 and 31) have not appeared in book
form before.

1. Fiction in History

This first appeared in The Times Literary Supplement with a companion, History in Fiction, by a writer of historical novels.

In most European languages 'story' and 'history' are the same word: *histoire* in French, *Geschichte* in German. *Quelle histoire* or *Was für eine Geschichte* does not mean 'What admirable history A J P Taylor writes' (even if he does) but 'What a far-fetched yarn'. It would save much trouble if we had the same coincidence of words in English. Then perhaps we should not be ashamed to admit that history is at bottom simply a form of story-telling. Historians nowadays have higher aims. They analyse past societies, generalize about human nature, or seek to draw morals about political or economic behaviour that will provide lessons for the present. Some of them even claim to foretell the future. These are admirable ambitions which have produced work of high quality. But there is no escaping the fact that the original task of the historian is to answer the child's question: 'What happened next?'

The past, or more precisely the past of literate mankind, is our raw material. In this past events succeed each other in order of time. This awareness of time came quite late in man's consciousness. Some civilizations do not have it. Early Indian chroniclers put in anecdotes higgledy-piggledy without caring which happened first. No true history can be written on this basis. We cannot change the order of time unless of course we or our sources have made a mistake, which is by no means unknown. We cannot have the events other than they are. Some historians like to play at the game 'If it had happened otherwise.' This only goes to show that they would be better employed writing romantic novels where dreams come true.

History is not just a catalogue of events put in the right order like a railway timetable. History is a version of events. Between the events and the historian there is a constant interplay. The historian tries to impose on events some kind of rational pattern: how they happened and even why they happened. No historian starts with a blank mind as a jury is supposed to do. He does not go to documents or archives with a childlike innocence of mind and wait patiently until they dictate conclusions to him. Quite the contrary.

His picture, his version of events, is formed before he begins to write or even to research. I am told that scientists do much the same. They conduct experiments to confirm their ideas. They do not sit openmouthed until an idea falls into it. Similarly the historian is after details to thicken up his picture and make it look intellectually convincing. Usually he finds them. Sometimes the opposite happens. He comes across events that upset his preconceived picture. The picture changes under his hand often without his realizing that it is doing so.

This happened with me when I wrote a book about the origins of the second world war. I set out with the firm conviction, inherited from my pre-war years, that Hitler planned it all. I discovered, or thought I discovered, that Hitler, though no doubt resolved to make Germany a world power, had no clear-cut plan how to do it and moved forward with the changing situation. Some critics were shocked by this and attributed to me all kinds of wickedness – apologizing for Hitler or justifying the later appeasement of Soviet Russia. I had no such aims. My historian's conscience simply carried me in an unexpected direction. I do not think any historian is worth his salt who has not had a similar experience.

Are we then to say that there is nothing to choose between the different versions of events produced by historians? It sometimes looks like it. Pieter Geyl whiled away his years in a German concentration camp by analysing the views of French historians on Napoleon : For and Against. In this country singing the praises of the Industrial Revolution or displaying its brutalities has itself become a major industry. Certainly these are very different versions, but they remain versions of events, and the historian who cheats on his events will be beyond the pale even if his version happens to be a welcome one. Take a photograph of the west front of York Minster if the scaffolding is now down. Take another of the interior. You will have different versions but both of York Minster. Slip in a photograph of Lincoln Cathedral, and you are cheating.

When an historian is working on his subject, the events or statistical data or whatever he is using change under his hand all the time and his ideas about these events change with them. He upgrades some of the evidence and downgrades other parts according to the changes of his outlook. Sometimes, I am afraid, he exaggerates the importance of a piece of evidence because it fits in well with what he is trying to say.

Sometimes he puts an unwelcome piece of evidence at the bottom of the pile. But, if he is any good, the omitted piece nags at him. He pulls it out and confesses : 'Oh dear, I was wrong.' Recently some younger scholars disproved my interpretation of Lloyd George's Mansion House speech at the time of the Agadir crisis. I was just ordering a very smart suit of sackcloth and ashes when another young scholar demonstrated that I was not all that wrong after all. Now I do not know where I stand. However I cannot say I was altogether pleased when one bit of my interpretation, or rather a guess, slipped into a television play on Lloyd George.

Certainly we guess. We are writing to shape into a version a tangle of events that was not designed as a pattern. 'Ceaselessly explain' was Lenin's motto and is also mine. Guessing is the only way of explaining when solid evidence runs out.

There are gradations of guessing. Consider a general conducting a battle. If we know from his later dispatch or from what others recorded at the time, we say: 'He saw the enemy advancing.'

If we can deduce what he saw from studying the map or ourselves reconnoitring the battlefield, we say: 'He must have seen the enemy advancing.' If we can only deduce what he saw from his subsequent actions, then we say: 'Probably he saw the enemy advancing.' If he behaved like a complete idiot, as generals often do, we fall back on what we know of his character or previous actions. This is the way we explain Gamelin's total failure to do anything about the German breakthrough at Sedan in May, 1940. One day evidence may provide a different explanation. Perhaps Gamelin had a heart-attack. Perhaps his staff concealed the news of the break-through from him. Then our version will change. All the time we are tied to the events though the connection sometimes becomes remote. We never actually invent, though we sometimes practise sleight of hand. History, just like historical fiction, is an exercise in creative imagination, though in our case the exercise is restrained by the limits of our knowledge. One essential ingredient we learnt from a writer of historical novels: the past is different from the present. This is quite a recent discovery. Until the beginning of the nineteenth century historians did not know it, though they sometimes appreciated it unconsciously. Machiavelli, for instance, wrote his *Discourses* in the belief that the political affairs of ancient Rome provided useful guidance for the Italian republics of his time. For that matter, the Greats school at Oxford assumed that the study of ancient history and philosophy was perfect equipment for the administrators of the Indian Empire. I do not think that even Gibbon, despite his superlative gift of narration, regarded the Romans as different from himself. He thought that Commodus was another version of Louis XV, though with less usual tastes, just as eighteenth-century statesmen did not feel it incongruous that their statues should be draped in togas.

True history began with Sir Walter Scott. He felt himself backwards into time. He did not always succeed. *Ivanhoe* is not a convincing picture of the Middle Ages : it is simply lay figures in fancy dress. But *Old Mortality* is a convincing picture of the later seventeenth century. It is the cloak from which we are all cut. That the past is different from the present is a hard doctrine. Though we try to operate it, we never wholly succeed. The historian who now looks at the English Revolution or Great Rebellion of the seventeenth century cannot help seeing in it a form of class war. So no doubt it was. But when I am told that Bunyan voiced the outlook of independent artisans, I cannot altogether forget that what he attached importance to was being a Baptist.

There is another difficulty that comes from our dealing with events that succeed each other in time. Maitland, to my mind the greatest of English historians, formulated it : 'It is very difficult to remember that events now in the past were once far in the future.' We know what is going to happen. The characters of our history did not.

Hitler maybe knew that he was going to aim at world power, and also knew incidentally that he had a pretty thin chance of getting it. But did Napoleon know that there would be a Napoleonic Empire of Europe? Did F D Roosevelt foresee that under his direction the United States would become the greatest power in the world? Cromwell made a boast of not knowing where he was going. Others often claim to know and end up somewhere quite different. The historian uses his mixture of information and creative imagination to sort out what was in men's minds : not attributing conscious design unless there is some evidence for it and yet admitting its existence sometimes all the same.

In spite of our virtuous resolves, we often stray from history into fiction. We never actually invent, though the temptation to do so is often great. Beaverbrook, an historian whom I greatly admired, played tricks that the more scrupulous would shrink from. Here is an example. In 1917 Lloyd George was having difficulties with Sir William Robertson, the CIGS. F E Smith was consulted. Beaverbrook records : 'He recommended an immediate reorganization of the high offices in the military command at the War Office.' That accords with the evidence. It is a drab statement. So Beaverbrook inserted on the proof : 'Sack him now,' said F E in effect.

The last two words, I suppose, just make the sentence allowable, but it was sailing very near the wind. A professional historian would not risk it. Certainly we speculate. We produce explanations that seem reasonable to us rather than being provided by the evidence. But we draw a clear line and warn the reader what we are doing.

Our fiction comes in quite another way and is all the more dangerous for being usually unconscious. We take the characters of the past too seriously. Most of our evidence until fairly recent times is about the thin top layer of society – kings, nobles, ministers and high clerics. They may be a poor lot but they are all we have, and we blow them up beyond their deserts. Experience teaches that hereditary succession is not a good way of producing ability. Yet we go on treating kings as though they possessed the sort of ability shown by men who had to fight their way to the top. Of course we acknowledge bad kings, according to the immortal phrase of Sellar and Yeatman, but we also find good kings and even great kings.

My late colleague Bruce McFarlane described Henry V as 'the greatest man that ever ruled England'. Great, say, compared with Churchill, let alone Cromwell? I do not believe it. I doubt whether he was much improvement on Ramsay MacDonald. Looking around the crowned heads who have bestrewn the European stage over the centuries, I cannot see any other than Frederick the Great as a man of more than common abilities, and even his abilities were on the thin side.

Of course many kings conducted the affairs of state in a reasonably competent way just as the wealthy man who inherits a great industrial undertaking makes a tolerable chairman of the board. But we cannot be content with that. We manufacture heroes simply because they occupy great positions. We forget that most of these heroes were mainly concerned to show off and enjoy themselves – hunting, running after mistresses, building palaces, collecting works of art, or merely eating and drinking. If they carry this too far, we rebuke our heroes for neglecting what we regard as their true historical duty of ruling.

In my opinion, most great men of the past were only there for the beer – the wealth, prestige and grandeur that went with power. What blinds us to this is the occupational disease of the historian : assuming, when we think back into the past, that we too will be in the top drawer. We shall be jesting with Queen Elizabeth I, building our own palace to rival Blenheim or running a faro bank with Charles Fox. My grandfather was a weaver, so I am less liable to this delusion. If I went back, I should more likely be working eighteen hours a day at a hand-loom or dying of starvation in a ditch.

Of course historians no longer neglect the common people as they did in the days when G M Trevelyan defined social history as 'history with the politics left out'. Now they are interested in how people lived and what made society work. Indeed 'political historian' has almost become a term of reproach. We of this despised class also try to bring in the people and, I fear, often slip into fiction when we do so. We invent national sentiments and attribute to past generations a conscious community of ideas that may exist nowadays. There is perhaps just enough evidence for us to say that in August 1914 the peoples of the major European countries were enthusiastic for war. Looking at that sentence again, I begin to doubt. Are we taking too seriously cheering crowds in the capital cities? It is not possible that they would have cheered just as vociferously an announcement that peace had been preserved?

In earlier times national sentiment is surely a fiction, though perhaps a necessary one. Were the ordinary people of England running over with eagerness to destroy the French Revolution? The governing classes did not think so. They believed that they were sitting on a Jacobin volcano. Take another example. Dr Johnson, a good judge though a Tory, said that if the people had been polled in 1714 the Old Pretender would have been restored. The riotous mobs at the time of Sacheverell's impeachment suggest that he was right. Did the common people really rejoice at Henry V's conquest of France? And what did they think of William the Conqueror's victory at Hastings? When did they even learn of it? Not until months, perhaps not even until years, afterwards. It is easy to forget that people once did not have newspapers, let alone television.

Such are the myths with which we try to give the historical record some sort of rational shape. Our work looks duller and less dramatic than the work of avowed fiction. So it is in appearance, with its scrabbling over sources, its footnotes, and its hesitations. But our material is often more dramatic than anything a historical novelist would dare to invent. Real life outdoes imagination. When Laurence Sterne wanted to put his father into a book, he had to make two of him; Walter Shandy and Uncle Toby. The real man was too much. No one would have believed it. No political novel has ever had a story as dramatic as the fall of Parnell. For that we go not to a novelist but to a modest work by F S L Lyons.

I recently saw a television play about Hitler in the bunker. Stuffed figures, dressed as German generals, delivered remarks taken from the sources. Bormann displayed an anonymity which would, it was said, enable him to vanish into thin air. But where was Hitler – the demonic character who carried a world into war and commanded the unquestioning allegiance of the vast majority of Germans to his last day? He had shrunk to a crazy neurotic, which of course he was as well. But we can find him again in the acknowledged masterpiece by Hugh Trevor-Roper, which leaves fiction far behind.

Marx was fond of quoting Heraclitus: *panta rei*, all things move. This is the one truth we seek to recapture when we write history. We know that our version, being set into words, is itself false. We are trying to stop something that never stays still. Once written, our version too will move. It will be challenged and revised. It will take on appearances that we did not expect. We are content to repeat the words with which Geyl finished his book on Napoleon: 'History is an argument without end.'

2. Tory History

New Statesman. A review of A History of England by
Keith Feiling (1950).

'Good people, I am the Protestant whore!' So Nell Gwynn quietened a mob which had taken her for one of her Roman Catholic colleagues. Professor Feiling is a writer with too many idiosyncrasies to be so simply docketed. Still, when a man writes a massive history of England, he challenges comparison with Trevelyan, with J R Green, even, his publishers think, with Macaulay. Compared with these Feiling is the Tory historian. Yet this is an elusive category. The Whig interpretation of history is easy to define; all our political thinking rests on it. It is the story of English liberty, founded by Magna Carta, consolidated by the Glorious Revolution, expanded by the great Reform Bill, and reaching its highest achievement with the Labour Government. In the words of

Ramsay MacDonald, 'Up and up and up and on and on and on'. It is the doctrine of history as Progress : men always getting wiser and more tolerant; houses more comfortable, food more plentiful; new laws always better than old laws; new ideas always better than old ideas; new wives, I suppose, always better than old wives (this last much practised by the Whig aristocracy).

Liberty ought to be a revolutionary doctrine, the creed of a minority; in England it has become traditional, respectable, universally accepted. This is a result of the Glorious Revolution. True Toryism perished in 1688 or, at any rate, with the Hanoverian succession. What sense had 'Church and King' in the age of latitudinarian bishops and German princes? For that matter, even in the twentieth century the Tories, despite their loyal phrases, were responsible for the only real subversion of modern times, the Ulster rebellion of 1914. If Toryism means anything, it rejects the sovereignty of parliament and the doctrine of the Social Contract, which underlay the revolution of 1688. In practice, as Macaulay observed, Toryism amounts to no more than defending Whig achievements of a previous generation. In the world of ideas, the Tories have had to make do with unprincipled adventurers, like Bolingbroke and Disraeli, or to borrow from the other side. Burke, whom Feiling calls 'the largest mind ever given to politics in our island' and 'the inspiration of a second party of Tories', was a corrupt Whig hack. A century later, the Tories learnt their Imperialism from the renegade Radical, Chamberlain. It would be unfair to blame Toryism for being short of ideas. Ideas are an affair of the mind, and Toryism distrusts the mind in politics. In essence, Toryism rests on doubt in human nature; it distrusts improvement, clings to traditional institutions, prefers the past to the future. It is a sentiment rather than a principle. Feiling carries this sentiment so far that he can even include Oliver Cromwell in it.

Though reason may be a good guide in politics, it is inadequate for the writing of history, and the very qualities which make Tories detestable as politicians should make them good historians. After all a historian should start by appreciating the past. It is true that Gibbon, the greatest of our historians, had nothing but contempt for his chosen subject; this merely shows that genius can disregard all rules. In lesser men Whig rationalism produces what has been well called 'the linotype school of history'; in which everyone behaves according to rule, the mysteries of human behaviour vanish and everything moves relentlessly towards infinite improvement – or to infinite disaster. Mr Feiling writes with a greater understanding of human affairs. He does not pretend to know the answer to every problem in the universe. In his book events remain, as they are, blurred and confused; it is like listening to a story told entirely in echoes. When we read the narrative of a cocksure historian, we tend to forget that the historian can never speak with first-hand authority; he can only piece together the accounts of others. A novelist creates his characters and therefore knows their every motive and action; Feiling never forgets that he did not create the English people. Very often he puts his narrative in the form of hearsay. 'We hear of Saxon invaders on the south coast'; 'there are reports of great acts of cruelty'. The effect is of news arriving late and contradictory to a remote country house, where a slow-witted squire is trying to make sense of events in the short intervals between hunting and fishing. It needs a writer of supreme skill, far from slow-witted, to create this impression, so much nearer to life than our neat explanations.

Toryism starts with the squire, the lesser landowner. Everyone knows that. Feiling emphasizes again and again the permanent elements in rural society. He recognizes, as few Whig historians have done, the importance of local government; indeed even parliament bulks largest in his eyes as a gathering of country gentry. The traditional 'liberties of England' rested on law and custom, not on rational dogma, and the man who maintained them, as in Poland or Hungary, was the country squire. He maintained them no doubt for his own profit and advantage, a point which Feiling is inclined to slide over; still England would not be a free country without him. The unique feature of our history is that the conservative defender of liberty had to take other classes into partnership and finally indeed found himself in the position of a tolerated minority. Feiling says rightly: 'in ages when everywhere in Europe public liberties were being quenched, English law defended freedom', but he also admits that this 'venerable common law' was by the end of the eighteenth century wholly unfit to deal with a new age.

Would these changes come by violence or by agreement? This was the great question of the early nineteenth century. As we know, they came by agreement or, at any rate, by constitutional process. This is usually regarded as the greatest triumph of the Whig spirit. The new Toryism may claim almost as much credit – meaning by this an attitude of mind rather than either the practical common sense of Peel or the flashy trivialities of Disraeli. Though Tory government of the early nineteenth century needed the votes of country squires, it did not represent their outlook nor was it run by them. The squires got the Corn Laws; in return they voted for a government of administrators and soldiers, the former 'King's friends'. This is a point which Feiling does not make explicit, but it conditions all the later part of his work. If by Liberalism is meant all those who try to apply reason to politics, and who enter politics in order to improve things, then it is not only Tory landowners who are on the other side. Conservatism becomes the party also of those who are in politics simply to make things work: to promote, no doubt, their own careers, but to promote it by public service. In a spendid Tory phrase, Feiling quotes the East India Company as declaring on its extinction that the Crown had inherited 'such a body of civil and military officers as the world has never seen before'.

Toryism is no longer a creed merely for the man in the country; it becomes the creed also for the man in the office. Further, when the enterprising capitalist ceases to be adventurous and becomes also a man in the office, Toryism becomes his creed too. Of course this knocks the remaining romance out of Toryism. As Feiling says regretfully of Peel, 'he was cold or deaf to some high sentiments in Tory tradition, whether religious passion or the vision of paternal government'.

Thus what may be called the Tory interpretation of history has no longer much to do with high-flown loyalty to the Crown or devotion to the Church of England : it is not even the exaltation of traditional institutions. The Tory spirit in history is shown by an emphasis on administration, by getting ideas out of history and putting humdrum personal motives and office routine in. Until reading Feiling's book I had thought that the opposite to Whig history was history as it really worked. I now see for the first time that when you take ideas out of history you put Toryism in. When Tout emphasized the administrative history of Edward II against Stubbs's search for the growth of the British constitution, he was not being a better historian than Stubbs; he was being a Tory historian. When Namier emptied Hanoverian Whiggism of principle and analysed the personal or family motives which took men into politics, he was not being a better historian than Macaulay; he was being a Tory historian. When Sir Charles Webster admired Palmerston for the efficient way in which he organized the Foreign Office instead of for the great liberal principles which he tried to apply, he, too, was unwittingly opening the gates to the Tory interpretation of history. In fact, as Sir William Harcourt might so wittily have said : 'We are all Tories nowadays.'

History is no doubt best conducted, like the British constitution, on the principle that Whig plus Tory equals eternal truth. This principle works only so long as it is clear that

Toryism is only half the truth, just as Conservatives are only a substantial minority of the nation despite the Union Jack on their platforms and their masquerade as the National party. Tory history becomes dangerous only when it is presented as impartial history. Feiling, for instance, appears extremely fair and detached until you look at his treatment of the Radicals. Try him on Wat Tyler, on the Levellers, on the Chartists, and you discover a point at which his English sympathies break down. It is revealing that the only spiteful remark in the book is about Major Cartwright, first advocate of universal suffrage. Characteristic also is the judgement that Tom Paine 'had not a rudiment of English feeling, nor was he a thinker', this of the author of *The Rights of Man*, the best statement of democratic belief in any language. The administrator sees the reformer and the agitator as disturbing elements, upsetting office routine and putting forward impractical ideas based on a Utopian faith in human reason.

It was no doubt inevitable that Tory history should gradually take the place of a Whig interpretation which had become traditional and formal. More than this, our whole educational system is now directed to turning out administrators, and these administrators want history with passion left out and machinery put in. Above all, Whig history was the work of an age which believed in progress. For Feiling, British greatness ended in 1918. The rest was 'aftermath', redeemed only by Neville Chamberlain. This is history written in the spirit of a Roman of the late Empire. The administrator still sits at his desk, the army officer still drills his men; but the wall is crumbling, the barbarians are breaking in, nostalgia has taken the place of hope. Yet even nostalgia is a human sentiment. If we survive at all, both Trevelyan and Feiling will be outmoded. What we must expect is history that will be neither Whig nor Tory, but Byzantine.

3. Cromwell and the Historians

New Statesman. Written for the three-hundredth anniversary of Cromwell's death.

Oliver Cromwell, the Lord Protector, died on 3 September 1658, a figure of stormy dispute for his contemporaries and for posterity. He rose higher than any other Englishman not of royal birth; rose indeed higher than a king, for he was king and chief minister in one – the only dictator in our history. He was buried in Westminster Abbey with sovereign honours. Little more than two years later his dead body was dug up and hanged at Tyburn. The head was struck off and set on Westminster Hall; the corpse was flung into a pit beneath what is now Connaught Square.

For almost two centuries the verdict of historians went unanimously against him: knave, hypocrite, fanatic; at best, in Clarendon's phrase, 'a brave, bad man'. Then Carlyle came to his rescue: 'not a man of falsehoods, but a man of truths'. Cromwell's speeches, with their turgid, groping sincerity, spoke to the Victorian spirit. In the later nineteenth century Nonconformity, rising again in the social and political scale, took Cromwell as its first hero and even transformed him into the founder of the Liberal party. In 1899 the man who knocked over parliaments faster than any Stuart had his statue set up at Westminster as the guardian of constitutional liberties.

The twentieth century has brought fresh praise – and new condemnation. Some Radicals have continued to admire Cromwell. After all, he cut off a king's head. Others, fortified by the evidence from the Clarke Papers, have echoed the Levellers and denounced him as the defender of oligarchy and social privilege. The Puritan revolution has been given a Marxist interpretation, and Cromwell has become the champion of capitalism against a feudal monarchy – an interpretation which would have surprised him. More recently, Professor Trevor-Roper has stood Marxism on its head and presented Cromwell as the spokesman of the declining gentry who, far from being revolutionary, resented the modernity of the Court and wished to restore the good old days of Queen Elizabeth. For some, Cromwell has been the founder of the British Empire; for others, the forerunner of Robespierre and Lenin.

In fact, Cromwell was Cromwell and no one else, a puzzled country gentleman of Puritan religion with no originality of view in either politics or economics, but courageous, sincere, and above all resolute. Where others doubted and reasoned, he acted. He gave the best explanation of his career in a phrase now unbearably hackneyed but inescapable : 'No man rises so high as he who knows not whither he goes.' He had no defined policy at the beginning of the civil wars and certainly no vision of his ultimate attainment. He knew only that the king had to be beaten in the field.

Though he never saw a battle until he was over forty, he became the best military leader in England, perhaps the best in Europe. Like Gustavus Adolphus, whom he much admired, he realized that the object of war was to win decisive battles, not to conduct manoeuvres. His strategy was Napoleonic in its daring. Time and again, but particularly in the campaign that ended at Worcester, he tempted the enemy into invasion so as to destroy him the more finally. Like Napoleon, and with more justification, he won the trust and affection of his men. A great cheer went up from the whole army when, before Naseby, 'Old Ironside' rode into the camp. He repaid this affection with an equal devotion, and the reluctance of the army twice prevented him from accepting the Crown.

Politically indeed he was conservative and unconstructive. Though he resisted the tyranny of the king, he disliked almost as much the dictatorship of the Rump. The theories of the Levellers were abhorrent to him. 'A nobility, a gentry, and a yeomanry – that is a good estate.' He wanted to restore the old constitution as he supposed it had existed in the time of the Tudors – crown and parliament bound together by mutual trust. It was lack of this trust which caused the civil wars and brought Charles I to the scaffold. Cromwell stepped into the vacant place and hoped by goodwill on his side to provoke goodwill in others – a hope never fulfilled. He was conservative, too, in foreign policy, dreaming of a great Protestant alliance that was long outmoded. In finance he was most conservative of all and stumbled from one expedient to the next like any Stuart.

Yet with all this he was a revolutionary too – a revolutionary in religion. He was the greatest of Independents, seeking the inner light not only for himself but respecting it in others. He 'did endeavour to discharge the duty of an honest man to God and His people's interest'. He was the first English ruler to make religious toleration the basis of his policy, even though this toleration reached its limits with Prelacy and Popery, and it is thanks to Cromwell that Dissent became a permanent element in English life. But this devotion to religion had its dangers. Cromwell sought always for God's providence, and he was only too ready to see God's hand in the victories of his own sword and the workings of his own will. God was for Cromwell what the general will was for Robespierre or the proletariat for Lenin : the justification for anything he wished to do.

Impatient in temper, choleric in disposition, he reined in his nature and strove for compromise. He had a noble record as ruler of England. No man has been a more reluctant dictator. Though power corrupted him – as it corrupts all men who touch it – there was a redeeming quality in him to the end. But in this record there stands one great blot. In the long story of crime and wickedness which comprises English rule in Ireland Cromwell has the blackest name. Ingenious apologists may excuse the massacres of Drogheda and Wexford as in accordance with the laws of war. They may even find explanations for the clearances and the transportations. But these acts were beyond all excuse or explanation. Cromwell regarded the Irish as wild beasts who should be hunted down and exterminated, and even Englishmen who opposed him followed him in this. The Curse of Cromwell will be remembered when all else he did has been forgotten.

4. Conquerors and Profiteers

This essay first appeared in The History of the British Empire, published by Time-Life Books in cooperation with the BBC, and is reproduced here by permission of © Time-Life International (Nederland) B.V., 1973. All rights reserved.

History began and prehistory ended when men learnt to read and write. Literate men produce a civilization, and almost every civilization has sought to extend its sway over others. Such is the essence of Empire and ancient history is a record of successive empires. Empires arose first in Egypt and Mesopotamia. The Old Testament tells the story of a people repeatedly conquered and yet surviving. The Medes, the Assyrians and the Persians all had their day.

Alexander the Great established a short-lived empire which encompassed the known world. The great Empire of Rome has left its marks on Europe to the present day. The Chinese Empire overshadowed the Far East for more than 2,000 years. When Europeans broke into the New World they encountered the Empires of the Incas and the Aztecs.

All empires were systems of domination, won by conquest and dependent upon superior strength. All, too, had a superior way of life or so the imperial people believed. The imperial system of politics, laws and religion was supposed to be uniquely inspired, and every empire claimed that it was bestowing benefits on those whom it conquered, even when the benefit took the form of extermination. In reality the imperial people took most of the benefits for themselves.

The empires of ancient times were land empires. Their power rested on armies, and they extended their sway by conquering adjacent territories. The legions, rather than political wisdom, held the Roman Empire together, and it fell when the legions lost their strength. Throughout the Middle Ages there was still a Roman Empire in eastern Europe and a shadowy attempt at one in the west. Even the English entered the imperial competition during the hundred years war when Edward III and Henry V attempted to establish an empire in France. That was an antiquated enterprise. During the fifteenth century the European peoples of the Atlantic seaboard developed a new form of power. They turned to the oceans. That was the beginning of modern imperialism.

The driving force behind maritime exploration was economic – with a dash of geographical curiosity thrown in. The merchants of western Europe wanted to break Venice's monopoly of the spice trade by opening a direct route to the Far East. They succeeded. The Portuguese circumnavigated Africa and crossed the Indian Ocean. As an almost accidental by-product they established an overseas empire – the only one the relics of which still survived until the other day. The Spaniards hoped to reach the same goal by crossing the Atlantic. Instead, they discovered America and set up there a vast empire, richly endowed with gold and silver.

Both Portuguese and Spaniards were also missionaries. In their empires they converted; they did not exterminate. Christianity in its Roman Catholic form, as well as trade, followed their flag. Wherever they ruled, Christianity has predominated to the present day – in Goa as much as in South America.

The English were late in entering the competition for overseas empire. Though John Cabot discovered Newfoundland in 1497, nothing followed from this for almost 100 years. For much of the sixteenth century England was hard pressed to assert her independence from continental powers. Protestantism was part of this assertion, giving the English a feeling of superiority over other races. From the moment that the English broke with Roman Catholicism in 1533, they regarded themselves as a Chosen People, authorized by God to override the ordinary laws of civilized behaviour. The sea-dogs of Elizabeth's time, so much admired by nineteenth-century historians, were in fact pirates.

The aim of Drake, Hawkins and the rest was to seize for themselves the loot which the Portuguese and Spaniards were deriving from their empires. As this became more difficult, their successors turned more or less casually to establishing overseas settlements of their own. And since the richest prizes had gone to others – or so it seemed – the English had to make do with North America, where there was neither gold nor silver.

Religion reinforced greed. In the seventeenth century, Puritans who could not worship according to their own fashion at home established New England. In their view the pursuit of wealth was a religious duty, and they did not neglect it. At the same time other Englishmen set up chartered companies to trade with Russia, the Levant and India. The last of these unwittingly led to the greatest overseas empire of all.

The Europeans had two great resources to assist them in building their empires. The first was the sea itself. They could move safely across it, fearing no enemy except other Europeans, until they arrived at their destination. They could thus inflict on the rest of the world the turmoil which the Vikings had once inflicted on them. Their second resource was gunpowder. They alone had the secret of firearms which gave them mastery over all other races. For more than 300 years firearms, not Christianity, guaranteed the predominance of European civilization.

The English had, in addition, a special resource which enabled them, in the long run, to win the race for empire. Though European in their origins and culture, they were detached from Europe geographically. England was an island and the English, when they were wise, could keep out of European conflicts. Europeans sometimes tried to invade England. None succeeded after William of Normandy in 1066. The English, on their side, did not seek European conquests after the hundred years war. Their last foothold, Calais, was lost in 1558. In later times, British statesmen pursued a European balance of power in their foreign policy. They kept the European powers in conflict as the guarantee of their own security and were thus free to expand their dominions overseas.

In the eighteenth century the British eclipsed all their rivals. Spain was in decay. France was distracted by European ambitions and emerged from a long series of wars with Great Britain second best. The British Empire extended over North America. Another less formal empire was established in India, where the East India Company grew from a trading enterprise into the territorial overlord. The British motive in India was entirely economic. The British did not seek to impose their way of life on the inhabitants. They merely wanted peace and security in order to extract wealth and remit it to London.

North America, on the other hand, was an empire of settlement. The British there exterminated the native inhabitants to the best of their ability, just as they had earlier striven to exterminate the native inhabitants of Ireland. No empire has marched forward with more savagery. Although the home

29

government often tried to stem the westward tide of settlement and to protect the Indians from settler depredations, the British in North America followed a simple rule: the only good Indian is a dead Indian. Indeed, this difference in attitude between the British government and the settlers was one of the causes of the American Revolution.

Why did the British overseas emulate Attila and his Huns? It is hard to answer. Perhaps their Protestant creed was peculiarly exclusive and intolerant – English Roman Catholics in America had a better record. Perhaps their comparative freedom from control by the home government enabled them to disregard the rules of civilized behaviour. Perhaps there is a simpler explanation: in the eighteenth century the British merchants had a virtual monopoly of the slave trade from Africa to America, and this brutalized them beyond redemption.

The British Empire of the eighteenth century – the first British Empire as it was often called – was a straightforward institution of plunder. It was 'a good thing' for those who profited from it and for no one else. No eighteenth-century nabob, as the plunderers of India were called, pretended that he laboured for the benefit of the Indians. He laboured in order to become a millionaire.

Similarly, the British government in London did not claim to run the North American colonies for the benefit of the inhabitants, even though they were populated by men of British stock. The colonies existed in order to provide cheap raw materials and preferential markets for British goods. No doubt the North Americans believed that they were extending the British way of life as they saw it – gentry society in the South, Puritanism in the North – but this did not much concern the British government.

One aspect of the colonies, however, concerned the British governing class very much. As the colonies developed into settled communities, they had to be administered, and this meant public offices – 'jobs for the boys', in the later phrase. All colonial posts, from that of governor down to customs officer, were reserved for the British aristocracy and its hangers-on. Needy noblemen were made governors. Subservient Members of Parliament were rewarded with colonial appointments for their relatives and dependents.

Much the same happened in India, where the administration, nominally still conducted by the East India Company, became a happy hunting ground for the British upper classes. Many a great nobleman added to his prestige and, of course, to his wealth, by serving as Governor-General of India. Successful generals, and unsuccessful ones also, received high posts in India instead of pensions. Hilaire Belloc has immortalized the system in the famous lines:

> We had intended you to be
> The next Prime Minister but three:
> The stocks were sold; the Press was squared;
> The Middle Class was quite prepared.
> But as it is! . . . My language fails!
> Go out and govern New South Wales!

Here was a new factor in the drive for empire. The British Empire was increasingly run for the sake of those who ran it. Not all were in the game merely for the high salaries they received. Many welcomed greater power and openings for achievement than they could find in serving as rural magistrates or backbench Members of Parliament at home. Some had an intellectual curiosity to explore the history or languages of India. Some were glad to escape from boredom. Whatever their motive, the administrators provided an imperial class. The Empire which provided them with jobs became for them a mission, a sacred duty.

As time passed, they came to believe that they were extending the virtues of British civilization, and their belief was not without foundation. What had begun as a trading venture turned into a moral cause. The administrators began to consider the interest of those over whom they ruled. They drew the line only at one point: they would do anything for the subject peoples except get off their backs.

The first British Empire of the eighteenth century did not last long. The American colonies revolted against their exploitation. They wanted to run their own economy without restrictions and they wanted to govern themselves. The Americans won their war of independence. The thirteen colonies of the Atlantic seaboard became the United States of America. In time, American settlers spread right across the continent, carrying with them institutions and laws that had English origins. The loss of the American colonies did not do much damage except to the pride of George III and his ministers. Culturally and economically the United States remained a British dependency until the beginning of the twentieth century. Here was a great discovery, made theoretically by Adam Smith and reinforced practically by the loss of the American colonies: that political overlordship was not essential for economic profit and that the straight pursuit of exploitation could therefore be laid aside.

Other developments contributed to the advance of this new outlook. For much of the eighteenth century the West Indies were by far the most profitable part of the British Empire. William Beckford, the richest Englishman of his time, derived his entire wealth from Caribbean sugar plantations, and he was only one among many. Towards the end of the century, however, the plantations showed signs of exhaustion from over-cropping. Beckford's son was a symbol of this decline. With his vast wealth he built himself a gimcrack Gothic abbey. The tower fell down, and Beckford finished as an impoverished valetudinarian in Bath. Here then was further evidence that exploitation was providing diminishing returns.

Far more significant was the rapid change in English

economic life itself. England had been a flourishing commercial country since the beginning of the seventeenth century. She had excelled in trade, not manufactures. A hundred years later machines and factories had transformed England into the world's foremost industrial community. Some economists have conjectured that the capital necessary for this industrial expansion derived from the exploitation of Empire – primitive accumulation, as Marx called it. Other economists assert that the capital reserves had been gradually built up at home, and this is the prevailing view at the moment. Whether capitalists flourished by robbing other Englishmen or by plundering the rest of the world is a point of no great moment. They had to rob someone if they were to come into existence at all.

The development of British industry, which for a time made Great Britain the workshop of the world, was a striking, even if negative, event in the history of Empire. For the profits derived from coal and cotton, iron and steel seemed to make Empire unnecessary. British industry did not need protected markets. Free Trade, which triumphed with the abolition of the Corn Laws in 1846, was implicitly a repudiation of empire. The British retained only a Free Trade Empire, which was almost a contradiction in terms. But not quite. The free trade which benefited the British was bestowed on the subject peoples, particularly of India, whether they liked it or not. In this high-principled way the Indian textile industry was made totally defenceless against that of Lancashire.

The Industrial Revolution, which made empire unnecessary in one way, stimulated it in another. For along with the growth of industry went a great increase in population. We do not know how closely the two developments were connected. Possibly the growth of industrial towns made better sanitation and health services essential. Possibly industrial workers, though miserably poor, were better fed than agricultural labourers. At any rate, the increased population was available for industry.

It was soon believed that there were too many people; both Australia and New Zealand originated as receptacles for this surplus population, Australia more specifically as one for criminals. This was a new feature in imperial expansion. Previously, men had gone to the colonies in search of gain. Now they went for space and, to some extent, for a freer life. The new steamships made emigration easy and cheap. In the mid nineteenth century something like a quarter of a million people left Great Britain each year, the majority for the United States, but many for the developing British colonies.

In this way British communities, complete with British institutions, established themselves almost within a decade. The home government exercised little control over them. It had learned a lesson from the revolt of the American colonies. Canada was the first to receive 'responsible government'. New Zealand and the Australian colonies soon followed. This was an unprecedented development in the history of empires. For all practical purposes, the colonies with responsible government were no longer under the authority of London. They were bound to Great Britain only by ties of sentiment. Of course, they received practical advantages as well. The Royal Navy, paid for entirely by the British taxpayer, gave the colonies an effortless security until well on in the twentieth century.

Great Britain also offered a profitable market for colonial foodstuffs and raw materials. Later, the London capital market was opened to the colonies on advantageous terms. The balance sheet of empire was reversed. Throughout the nineteenth century the British colonists benefited from the imperial connection, and Great Britain drew no great profit from it. The possession of an empire brought prestige. It still provided agreeable jobs for the upper classes. But the British capitalists made most of their wealth by their own activities at home. Great Britain would have been no poorer, perhaps even a little richer, if the colonial Empire had not existed.

India was a different matter. Direct exploitation in the old plundering fashion came to an end. The nineteenth century saw no more nabobs. The administrators became more powerful than the traders and also developed a new high-mindedness. There were two causes for this. The first was a change in political ethics. Corruption fell out of fashion. Public service took its place. Politicians no longer sought direct financial rewards from their activities, and the same spirit extended to administrators in India as well as at home. The second cause for this change was a revival in the British governing classes of Evangelical Christianity.

Victorian England was an intensely religious country. The British generals and administrators in India saw themselves as soldiers of God. Though they could not actually convert the Hindus and Muslims to Christianity, they could impose on India the Christian virtues. The British suppressed such practices as *suttee* – the burning of widows at their husband's funerals. They imposed a rigorously honest system of government. They began a laborious struggle against disease and famine. They ended the wars between the Indian states, usually by the simple process of annexation.

The rule of the Indian Civil Service brought great benefits to the Indian people. India was more peaceful and orderly, more fairly administered and better endowed with hospitals and railways than it could have been without British rule. But there was a heavy debit to be set on the other side. The more efficient and honest the British rulers of India became, the greater grew the cleavage between them and those over whom they ruled. The eighteenth-century adventurers had not regarded the Indians as different from themselves. They spent many uninterrupted years in India, and it was a normal practice for them to marry Indian women. A servant of the East India Company who married a rajah's daughter would have thought himself in luck's way.

Now all was changed. The virtuous administrators of the

nineteenth-century Indian Civil Service regarded the Indians as inferior. Indians took bribes. They put the interest of their family before that of the state. They neglected the drains. They worshipped many gods of a most peculiar sort. The British administrators have been described by an admirer as Platonic Guardians. To a less enthusiastic eye they appear to be complacent prigs. After all, if they were so keen on improvement, there was plenty to improve in their own country without interfering in the affairs of a distant civilization which had done them no harm.

The Indian Civil Service provided the richest outlet for the products of the public-school system which was now flourishing in England. These so-called public schools – actually expensive private schools – grew up in order to provide the sons of the gentry and wealthy middle classes with what had previously been an aristocratic education. Those who passed through the public schools were known as 'gentlemen'. Unfortunately, having acquired a gentleman's culture and tastes, they also needed a gentleman's income. Where were they to acquire it? Certainly not by trade or industry, in which most English people made their livelihood.

The Indian Civil Service was the perfect answer. Its members, qualified mainly by their command of Latin and Greek, were safely immune from any taint of trade. They felt that they were discharging a religious mission. At the same time, they led the life of gentlemen, with households of fifteen to twenty native servants. Retiring at an early age on a high pension, they returned to gentlemanly ease in England with their sons following the same careers.

It is thus easy to decide who benefited from the Indian Empire. Its administration helped to perpetuate the English class system throughout the nineteenth century. The benefit for British society is less obvious. The public schools were conservative institutions. Their outlook sapped the spirit of enterprise and invention that had carried Great Britain forward during the Industrial Revolution. As the nineteenth century advanced there was increasing speculation about what was wrong with Great Britain. Why was her economic growth slowing down? Why did she not predominate in the new industries of electricity and chemicals as she had done in coal and cotton?

The simplest answer, which remains true to the present day, was the public schools. They taught the classics when they should have been teaching the sciences. They sustained outlooks unsuited to a progressive industrial community. And these in their turn were sustained by the Indian Empire.

The British rulers of India claimed to be there for the benefit of the Indians. In 1857 the Indians disputed that claim. The Indian mutiny was the greatest challenge to the British Empire since the revolt of the American colonies. No doubt it was a rebellion in favour of ancient ways, not an explosion of modern nationalism. There were massacres on both sides. The British, in their alarm, were as savage as the mutineers. The Mutiny revealed the underlying truth about the Indian Empire: the British were not there because they were wanted, but because their troops had superior discipline and superior weapons. Armed force was the fundamental resource of the British in India as it was for all other empires.

The Indian Mutiny completed the estrangement between the British and their Indian subjects. Henceforth the British ruled India as if it were another planet. Any idea of educating the Indians into self-government was postponed to an extremely remote future. India became the brightest jewel in the British crown and in 1876 formally an Empire. Queen Victoria became Empress of India – an imperial title never taken for any other of her Dominions.

It was in this period that India brought most profit to Great Britain. Internal peace made India a rich market. Lancashire continued to prosper with the Indian demand for cotton goods.

India brought also great advantages in power. The Indian Army, paid for by Indian taxes but officered by Englishmen, provided Great Britain with military resources. Many of the later imperial conquests were made by Indian troops serving overseas in Africa or the Persian Gulf. In addition, about half of the British Army was regularly stationed in India, again at Indian expense. Altogether the Indian Empire was a wonderful device for maintaining armed forces on the cheap.

Until the end of the 1870s the British Empire was the only one of its kind in the world. The Spanish Empire in America had been lost. The Portuguese and Dutch Empires were remnants, though the Dutch was a very profitable one. The French Empire was also not much more than a collection of relics except in North Africa. The British Empire, however, encompassed the globe. The white communities were growing in population and resources. British control of India seemed unshakable. All this rested essentially on the British command of the seas. Though there were occasional alarms, the Royal Navy was never seriously challenged between the battle of Trafalgar in 1805 and the building of a great German navy in the early twentieth century. Sea power was the key to empire.

A new epoch opened in the 1880s. Other European powers began to covet colonies and turned to Africa, the one continent that had not been seriously penetrated by Europeans. Curiously, Belgium, by no means a great power, started the race when Leopold II set out to acquire the Congo basin as an individual venture. France, Germany and even Italy soon joined in. The British would have preferred to leave Africa alone and acquired vast African territories mainly to keep others out. There was also a strategic motive. The British now controlled the Suez Canal as their route to India and extended their rule over much of Africa in order to make this control more secure.

The imperialism of the late nineteenth century has been

much discussed by historians. It had many causes, not all of them political. Explorers were eager to chart the Dark Continent and often used patriotic motives as an excuse for purely academic curiosity. Christian missionaries wished to rescue the Africans from paganism. Philanthropists wished to end the Arab slave trade. Empire became a demagogic cry, if only to divert the working classes from their economic and social grievances at home.

On a more practical basis, colonies were supposed to offer profitable markets as they had done in the eighteenth century. More than this, they were supposed to offer profitable openings for investment. According to an ingenious view, first propounded by the English economist J A Hobson, and then taken up by Lenin, the yield on capital was diminishing at home as industries became fully developed and production outstripped demand. Investment in the undeveloped colonies provided what Lenin called 'super-profit'. Hence the motive behind imperial expansion was the old search for wealth.

This view has been sharply discredited in recent years. It has been clearly shown, for instance, that the direct connection between overseas investment and the new imperialism, as laid down by Hobson and Lenin, has been grossly exaggerated. British overseas investment certainly increased greatly at this time, but most of it went to South America, the United States and other independent countries, not to the newly-acquired African colonies. Few of these colonies indeed 'paid' the countries which acquired them.

The annual cost to Germany of administering the Cameroons was five times as great as her total trade with the colony, and much the same applied to other countries. Nor is there any clear evidence that the yield from colonial investments was higher than that from investment at home. On the contrary, the dabbler in overseas shares was far likelier to lose his money. In almost every case, European countries spent a great deal of money in acquiring colonies which proved of little economic value.

These arguments, though true, are also irrelevant. They treat European countries as communities in which policies were conducted for the benefit of all, much as companies are conducted, or are supposed to be, for the benefit of the shareholders. This was not so. Benefit went to the few who determined policy and shaped public opinion; it was of no concern to them that this was achieved at great loss to the many. James Thurber, the American comic artist, drew extremely ugly women. When told that his women were not attractive, he replied: 'They are to my men.' Similarly, when we are told that imperialism was not profitable, we can reply: 'It was to the imperialists.' The humble investor might lose his money, but the mighty company promoter did not go away empty-handed even if the company he promoted went bankrupt.

Overseas railways often did not pay those who invested money in them, but they paid those who built them and those who peddled the shares. The Boer war cost the British taxpayer a great deal of money, but South Africa also produced many millionaires. In Edwardian times these millionaires occupied most of the houses in Park Lane. Clearly, imperialism brought economic gain to some people, if not to the imaginary national community, and the lucky few could hire journalists and historians to bamboozle the many.

Economic imperialism was a striking example of conspicuous waste, the doctrine laid down by Thorstein Veblen. According to Veblen, capitalism needs a steady increase in expenditure to keep going, and the great problem is to find new excuses for spending money. Imperialism was a splendid way of doing it. If some great nobleman had offered to stay at home instead of becoming Viceroy of India on condition that he was given a rise in the peerage and £200,000 this would have been an excellent bargain for the British taxpayer. But, of course, no one considered it, and the nobleman duly went to India. James Mill said early in the nineteenth century that the Empire was a system of out relief for the British aristocracy. By the end of the century it had become a system of out relief for British capitalists also.

Economic imperialism did not last long as the predominant tone. The first world war again changed the spirit of British imperialism. The supposed strategical danger from the German colonies revived Britain's desire to lay hands on more of the world for herself, and at the end of the war this desire was strengthened by a new alarm over Bolshevik Russia. The British Empire acquired a new empire in the Middle East, stretching from Egypt to India, to serve as a barrier against Russia.

There was also a change in a different direction. Germany was deprived of her colonies on the excuse that she had ruled them brutally. The British acquisitions in Africa and Asia were disguised as 'mandates', allegedly administered for the good of their inhabitants. The British had to be on their best behaviour. Often they took their high professions seriously.

Yet, at this late stage of empire, the British reverted to old ideas of direct exploitation. Free Trade no longer brought automatic prosperity and in 1932 Great Britain reverted to Protection. Lord Beaverbrook preached Empire Free Trade – in reality, an economic system closed against foreigners – and an attempt was made to realize this at the Ottawa Conference. The self-governing Dominions would not accept it. The colonies administered from Whitehall had no choice. In the years before the second world war these colonies became protected markets for British goods exactly as the American colonies had been in the days of mercantilism. This brought no benefits to the colonies, and most economists now hold that it also brought none to Great Britain. Her principal competitors, the Japanese and the Germans, being excluded from the colonies, merely became fiercer rivals elsewhere.

There was a deeper underlying change. In 1922 Ireland, the oldest of British colonies, won her freedom. She did so by rebellion, not by conciliation and consent. The Sinn Feiners succeeded where the parliamentary Home Rule party had failed. This was an example for other colonial peoples. In India especially the party of independence, led by Gandhi, moved from conciliation to resistance even though on Gandhi's insistence this was non-violent.

The British were challenged at their most vulnerable point. They had held their Empire by the possession of superior force. Now the balance of strength was turning against them. During the inter-war years they were still strong enough to retain their hold on India and only made concessions which involved no surrender of power. But they were increasingly strained by the mounting challenge from Germany and Japan. In 1939, and then more decisively in 1941, they were again plunged into war.

Though the British entered the war in order to destroy Nazi tyranny in Europe, it became, in effect, mainly an imperial venture. Britain fought Germany and Italy in North Africa and the Mediterranean. She fought Japan on the eastern borders of India. Paradoxically, she fought this war for the sake of an Empire which she had already decided to relinquish. The Indians were offered their freedom if they would wait until the end of the war and, though they refused the offer, they got this freedom afterwards all the same. Withdrawal from India was really the end of the British Empire. It had been the central focus of the whole system and, once it went, there was little point in hanging on to the rest.

It took the British some fifteen years to appreciate this. Then, in the early 1960s, the British colonial Empire vanished overnight. The British maintained that they were no longer strong enough to maintain their Empire. It would be truer to say that they no longer believed in it. There is no explaining a loss of belief of this kind. It happened. One day the British believed that they were a great people because they had an Empire. The next day they regarded the Empire as a worthless burden and discarded it without further thought.

Imperial collapse had an unnecessary and unfortunate accompaniment. The colonies and the dominions really had little in common, though they were lumped together as British. The dominions were independent communities, associated with Great Britain by their own free will. As such they were the only allies of Great Britain who went through both world wars with her from the first day to the last. They imposed no conditions. They asked no reward. They responded instinctively to the call of their kith and kin – a phrase now discarded as ridiculously sentimental, but once full of meaning. Commonwealth aid in wartime was economic as well as financial. The United States demanded hard terms when they provided Lend-Lease. Canada gave Mutual Aid unconditionally. Here was the living reality of Commonwealth feeling.

Yet nothing was made of it. Once the second world war was over, British opinion turned against the Commonwealth as much as it did against the Empire. Admittedly, the Royal Navy could no longer provide the effortless security which the dominions had received in the nineteenth century, and Australia, for one, turned to the United States for military protection. Admittedly, too, there were elements, such as the French in Canada and the Boers in South Africa, who did not feel the tie with Britain. But essentially the Commonwealth was a union of hearts, not a union of interests. The British political leaders deliberately threw it away. By the 1960s Commonwealth citizens, as much British as the inhabitants of Lancashire, were denied free entry into their own home. The Commonwealth Immigration Act of 1963 was the real end of Empire.

There is a curious posthumous relic. The British nc longer have an Empire: but in one important way they behave as though they had. Only two countries maintain expensive military establishments outside their own territory. One is the United States, which spend well over £1,000 million a year in foreign currencies. The Americans now regard themselves as one of the two remaining imperial powers in the world and presumably know what they are doing. Great Britain spends £300 million a year in foreign currency for the defence of an Empire which no longer exists. No other country does this. Germany and Japan actually make a profit out of being defended by others. Nor did the defence of the British Empire cost anything in foreign currency before the second world war. It showed a profit, thanks to some £200 million levied on the people of India.

Were it not for this persistence in spending foreign exchange on military purposes there would never have been a balance of payments problem in the British economy, and everyone in Great Britain would have been remarkably the richer as a result. We may debate interminably whether the possession of Empire ever showed a profit to the national community. Continuance of imperial habits when there is no Empire certainly produces a considerable loss. But such debate is pointless. The British Empire was run for the sake of those who administered it, defended it and speculated in it. No doubt the non-existent Empire brings similar advantages, in prestige if not in profit, to those who run it now.

There remains a final question. Did the British Empire benefit its former subject peoples? There is no simple answer. The Empire carried British institutions overseas in the dominions and made Africans and Indians, at least superficially, European in their ethics, politics and customs. If European civilization in its British guise be accepted as superior to African and Asian, then the British Empire was clearly a good thing. It all depends on the point of view. Anyone who regards industrialization and pollution and nuclear weapons as evil may regret that they are now spread throughout the world. That is what the British Empire helped to do.

Perhaps the subject peoples would have found a way of life more suited to their needs if they had been left to themselves. They were given no choice. For that matter, the Japanese have been the most successful imitators of Europe without any imperial assistance. The British thought that they were discharging a mission of civilization. Their real mission was to extract profit for themselves, and it is not certain that they managed to do even that successfully.

5. *Charles James Fox*

Manchester Guardian. Written for the hundred-and-fiftieth
anniversary of Fox's death. This was the last piece
commissioned from me by A P Wadsworth, editor of the
Manchester Guardian, who died soon afterwards.

On 13 September 1806 Charles James Fox died in the Palladian villa of the Duke of Devonshire at Chiswick. His last words echoed the royal ancestor whom he rivalled in charm: 'It don't signify, my dearest, dearest Liz.' Charles Fox was a legend even in his lifetime. No public man has been so loved by his associates. He was the first statesman, incidentally, to be universally addressed by his Christian name. His picture in the National Portrait Gallery conveys something of his unique fascination – a flushed stout man, sitting on a stile in disarray amid the delights of Nature; a welcome contrast indeed to the formal figures who surround him on the walls. Many historians have seen in Fox a charmer and nothing more; a blundering tactician greedy for power; an irresponsible declaimer who drove himself and his followers from one disaster to another.

The picture has a touch of truth. Fox had an incurable love for members of the great Whig families. There was something absurd in a champion of the people who set up a ministry composed predominantly of dukes and marquises. His private life did not show the austere morality that the British public expects from its leaders. Other Whigs, including his father, made fortunes from the service of the state; Charles Fox lost an even vaster fortune on the race course and at the gambling tables. His father, Lord Holland, brought him up on the doctrine: 'The young are always right; the old are always wrong.' Everyone knows the story of Lord Holland's remark when Charles smashed a gold watch: 'If you must, you must.' On the same principle Lord Holland provided £300,000 to pay his son's more pressing debts. Charles himself tried to meet this same need by running a faro bank at Brooks's – a bank which he continued to run even when he was secretary of state for foreign affairs.

When all else had failed, his aristocratic friends had a whip round and provided him with £3,000 a year. 'How will he take it?' one of them asked anxiously. Another gave the correct reply: 'Quarterly, I suppose.' Gambling, drinking and late hours did not exhaust his vices. He had a number of natural children, all of whom he adored. He lived with Mrs Armitstead, 'dearest Liz', for nearly twenty years before he married her – she had grown rich by living previously with other men. Then he kept his marriage secret so that he might continue to flaunt the immorality that he was no longer practising. If there was only his love of Nature and the classics to set off against all this, we should say that he was a curious character, an amusing period piece, no more; certainly not worth commemoration.

But there is a great deal more. For one thing, Fox invented the modern British constitution – invented, that is, the two-party system and the doctrine that the crown must accept as prime minister the political leader favoured by a majority of the House of Commons. Earlier politicians had in fact 'opposed', but they wrapped up their opposition as patriotic advice or took shelter under the patronage of the heir apparent. Fox criticized whatever was done by the government of the day and claimed on every issue that he could have done better; he was the first leader of a formed and avowed Opposition. Again, earlier politicians had forced their unwelcome services on the King, but always with loyal apologies and in the belief that the favour of the Crown would bring with it support from the House of Commons, not the other way round. Fox, with a gambler's extremism, resolved to win or lose all. He regarded George III as Satan and held that the Crown should be reduced to a cipher. 'The Crown is endowed with no faculty whatever of a private nature.'

Charles Fox lost in his lifetime, but he won the future. In the words of Richard Pares: 'George III undoubtedly beat Charles Fox in 1784, and trampled on his ghost in 1807; but our politicians act, today, on Charles Fox's constitutional principles.' It was evidence of Fox's triumph when Victoria had to accept Gladstone as prime minister in spite of her violent protest, and even more striking evidence when George V sent for Ramsay MacDonald in 1924 with no protest at all. We are supposed to owe the British constitution to the wisdom of our ancestors. It would be truer to say that in its present form it sprang fully grown from Charles Fox's personal hostility to George III. The 'Whig interpretation of history' is a horse from the same stable. Fox asserted, quite wrongly, that his view of the constitution had flourished ever since the Glorious Revolution. His Whig friends echoed this belief, and historians followed suit until they were put right in our own day by Sir Lewis Namier.

This political doctrine makes Fox interesting, important, even great; it does not make him admirable. What gave him a unique place in English history was his championing of liberty, both individual and national. He was a long time

coming to it. In his early days he had a wrongheaded enthusiasm for the House of Commons – even defending its right
to expel and disqualify Wilkes. The revolt of the American
colonies taught him that there were more important things
than legal niceties or the struggle for political power. Fox
was among the first to advocate the complete independence
of America, and he staked his political career on this cause
until it was won. The impeachment of Warren Hastings,
which he shared with Burke, took him a stage farther. However doubtful the detailed charges, that case established the
principle that the British Empire was something more than an
empire of exploitation.

Fox's finest hour came with the war against the French
Revolution. All calculation of personal advantage was swept
aside. Fox could have been a leading war minister. He, not
Pitt, would have been 'the pilot who weathered the storm'.
Fox never considered this course for a moment. He was convinced that the war was unnecessary and morally wrong.
Almost alone among Englishmen of the governing class, he
recognized the principle of liberty in France in spite of the
violence of the Terror and was convinced that Great Britain
was fighting on the side of tyranny. He broke with his closest
friends and for five years argued against the war almost single-
handed. There is no more glorious story in our history. Sixty
years later Richard Cobden, contemplating a similar course of
action himself, wrote of Fox:

It is impossible to read the speeches of Fox at this time without
feeling one's heart yearn with admiration and gratitude for the
bold and resolute manner in which he opposed the war, never
yielding and never repining, under the most discouraging defeats.
The annals of Parliament do not record a nobler struggle in a
nobler cause.

Here again Fox lost the present and won the future. He
saw his supporters in the House shrink from fifty to twenty;

he was struck off the Privy Council for toasting 'Our Sovereign Lord, the People'; police spies were set on him, and Pitt considered sending him to the Tower. But posterity has confirmed his judgement on this war for despotism, and in the nineteenth century British policy welcomed the liberal revolutions which Pitt had tried to suppress. The spirit of Fox prevails whenever England stands on the side of Freedom. The independence of Ireland and India are his memorials, and those who now champion the peoples of Africa are only the latest who belong to 'the party of Mr Fox'.

6. *William Cobbett*

New Statesman. Ostensibly written as a review of
A Bibliography of William Cobbett's Writings by M L Pearl
(1953). The reference to sponsored television indicates that
the essay was written during the controversy that preceded
the introduction of commercial, or as it is called,
independent television. The essay contains, I think, the first
use of the term, The Establishment, an invention usually
attributed to Henry Fairlie.

Trotsky tells how, when he first visited England, Lenin took him round London and, pointing out the sights, exclaimed: 'That's *their* Westminster Abbey! That's *their* Houses of Parliament!' Lenin was making a class, not a national, emphasis. By *them* he meant not the English, but the governing classes, the Establishment. And indeed in no other European country is the Establishment so clearly defined and so complacently secure. The Victorians spoke of the classes and the masses, and we still understand exactly what they meant. The Establishment talks with its own branded accent; eats different meals at different times; has its privileged system of education; its own religion, even, to a large extent, its own form of football. Nowhere else in Europe can you discover a man's social position by exchanging a few words or breaking bread with him. The Establishment is enlightened, tolerant, even well-meaning. It has never been exclusive, rather drawing in recruits from outside as soon as they are ready to conform to its standards and become respectable. There is nothing more agreeable in life than to make peace with the Establishment – and nothing more corrupting.

The Establishment made nearly all our history and nearly all our literature. But what of those outside, the nameless many? It is characteristic of their fate that even when they found a name for themselves as the Commons of England, this was at once appropriated by the most privileged assembly in the world. Not only anonymous, they are also silent: 'we are the people of England, that never have spoken yet'. Yet silent is the wrong word; inarticulate would be better. For outside the snug structure of the Establishment, there is always a vague movement – sometimes no more than a rustle, often a breeze, occasionally a real storm. But rarest of all are the moments when the sound becomes an articulate voice, pronouncing recognizable words. It is not enough to be risen from the people; the writer must still think as they do, though expressing himself more clearly. There was never a writer of more impeccably popular origin, for instance, than D H Lawrence, but his spirit soon took on an alien tinge, and his later inarticulate phase was not at all like public-house conversation. Nor is it enough to have advanced or revolutionary ideas. Republicanism has often been aristocratic since the days of Algernon Sydney, and our most revolutionary poet was the son of a baronet. It is not really possible to rouse a working-class audience by reciting either Shelley or Swinburne, though I have seen the experiment tried; the audience preferred Ella Wheeler Wilcox.

The spokesmen of the Commons of England can be numbered on the fingers of one hand; they earn recognition even if they speak only a few words. John Ball has to carry the Middle Ages almost alone. We have to wait until the seventeenth century for a real democratic movement, obtruding itself into the civil war between the king and the magnates. Our own preoccupation with social questions has led us to exaggerate the importance of the Diggers. We fail to see that the more profound revolutionaries are to be found in the religious sectaries. John Bunyan was the first great English writer who owed nothing to the Establishment, and Pilgrim's Progress is the most subversive tract ever written. For Bunyan did not merely hate Vanity Fair : he rejoiced to be outside it. This democracy made but a brief stir. After the battle of Sedgemoor the people of England disappear from history for more than a hundred years, and we shall never discover the subterranean channels which connected the Independents of Cromwell's time with the Radicals of Peterloo. Tom Paine was the first to break the long silence and broke it so effectively that he is still frowned on by respectable historians.

He was followed by a greater writer, though an inferior thinker. William Cobbett was the common man suddenly grown articulate. Apart from a supreme gift of expression, he had nothing – no ideas, no policy, not even the ability to get on with others. Cobbett was a torrent of printed words. He began as a Tory; he became a Radical reformer. Both political descriptions are irrelevant to his real outlook. He hated the Establishment – the THING. At first he hoped to escape from it by returning to an imaginary past; later he hoped to destroy it in an equally imaginary future. But he was more concerned to strike against it in the present. His first appearance was as a barrack-room lawyer, and he had always the popular taste for litigation. He went to law with his printers, his partners, his creditors, with great statesmen, finally with members of his own family. He was self-taught in law and in politics as well as in writing and always unshakably self-confident in his own cause. Not only did he know best how

England should be run. He also knew best how houses should be heated, what crops should be grown, what clothes should be worn. The reader who is to enjoy his writings must accept unquestioningly that Cobbett is always right – as much in his obscure feuds as in great issues of public policy. Lord Sidmouth and the Botley parson, Sir Francis Burdett and Sir Robert Peel – all must be consigned to outer darkness. Cobbett was always being cheated, always battling against great odds, always being threatened with the majesty of the law – yet always turning up remarkably successful in no time.

The Political Register was the first popular newspaper. Its secret was to express, clearly and forcefully, what every labouring man obscurely felt. Cobbett's political programme was simple: government should cease to exist, and the THING along with it. The National Debt should be repudiated – with some compensation to small holders; the army disbanded; the civil service wound up. Then taxes could be ended and everyone would be prosperous. It is only our unconscious allegiance to the THING which makes us think these ideas preposterous. In reality, they are the politics of every natural man. Andrew Jackson applied them almost contemporaneously in the United States with extreme success; the Capital Levy was a basic part of the Labour Party's programme in the days when it was Socialist; and even to the present day the Swiss manage to be the best-defended state in Europe without an army in our sense at all. If we did not have to carry the incubus of the gentry, the clubs and bishops, The Times – Cobbett's 'bloody old *Times*' – and the public schools, we should be nearly as prosperous as Cobbett wanted us to be. Unfortunately, if you knock one THING down, another bobs up. The United States and the Soviet Union both prove it in their separate ways.

Cobbett was against the THING; he was on the side of the labouring people. This is far from saying that he had any idea of a new social order or indeed of any social order at all. He thought that the farmer and his labourers, or for that matter the factory owner and his workers, were on the same side. He, too, was a master and an employer. Though he refused to accept letters addressed to 'William Cobbett, Esq.' and always described himself in his writings as 'Mr Cobbett' yet, when he wrote to his farm-labourer, he began abruptly, 'Marshall!' Attwood argued rightly that his insistence on an undiluted gold currency would retard the development of industry. Cobbett thought this all to the good. He always refused to admit that the population of England was increasing. He held that it had been greater in the Middle Ages and proved it by calculating how many people the village churches would hold if they were packed to the doors. He invented an extraordinary version of the past in his History of the Protestant Reformation. His Advice to Young Men is advice about how to have a good life without being associated with the THING. Cobbett did not advise his young man to be educated at Winchester or to join the Fabian Society or to oppose sponsored television; in fact he did not give good advice for those who wish to become Labour Cabinet ministers.

Yet it will not do to turn Cobbett into a popular saint. The THING gets hold of you, even if you kick against it; indeed the THING shows its greatest skill in rewarding its opponents. Cobbett became a respected and admired character even in his lifetime. Hazlitt canonized him as the representative Englishman; the Steam Intellect Society reprinted his pamphlets; and he ended as a member of parliament, put in by a wealthy radical millowner. His son, starting as a Chartist delegate, ended as a Conservative MP, supporting Disraeli, and his descendants were pillars of Manchester conservatism. Cobbett always presented himself as a farmer, who had taken to writing as a side line. Like most agricultural experts, he does not seem to have known much about practical farming. His various farms were no great success, and he made money, apart from journalism, by running a seedsman's shop in

Kensington. Rural Rides is one of the greatest books written in English, but its title gives it away. It describes the visits of a town dweller to the country, not the country seen and felt from inside. It is the hiker's pocket companion. Anyone who tries to follow the advice of Cottage Economy condemns himself to a laborious life, and Cobbett himself got up early in the morning to write pamphlets, not to brew beer.

The contradictions of Cobbett are best shown in the parable of the Indian corn. Cobbett came back from America as great an advocate of maize as of democracy, and in subsequent years he put as much energy into preaching its virtues as into attacking the THING. Maize is not a reliable or profitable crop in the English climate, as Cobbett could have learnt from any practical farmer. It has never been grown extensively in our fields. But seedsmen produce a delicate variety for private gardens, and what Cobbett advocated as a staple food for the labouring poor has become an exotic delicacy at the tables of cosmopolitan epicures.

7. *Macaulay and Carlyle*

A talk given on the Third Programme of the BBC and published in The Listener, somewhat reinforced by passages from a review of an anthology of Macaulay's writings which appeared in The New Statesman.

Critics used to have a trick, now rather gone out, of matching two contemporary authors like prizefighters in a ring. Dickens and Thackeray, Fielding and Richardson, Meredith and Hardy – there was not much sense in it. These contrasted pairs do not demonstrate anything except that it takes all sorts to make a world, especially the world of literature. They are a warning against taking any writer, however great, as typical of his age;

there is always someone equally great who is his exact opposite. Macaulay and Carlyle were the two greatest writers of history in nineteenth-century England. It is all that they had in common. There are only two other historical works in English which can match Macaulay's History of England and Carlyle's French Revolution for literary and intellectual pleasure. It is not difficult to guess one, though it is unlikely that you will guess the other.

Though Macaulay and Carlyle were both great historians, they were not only historians, indeed not even primarily historians. Macaulay was a politician, Carlyle a prophet. This is not unusual. Most historians are amateurs in that they write in their spare time – nowadays the time that they can spare from teaching or administration. Paradoxically those who devote all their lives to writing are usually the most amateurish. Macaulay came to history as a journalist. I do not mean that he knew little history – many journalists know a great deal of history, and Macaulay's mind was stocked with historical information in a way without parallel. His mind ranged over the centuries. He could match the decline of the Moghul empire with incidents from the Carolingian eclipse, and in a single speech in the House of Commons he brought in Edward I and Constantius Chlorus, the Rump and the Plebeians of Rome, Socrates and Mr Burke. But he used the past as Machiavelli and the men of the Renaissance had done : it was a storehouse of anecdotes and events, which illustrated the character of individuals. As an essayist his subjects were chosen for him by the books which he had to review. He took a theme, made up his mind about it, and wrote down his ideas fast, in time to catch the press. He had no time to hesitate and there has never been a historian who doubted so little.

Politics reinforced the same habit. In politics there can only be one of two answers – Yes or No, For or Against. As an historian, too, Macaulay always chose his lobby and stuck to it. The complexity of history is very different. Time and

55

again the evidence does not allow us to make a firm conclusion and even when it does, we cannot say that one side was right and the other wrong – the two sides were merely different. We cannot even say that there were two sides. Parties and sects shade into each other, and the historian who is trying to recapture the past must often leave his reader with an impression of muddle and confusion. Macaulay never did this. He was always cocksure. He never doubted what had happened or which side was in the right. His characters were all drawn in black and white, the good very good, the bad very bad. Those who are not bad but whom Macaulay does not like turn out to be very silly. James II and those who supported him were villains; William III and the Whigs were enlightened statesmen who could do no wrong. This is, to say the least, a very simple view of human nature. But then Macaulay had a very simple outlook. He thought that the England in which he lived – the England of the Reform Bill – was as nearly perfect as a country could be. Therefore he found no difficulty in judging the past. The people and events that had helped to produce early Victorian England were in the right of it. Everyone else had gone off the rails. This 'Whig interpretation of history' comes in for a good deal of criticism nowadays, and it is suggested that Macaulay and his school only picked out the bits of history that suited their doctrine. As a matter of fact, all historians do that, and the most dangerous are the ones who do not realize how selective they are.

In any case I am not sure that Macaulay and the Whig view of history were all that mistaken. He thought that the British constitution was a unique display of political genius. But wasn't it? The revolution of 1688 was truly a Glorious Revolution. George Orwell once pointed out that in this country we do not kill each other for political reasons. Is there any other great community where this has ever been true? Those who criticize Macaulay either do not care about liberty or they think that it can take care of itself. Macaulay was a good deal more sensible. Not only did he regard liberty as supremely important; he knew that it needs ceaseless defending. In recent years we have had a number of books on the eighteenth century which assume that profit and jobbery were the only things the Whigs cared about. They certainly cared about them a good deal, but I think that they also cared about parliamentary rights and the liberty of the subject. The father of Charles James Fox was the most corrupt of eighteenth-century politicians. It is more important that he himself was the founder of modern Liberalism. If men are to have a hero, it is better to find him in William the Deliverer than in Frederick the Great, though no one would have been more surprised than William III himself at this heroic role.

Macaulay's views did not make him a great historian. His unrivalled gift was his power of narration. No one ever told a story better. Tastes have changed. Now we want analysis, not narrative – what made things happen, not the record of events. You can see it even in our attitude to what goes on from day to day. We give a glance at the headlines, and then turn to the centre of the paper for the explanation. The great figures of journalism now are commentators, not reporters. And the historian, too, is expected to give us 'the low-down'. Macaulay does not; he gives us drama, sometimes unreal drama. He had lived too long in the political world. When he came to write of the past he was still present as a participant. He felt again the excitement of the great debates, knew afresh the importance of the great decisions. Everything he wrote tingled with life, but the life was artificial. The member of Parliament has to believe that the destiny of future genera-tions depends upon his vote; the historian acknowledges this belief but knows that it is not true. The politician performs upon the stage; the historian looks behind the scenery. Macaulay often forgot that the scenery was not real even when he had painted it himself.

This is why Macaulay never got inside his characters. For

him they were simply actors on the political stage. He did not attempt to read their minds. He ignored religion. This is extraordinary when you reflect that the great struggle of the seventeenth century was even more a struggle between Anglicanism and Dissent and between Protestantism and Roman Catholicism than between king and parliament. It never crossed Macaulay's mind that any honest man could be a Roman Catholic; therefore James II and his supporters were stupid and wicked. Nor did he inquire into the social and economic background of his characters – except to remark that the Tories were ignorant. You would not be aware from his History that the great Whigs were great landowners, yet it surely makes a considerable difference to a man when he owns thousands of acres. Certainly he tried to show how people lived as well as how they acted. But for him as for his great-nephew, G M Trevelyan, social history was 'history with the politics left out' – agreeable anecdotes, not the essential foundation which gives shape to everything else. It is an odd view that the way you make your money or the size of your family does not matter politically, and equally odd that a seat in parliament has no social importance. In short, what Macaulay did incomparably well was to write the political history of the governing class.

In this, as in everything else, Carlyle was Macaulay's opposite. He was the greatest master of English prose to spring from the people. This does not mean that he admired the people or got on with them. He despised the class to which he belonged and ran after Lady Ashburton as eagerly as D H Lawrence, his twentieth-century equivalent, cultivated Lady Ottoline Morell. Yet there was no escaping his origins. Though he called Christianity 'Hebrew Old Clothes' and railed against 'the multitudinous *canaille*', he remained a Scotch Calvinist with a stonemason for his father. His style is like nothing else in English. Carlyle acquired it by translating Goethe, and his writing is, in fact, German put into

English word for word. If put back into German, it appears simple and unaffected. It sheds a quaint light on the two languages that Goethe, the most classical of German writers, should have inspired the most uncouth writer of English. Carlyle did not learn ideas from Goethe as well as style. His ideas are those of a man of the people who has suddenly become articulate – if only in Anglo-German: ideas spluttering and half-formed, ideas of revolt and rejection with nothing constructive to follow, but rooted in humanity, not in class feeling or good taste.

Carlyle sensed the masses as no other writer has done. He expressed their outlook, against his own conscious convictions. He was shaped in the turbulent years when the masses of England straightened their backs and shook off respect, the great age of the Chartists. Carlyle had all the Chartist hatred of privilege, their contempt for 'the grouse-shooting aristocracy'. He knew what was at stake in 'the Condition-of-England question'. But when Chartism really stirred, Carlyle backed away. He should have been the greatest of Chartists. Instead he went sour. Betrayal is too common to need an explanation, but few have paid so high a penalty. Emerson once asked an anti-slavery agitator in prison: 'Friend, why art thou here?' The other answered: 'Why art thou not here?' The question rang through Carlyle's mind. Why was he not there? All his writings sprang from the goad of this question. To escape self-reproach, he had to reproach all the world. Too Calvinist to turn Roman Catholic, he set up as a self-made Jehovah, thundering out more violent commandments. Like the Hebrew prophets, he preached woe. He defended slavery and preached the worship of Force. He ran round the world looking for a Hero and found some odd ones. He called Bismarck 'a magnanimous, noble and deep-seeing Man', and wanted Sir Garnet Wolseley to shut up the House of Commons, sword in hand. He wasted years of his life trying to make a hero out of Frederick II of Prussia – as perverse a task as was ever attempted. He anticipated every trick of the twentieth-century demagogue – prejudice against negroes and Jews, admiration of the Germans. The abolitionists were 'rabid Nigger-Philanthropists'; Heine 'a slimy and greasy Jew'. The 'hopefulest public fact' in his time was that 'noble, patient, deep, pious and solid Germany' had become Queen of the Continent instead of 'vaporing, restless and over-sensitive France'. The Victorians, themselves full of doubt, enjoyed his reproaches and imagined that his strenuous exhortations had a concealed message. Even Huxley supposed that he had learnt from Carlyle to work harder.

In reality Carlyle spent his life denouncing the things that he himself did well. He despised writers, particularly of long books; no one wrote longer. He admired toil, honest work; he did none. He never handled a spade; he was not horny-handed. He preached the virtues of a humble, obscure existence, far from towns and factory chimneys. He won fame and wealth by writing successful books for rich industrialists. The rage in his books is rage against himself. The hero that he worshipped was his own opposite – silent, imperturbable, a man of action; and his praise of force was a protest against his own impotence – his social impotence, not the unsatisfactory sexual relations with his wife which everyone inquires into so eagerly nowadays. This conflict made Carlyle an unhappy man, but it made him a revolutionary writer. You do not read his books; you experience them, and what you experience in them is the storm of the world. He was a nihilist, a destroyer, despite his doctrine of toil and the heroic virtues. He once found a perfect subject, the French Revolution. That really was the end of a world, and Carlyle wrote of it like a man possessed. There is little narrative; a great many inaccuracies; none of that simplifying that we expect from the ordinary historian. Though he worked hard before he wrote it, he did not even keep up with the scholarship of his time, and Darwin was no doubt right when he said: 'As far as I could judge, I never met a man with a mind so ill adapted for scientific research.' No matter, The French Revolution is the only work in which the past is not merely narrated, but re-created. Carlyle has no gift for historical movement; he never describes how one situation developed into another. There is the lightning flash of genius, in which every detail stands out to remain vivid in the memory for ever. And, after it, new darkness, until broken by another vivid flash. The French Revolution is the most frightening of all works of history; and Carlyle was as frightened as any of his readers. He had meant to escape from Chartism into history; instead he found a Terror worse than before.

It needed the end of a world to find a use for Carlyle's gifts. There is nothing more impressive than the prophet who comes off; nothing more absurd than the prophet who does not. And for most of the time Carlyle did not come off. The world he lived in was not coming to an end. It was not being ruined by democracy and materialism. On the contrary, it was becoming more sensible, more tolerant, a better place to live in – and no thanks to Carlyle. He was a seer and a visionary, an iconoclast and a revolutionary. He exposed pretences, weighed everything anew. Macaulay was a man of commonplace mind, complacent, ordinary in everything except in his knowledge and his gift for writing. Yet Macaulay judged more wisely than Carlyle – had a better scale of values in the present, looked more accurately into the future. And we do not need to puzzle for an explanation. Macaulay had a talisman to guide him: his belief in liberty. He made liberty the theme of all his writing and looked forward to a time when everybody would care for it as he and his friends at Holland House did. Carlyle regarded liberty as an aristocratic fad which would be blown away when the people came into their own. Liberty is indeed the touchstone of every man's career. Do you respect the judgements of others as much as your own? Or are you so confident of your own judgement

that you would trample that of everyone else under foot?
Macaulay gave the answer for liberty, Carlyle for tyranny.
The worse cause had the more powerful advocate. All the
same, it was the worse cause.

8. Queen Victoria and the Constitution

Manchester Guardian. Written for the fiftieth anniversary
of Queen Victoria's death.

A monarch who occupies the throne for fifty or sixty years
becomes inevitably a symbol of stability, and at the end of his
or her death an age seems to end. So it was long foretold that
the Habsburg monarchy would not survive the death of
Francis Joseph; so Mrs Arbuthnot felt that the old world had
passed away with the death of George III, even though he had
been hopelessly insane for nine years; so, most of all, the
Victorian age was universally felt to end on 22 January 1901.
It is easy to agree that the symbolic character of the British
Crown was greatly strengthened during the reign of Queen
Victoria, especially in relation to the self-governing dominions; it is more difficult to assess the individual behind the
symbol. Yet the crown is not just a symbol in the British
constitution; it plays an individual and sometimes a decisive
part.

The reputation of Queen Victoria has known some sharp
vicissitudes since her death fifty years ago. At the time of her
death, and indeed for many years before it, she was popularly
regarded as the perfect constitutional sovereign, discharging
with impartiality the tasks defined by Bagehot: 'To advise, to
encourage, and to warn.' The publication of her letters, which
began in 1907, revealed a different picture of a sovereign more
active and more partisan than had been supposed. The first

series, which ran to 1861, was edited with an excess of tact, and it needed the genius of Lytton Strachey to bring them to life. The later volumes were increasingly frank and there was little left of the impartial queen when readers learnt of her ceaseless conflicts with Gladstone or of her intrigues with the leader of the Opposition to overthrow the Liberal Government in 1893.

Historical authorities of the Left, such as Harold Laski and Berriedale Keith, spoke sternly of her unconstitutional actions. The phrase seems meaningless : in our flexible system any practice is constitutional which is tolerated by contemporaries, and these authorities, to adapt a phrase of Romney Sedgwick's, were condemning Queen Victoria for acting like George III when she should have been acting like George VI. It is more important for the historian to discover what Queen Victoria did than to condemn her for doing it, and we have enough material to form an estimate for her position in constitutional history, though the royal archives at Windsor will no doubt reveal more.

The essential prerogative of the British Crown is the appointment of the prime minister, and this was exercised as a matter of personal choice by the four Georges and even by William IV. The great Reform Bill itself owed its origin to the fact that William IV preferred Lord Grey as prime minister, not to any violent swing of public opinion. Queen Victoria meant to continue the same system and regarded Melbourne as her personal appointment. The general election of 1841 marked an epoch in British history; in Croker's words, 'For the first time the people chose the First Minister for the Sovereign.' Peel, a Conservative, managed to perform the feat that had been beyond all the great Whigs of the eighteenth century and 'forced the closet'. The last Government to be brought into existence by the independent initiative of the Crown was Aberdeen's coalition of 1852, and royal favour could not sustain it against the stresses of the Crimean War.

Thereafter, as party feeling solidified, the Crown could occasionally choose between individuals but no longer between parties. The essential condition here was rigid party organization. When this weakened or broke down initiative returned to the Crown. It was not unreasonable for Queen Victoria to suppose in 1886 that, with the split in the Liberal party, it was her duty to promote a Unionist coalition rather than to let Home Rule be carried by a minority Government. George V certainly did not take the advice of the outgoing prime minister when he appointed Lloyd George to succeed Asquith in December 1916; he acted, as his ancestors had done, according to his independent judgement of what would be best in the national interest.

In 1940 Neville Chamberlain advised George VI to send for Mr Churchill; but this advice was tendered at the king's request, and the subsequent discussion between Chamberlain, Churchill and Halifax was an informal meeting between friends, not of ministers formally advising the Crown. The old Whigs sometimes dreamt of turning the Cabinet into an autonomous body which should elect its own head. This was not what happened in 1940. The king retained the initiative; only, being anxious to save time in view of the military crisis in France, he himself asked for Chamberlain's opinion, instead of leaving inquiries to his private secretary, and Chamberlain gave his opinion as leader of the Conservative party, not as outgoing prime minister.

Queen Victoria also refused to accept certain individuals as Cabinet ministers. Sometimes she objected to their views, more usually she was offended by their having opposed the grants to her sons and daughters – an intrusion of maternity into politics. George V excluded Lansbury from the first Labour government, and George VI is said to have intervened in Cabinet-making on one occasion. But this was influence rather than prerogative. It has been used discreetly, and there is no doubt that the prime minister can get the Cabinet of his choice if he insists on it.

It seems clear that the Prince Consort early foresaw the approaching change in the British system and intended the Crown to exert its influence on policy rather than on personalities. Disraeli indeed said that if the Prince Consort had survived 'we should have enjoyed the blessings of absolute monarchy': all he meant by this was that the Crown would have made an independent contribution to policy, as it has done in other constitutional monarchies, successfully in Sweden, less successfully in Belgium. This is probably the greatest importance of Queen Victoria's reign: the Crown failed to establish its claim to a share in policy-making. After the death of the Prince Consort, Queen Victoria was at first too withdrawn and then too erratic in her interventions to count for anything.

One of the greatest legends of our recent history is that the queen's favour was an advantage to Disraeli. He enjoyed flattering elderly ladies and got this pleasure in high degree from his relations with the queen; apart from this, her criticisms were as much trouble to him as they were to Gladstone or to Lord Salisbury. Dr Hammond preserved a tradition from Gladstone's last Government that the prime minister would open almost every Cabinet meeting by saying, 'Gentlemen, I have a message from the Queen.' He would then read a letter full of violent criticism and complaint. At the end he would fold the letter and put it back in his pocket; there would be a short silence; then the old man would exclaim, 'And now gentlemen, to business.' This, in fact, is all that the queen's influence amounted to. There is nothing to suggest that Home Rule would have been carried if she had been as strongly in its favour as she was against, nor would the queen's support have made the Liberal Government of 1892–5 anything other than a collection of warring elements.

The system envisaged by the Prince Consort demanded a ruler who should be intelligent as well as industrious; this was beyond Queen Victoria. While the Prince Consort lived all the greatest figures of the age were to be found at Court – artists, scientists, philosophers, novelists; after 1861, the Court became the centre of society in the formal sense and has so remained. A woman on the throne must always find it difficult to establish personal contacts with her subjects, and Queen Victoria did not make the attempt. Moreover the reign of a woman always involves a decline in the power of the crown. The reign of Queen Elizabeth, in spite of Mr Rowse, is no exception to the rule. English history would have been very different if Edward VI, instead of Elizabeth, had reigned for fifty-five years.

Queen Victoria did not by any means intend to create a new type of monarchy. To adapt Romney Sedgwick again, she tried to carry on the system inherited from her grandfather to the best of her limited ability. These very limitations made it easier, as well as more necessary, for statesmen to exclude her from the practical workings of politics and the effect was completed when she was succeeded by a king too lazy, and too elderly, to make any serious attempt at recovering the lost ground. In short, our modern constitutional monarchy was devised by accident and much against the will of the queen who made it.

9. Lord John Russell

A talk given on the Third Programme of the BBC and then
published in The Listener.

Lord John Russell as prime minister, leading and inspiring a
Government, was not a success. Indeed, his Government of
1846 to 1852 was the ruin of the Whig party : it never composed a Government again, and his Government of 1865 to
1866, which might be described as the first Liberal Government, was very nearly the ruin of the Liberal party also. He
was certainly not a great leader : he was not 'outsize' – I do
not mean in stature, though he was tiny, I mean in character.
He was not more than life-size as really great political figures
are – Gladstone, for instance. He spoke aridly, with a dry
pedantic voice, and made no effort to win the affection of his
followers. He was the first prime minister not to take direct
personal responsibility for the public finances, and the
finances of his government (it was their worst feature) were
always rickety – like those of a spendthrift Whig peer. He
was too sensitive, too, to be a successful politician, so upset by
the criticisms of his diplomatic muddles during the Crimean
war that he had to take to buying land as a distraction. He
had too much pride to get on with his fellows : pride of the
House of Russell, of being a son of the sixth Duke of Bedford,
pride also at having a better intellect and a better education
than most politicians. Still, these are both things worth being
proud of, and they are the things which give Russell his place
in history.

His life spanned the change from aristocratic to middle-
class England, from the England of broad acres to the England
of factory chimneys. Russell was the man of the transition,
the link between the old order and the new, belonging to the

old order by birth, carried over to the new order by his ideas. He was the last great Whig; he became the first Liberal. Russell, more than any other single man, created the Victorian compromise; he made the England that we know, or knew rather, the England that is vanishing before our eyes.

The unique thing in our political history is the way that we have been able to carry through great changes without violent revolution, going fast enough (just) to satisfy rising social classes without driving the possessing classes into open resistance. Someone has just ascertained that a third of the members of the present House of Commons are the sons of manual labourers; a little more than a hundred years ago five members of parliament out of six were landowners – that is the measure of our revolution. The symbol of that revolution was the reform of parliament in 1832. The Reform Bill does not look much in itself: the vote was still limited to quite a small electorate, and the House of Commons remained much as it had been before – in fact, for some years, there were rather more aristocrats and landowners in it. But the Reform Bill was a promise, a guarantee that the constitution would not be treated as something rigid and fixed for ever but as a set of habits which would change as public opinion changed. The Reform Bill was not intended to prepare the way for democracy; indeed, its purpose was to win over the prosperous middle classes to the side of the governing order and so bar the way against democracy, the rule of the people. Russell, its principal architect, defended it for years as a final settlement and opposed, for instance, the radical demands of the Chartists. All the same, it was the vital and decisive concession which set the pattern for the political changes which have followed. Russell himself, in 1866, at the end of his political life, started the discussions for the second Reform Bill, which granted household suffrage in the towns – and so accepted the principle of democracy.

I have called Russell the principal architect of the Reform

Lord John Russell

Bill. That is true in the sense that, although a junior minister without a seat in the Cabinet, he was one of the three who drafted the original Bill in 1831 and also in the sense that he was chosen to introduce the Bill into the House of Commons. It is true in a deeper sense that Russell, more than any other, represented the willingness of the great Whig families to surrender their position of privilege in the state. No, that is wrong: they thought that the more they surrendered of their legal privileges the more their claim to political pre-eminence would be recognized. Russell himself never forgot that he was a member of one of the greatest ducal families and, I dare say, ranked the House of Russell higher than most royalty. When, as a young man, he visited Napoleon on the Island of Elba, they discussed these topics in order of their importance; the political influence of the Duke of Bedford; the allowance which the Duke paid to his son; and third, the condition of France and Italy. Despite his own intellectual ability, he never supposed that ability was a qualification for office – look at the colleagues he chose for his government in 1846. Long after the Reform Bill, Russell never imagined that high office would cease to be a monopoly of the Russells and Cavendishes and Stanleys, the 'Venetian oligarchy' which Disraeli wrongly supposed to have existed in the eighteenth century, but which really existed in the early reign of Victoria.

All the same, and this was his redeeming quality, Russell believed in liberty. No doubt he regarded this, too, as a sort of family property. He never forgot that Lord William Russell, who was the founder of the family greatness and whose life he wrote, had died on the scaffold for conspiring against Charles II; for the sake of this ancestor, Russell, too, had to be on the side of radicals and rebels. The ideas of the Glorious Revolution of 1688 were still to Russell living ideas, and the guiding idea of 1688 was certainly liberty. Liberty meant then – and often still meant to Russell – the liberty of the property owner to do what he liked with his property, but it had been justified by appealing to the will of the people and therefore when a popular cause arose, Russell, despite his whiggish narrowness, had to come down on the popular side. Russell took the lead in turning the Whigs into political reformers. The results of these reforms, as we see them today, would often have surprised him. But if you ask why there are still dukes, why there is still a House of Lords and why we still listen, sometimes with respect and always with patience, to the opinions of members of the House of Russell, the answer is: Lord John Russell and his devotion, in his own phrase, to 'the cause of civil and religious liberty all over the world'.

Russell led the Whigs in their conversion to reform; he was not, though, the only reformer among the Whigs. In a different sphere of public affairs he took the lead more on his own: he was, I think, the link between the governing classes and the new economic idea of individualism, of *laissez-faire*. Two tremendous changes took place in England in Russell's lifetime. One was the political change. The other was a change in economic outlook, which cleared the way for the fabulous prosperity of this country later in the nineteenth century: the change from the traditional pattern of life in which every man had his allotted place in society:

> The rich man in his castle
> The poor man at his gate
> He made them high and lowly
> And ordered their estate,

a society in which even the poorest had some sort of assured existence, the change from this to the view that men were 'hands', that their labour was a commodity, the price of which (like any other commodity) should be determined by the law of supply and demand. This was the great revolutionary discovery of the early nineteenth century: that there were so-called natural economic laws (actually extremely unnatural) and that the only job of government was to get out of the way and let these laws work. Everything, even human beings, had to be subordinated to the 'price mechanism', that terrible Moloch to which old-fashioned economists still bow down. We do not care for the 'law of the market' now that it has become the 'American way of life'; it looks too much like the law of the jungle. But in its day it was a tremendous instrument of progress. In fact, as a result of it, human productivity increased more in a century than in all the rest of recorded history.

It is easy to trace the growth of these new ideas in writers and thinkers, not so easy to see how they were translated into practice. It was a bigger question than merely Free Trade – the part of the change which Peel came to understand. It was the transformation of the whole of social life. Russell was the only member of the ruling classes, the only man in really high office, who understood what Bentham and the economists were driving at. He had been educated : instead of going to Cambridge, where he might have learnt a little mathematics (and that would have done his finances, private and public, no harm), or to Oxford where he could have learnt only theology and classics, the two most useless studies known to man – instead he went to Edinburgh and learnt economics and political theory.

Later in life he was a friend of Nassau Senior, the leading orthodox economist of the day, and swallowed his doctrines open-mouthed, as recently our rulers tried to keep up with every flash of Keynes's nimble brain. Therefore it was no accident that Russell introduced the new Poor Law in 1834, the most revolutionary economic measure of the early nineteenth century. The new Poor Law swept away the old principle of the right to work or maintenance, the idea that society had some responsibility for its members; it substituted the idea that men must be driven to work by hunger – the basic idea without which capitalism will not work. We are trying to work capitalism without it now; hence all our present troubles. The new Poor Law and all that it implied – treating human beings as individuals who must struggle for themselves or else succumb – all this was Russell's work. He showed this in his attitude to the Irish Famine of 1846, which took place when he was prime minister. Russell was a tenderhearted man and was made wretched by the thought of all the suffering of the Irish, but he set his face against any measure of relief which would interfere with the workings of natural economic law. He was the man who translated the theories of the economists into practice.

Russell himself would have added other claims to fame. He attached great importance to his fight for religious freedom, by which he meant, to put it crudely, keeping the churches in their place, a very subordinate place. His own religion was a vague benevolent Deism and he had no patience with deep religious feelings. He made a famous reply to a Dean of Hereford who had scruples against electing as Bishop someone whom Russell had nominated: 'Dear Sir, I have received your letter in which you inform me of your intention to break the law.' The most popular act of his life was not the Reform Bill, but the Ecclesiastical Titles Bill of 1851, which forbade Roman Catholic bishops to take territorial titles of places in England – an odd way of defending religious liberty. Even odder, the last public act of this soldier of liberty was to congratulate Bismarck on his campaign against the Roman Catholic Church in Germany. In fact Russell was a Protestant, in the sense of being hostile to the Church of Rome, but not a Christian; a combination formerly common, though now, I think, extinct.

Russell was proud, too, of his record as foreign secretary between 1859 and 1865, when Palmerston was prime minister. He had objected to Palmerston's wildness, when he had been prime minister and Palmerston foreign secretary. Curiously enough, Russell was much wilder when the roles were reversed. Russell's stock-in-trade as foreign secretary was the hectoring lecturing dispatch, when he told foreign rulers the awful things that would happen to them if they did not follow the British constitutional pattern. He lectured the Tsar on how to govern Poland; he lectured the Emperor of Austria on the way to treat Hungary; he lectured Bismarck for daring to attack Denmark; he lectured the United States for having a civil war; he lectured the whole of Europe on the virtues of Italian Nationalism. In fact he started the tradition that it is part of the duty of a British foreign secretary to tell other countries how to run their affairs. Russell never followed up his lectures with any kind of action; he thought it would be quite enough to threaten tsars and emperors with his displeasure, the displeasure of a member of the House of Russell. He only succeeded in bringing the name of Great Britain into contempt. Still, if only these rulers had listened, Russell, in his pedantic way, had something to tell them: this country had hit on the secret of making great social and political changes without revolution, and it was Russell who had shown how the trick was done.

10. Genocide

New Statesman. A review of The Great Hunger by
Cecil Woodham-Smith (1962).

When British forces entered the so-called 'convalescent camp' at Belsen in 1945, they found a scene of indescribable horror: the wasted bodies of 50,000 human beings who had died from starvation and disease. Kramer, 'the beast of Belsen', and his assistants were hanged for this atrocious crime. Only a century before, all Ireland was a Belsen. Nearly two million Irish people died of starvation and fever within five years; another million fled, carrying disease to Liverpool and the New World.

The story can be told in general terms, presenting the famine as a natural catastrophe like an earthquake. The population of Ireland had greatly increased in the preceding years – why, no one knows. Most of the people depended almost exclusively on the potato. In 1845 potato blight arrived, apparently from America. It was a fungus that rotted first the plants and then the potatoes in the clamps. A run of wet summers helped the spread of the blight. The potato harvest failed four years running. The Irish peasants had no reserves to fall back on. Many of their landlords were harsh; some almost as impoverished as their peasants – though it is not recorded that any landlord died of starvation. It all happened because it had to happen.

This is how historians usually treat the past. We explain, and with that our duty is finished. The dead are dead. They have become so many figures in a notebook. But they were once human beings, and other human beings sent them to their death. The blight was 'natural'; the failure of the potato crop was 'natural'. After that, men played a part. There was food available to save the Irish people from starvation. It was denied them. Nor did Ireland stand alone. Ireland was at this time part of the United Kingdom, the wealthiest country in the world. The British Government had insisted on under-taking responsibility for Ireland. When crisis arose, they ran away from it. The men in Whitehall were usually of humane disposition and the bearers of honoured names: Lord John Russell; Sir Charles Wood, later first Viscount Halifax; Sir Charles Trevelyan. These men, too, were in a sense victims. They were gripped by the most horrible, and perhaps the most universal, of human maladies: the belief that principles and doctrines are more important than lives. They imagined that rules, invented by economists, were as 'natural' as the potato blight. Trevelyan, who did most to determine events, always wanted to leave Ireland to 'the operation of natural causes'. He refused to recognize that only the gigantic operation of an artificial cause – the exertion of British power – prevented the Irish people from adopting the natural remedy and eating the food which was available for them. Like most members of the comfortable classes of all times, he regarded the police and the law courts as natural phenomena.

Mrs Woodham-Smith in her most admirable and thorough book writes : 'The 1840s must not be judged by the standards of today.' Of course she is right, even though she goes on to judge, and to condemn, the British Government. Russell, Wood and Trevelyan were highly conscientious men, and their consciences never reproached them. Nor are the standards of today much to rely on. The British rulers of the 1840s were no worse than those who later sent millions of men to their deaths in two world wars; no worse than those who now plan to blow all mankind to pieces for the sake of some principle or other. But they were also no better. Though they killed only two million Irish people, this was not for want of trying. Jowett once said :

I have always felt a certain horror of political economists since I heard one of them say that the famine in Ireland would not kill more than a million people, and that would scarcely be enough to do much good.

The successors of these economists are the same in spirit. They preach the virtue of a little healthy unemployment, and do not rely on the whip of starvation only because it has been taken from their hands. If the particular crime committed in Ireland a century ago could not happen now, it is not because present-day statesmen are an improvement on their predecessors. It is because the common conscience of mankind no longer allows statesmen to live up to their principles.

Here was the peculiar tragedy of the Irish famine. The common conscience failed to work, or at least did not work effectively. It is easy to understand how Trevelyan and the rest thought that they were doing their duty. They were handling human beings as ciphers on a bit of paper. They looked up the answers in a textbook of economics without ever once setting eyes on the living skeletons of the Irish people. They invented a distinction between those who were starving because of the potato blight and those starving from normal distress. They excused the Irish for being hit by the blight once. They condemned them for persisting in planting potatoes after blight appeared – as though the Irish could do anything else. Most of all, these enlightened men feared that the whole social structure would topple down if men and women were once given food which they could not pay for.

Not all Englishmen were enlightened in this way. This was already the England of good works, the England which emancipated the slaves and ended child labour, the England that repealed the Corn Laws and brought sanitation to the towns. The public conscience was in many ways more sensitive, quicker to respond, than it is now. It responded over Ireland, though not enough. The British Government did much when it was in the hands of Sir Robert Peel. They contributed the stupendous sum of £8 million to meet the first disaster of 1845, set up relief organizations and provided public works on a scale never attempted before. Peel's fall from office in 1846 was an additional disaster for Ireland. He was never one to confess impotence, and he might have been powerful enough to override even the principles of Sir Charles Trevelyan.

Official and private individuals in Ireland did all that men could do. Doctors died of fever. Administrators drove themselves to death and often provided relief out of their own pockets. Trevelyan complained that his Commissariat officers could 'bear anything but the ceaseless misery of the children'. The British Relief Association raised large sums, including £2,000 from Queen Victoria. The Society of Friends had a record of spotless honour, as it often does, when men are suffering. Quakers contributed money, ran their own system of relief, sacrificed their lives. All these efforts touched only the edge of the famine. Everything combined against the Irish people. Ignorance played a large part. Even capable Irish administrators did not grasp that there were no harbours on the west coast which could discharge cargoes of food. No enterprising newspaper correspondent described the horrors in Ireland for the English press as Russell was to describe the lesser horrors in the Crimea nine years later. Nearly all Englishmen regarded Ireland as an inferior version of England, inhabited by lazier and less efficient people. The Irish administrators themselves were bewildered that the problems of Ireland could not be somehow solved by the well-tried methods of the poor rate, boards of guardians and the workhouse test. In many districts there was no one to pay the poor rate or to sit on the board of guardians: most of the Irish would have regarded an English workhouse as a haven of luxury.

The ignorance was often wilful. Men make out that a problem does not exist when they do not know how to solve it. So it has been in all English dealings with Ireland. Again, the famine went on so long. English people, and even the British Government, were ready to do something for one hard season. They were exasperated out of their pity when the blight reappeared year after year. How were they to understand that the blight, hitherto unknown, would settle permanently in the soil and flourish every wet summer? It was easy to slip into the belief that the blight was the fault of the Irish themselves. They were a feckless people; the blight was worse in Ireland than in England; the self-righteous conclusion was obvious. English antagonism was not turned only against the Irish poor. Though the landlords are often supposed to have represented a common Anglo-Irish interest, Englishmen and their Government were as hostile to Irish landlords as to Irish peasants. At the height of the famine the full system of the English poor law was extended to Ireland. This was quite as much to make life unpleasant for the landlords as to benefit the starving. The Irish landlords were 'very much like slave holders with white slaves . . . they had done nothing but sit down and howl for English money'. Lord John Russell doubted whether 'taken as a whole the exertions of property for the relief of distress have been what they ought to have been'. The starving tenants could not pay their rent. Yet landlords were told to relieve them out of the rents which they could not pay. Some landlords were still prosperous. A few contributed honourably. Most did their duty by keeping up a sumptuous estate, which is what landlords are for.

The Irish people were driven off their land. They were starved, degraded, treated worse than animals. They lamented, they suffered, they died. Yet they made hardly an attempt at resistance. This is perhaps the most dreadful part of the story – a people allowing themselves to be murdered. Mrs Woodham-Smith suggests that the Irish were physically too weak to resist, that famine only gave a final push to their perpetual course of misery and want. Surely it was more than that. Centuries of English tyranny had destroyed Irish will and Irish confidence. O'Connell told the House of Commons in his last speech : 'Ireland is in your hands, in your power. If you do not save her, she cannot save herself.' The few political leaders in Ireland themselves accepted the economic doctrines of their conquerers. They demanded Repeal of the Union, not a reform of the landed system, and Repeal was the cause which brought Smith O'Brien to the widow McCormack's cabbage patch in his attempt at rebellion in 1848. This provided a farcical note at the end of the tragic story.

Yet not quite the end, which was more farcical still. The English governing class ran true to form. They had killed two million Irish people. They abused the Irish for disliking this. Lord John Russell said in 1848 :

We have subscribed, worked, visited, clothed, for the Irish, millions of money, years of debate, etc., etc., etc. The only return is rebellion and calumny.

Lastly, as a gesture of forgiveness no doubt by the British

Government for the crimes which they had committed in Ireland, royalty was trundled out. Queen Victoria and Prince Albert visited Ireland. They were received everywhere with great enthusiasm.

The famine did not end in Ireland. It was repeated year after year, sometimes in milder form. Natural causes did their work. The Society of Friends alone saw the condition of Ireland in its true light. In 1849 they refused to act any longer as a relief agency. Only the Government, they wrote, 'could carry out the measures necessary in many districts to save the lives of the people'. 'The condition of our country has not improved in spite of the great exertions made by charitable bodies.' It could not be improved until the land system of Ireland was reformed, which was a matter for legislation, not philanthropy. The British Government ignored the Quakers' advice. Nothing was done for Ireland until an embittered and more resolute generation of Irishmen acted for themselves.

11. *John Bright and the Crimean War*

This was first given as a lecture at the John Rylands Library, Manchester. The lecture was the only one I ever gave with a prepared script. It was an offshoot from The Struggle for Mastery in Europe 1848–1918. If I were to deliver the lecture again, I should be less critical of John Bright and more critical of British policy.

John Bright was the greatest of all parliamentary orators. He had many political successes. Along with Richard Cobden, he conducted the campaign which led to the repeal of the Corn Laws. He did more than any other man to prevent the intervention of this country on the side of the South during the American civil war, and he headed the reform agitation of 1867 which brought the industrial working class within the pale of the constitution. It was Bright who made possible the Liberal party of Gladstone, Asquith and Lloyd George, and the alliance between middle-class idealism and trade unionism, which he promoted, still lives in the present-day Labour party. Yet his noblest work, as certainly his greatest speeches, were made in a campaign which failed – a campaign which brought him much unpopularity and led finally to a mental collapse; his opposition to the Crimean war. His attitude caused him to lose his parliamentary seat at Manchester in 1857 and so severed his political connection with this city for ever. Bright blamed the merchant princes of Manchester for his defeat, and it is therefore especially fitting that we should look again at Bright's stand during the Crimean war on a foundation established to commemorate one of the greatest of these merchant princes.

I have personal reasons, too, for this gesture of atonement. At Bright's old school, where I was educated, there was an annual prize for a Bright oration, and I have heard his great speeches against the Crimean war recited a score of times in the school library which bears his name. I, in revolt as usual against my surroundings, sought only something to Bright's discredit and proposed to offer one of his speeches against the Factory Acts. But these were not included in his collected speeches, and I was not used, as I am now, to going through the columns of old Hansards. I therefore remained silent, and it is only now, thirty years later, that I come to repeat the greatest sentences ever uttered in any parliamentary assembly. I am not, however, concerned to defend Bright, much as I now admire him. I have also learnt to admire the diplomatic skill and judgement of 'the aged charlatan', Palmerston. Bright said of him :

I regard him as a man who has experience, but who with experience has not gained wisdom – as a man who has age, but who, with age, has not the gravity of age, and who, now occupying the highest seat of power, has – and I say it with pain – not appeared influenced by a due sense of the responsibility that belongs to that elevated position.

I do not think that any historian who has examined the record of Palmerston's foreign policy would now endorse that judgement, though he would still be struck by Palmerston's jocular self-confidence and even occasionally by his levity. It is my intention – and I can say in all sincerity that I did not know when I started how the conclusion would work out – to examine Bright's criticism of the Crimean war in the light of later events and of the more detailed knowledge which we now possess, rather than to vindicate or condemn him.

When I began this inquiry, I was struck and indeed surprised by the material for my theme. I have some experience of public agitation on issues of foreign policy. I have sat on committees for Aid to Spain and Czechoslovakia and for Anglo-Soviet friendship. I can remember vaguely the pacifist movement of the first world war. I expected to find the same hubbub of public meetings, pamphlets, letters to the press, articles in newspapers and periodicals, which serve as the undertone for debates in Parliament. Gladstone used all these weapons in his attacks on Disraeli's eastern policy only twenty years later. Indeed, he did better than we. He used to stick his head out of the railway carriage and address waiting crowds at every station he passed through. Here was Bright engaged in the greatest political conflict of his career, yet he used none of the means that we should think essential. He did not write a pamphlet. He did not address a single letter to the newspapers. He wrote one letter to Absalom Watkin, designed for publication and stating his case against the war, on 29 October 1854, when the war had already been raging for six months. He attended in all three public meetings, over a period of nearly two years, and all in Manchester. They were designed to explain his attitude to his constituents, not to appeal to public opinion. The first, held on 18 December 1854, was not organized by Bright, but to declare against him. Neither he nor his opponents could get a hearing. At the second, on 5 April 1855, he spoke for an hour. The third was held on 28 January 1856, after the peace preliminaries had been signed. Bright, speaking for two hours, defended his past conduct and collapsed at the end. Thus he made one public speech against the war while it was on, and this was to a limited audience.

We have therefore to look solely at Bright's speeches in the House of Commons. And here is another surprising thing. He never spoke against the war before it was declared. Let me refresh your memory with some dates. The diplomatic conflict between Russia and the Western Powers, Great Britain and France, began at Constantinople in May 1853. Russian forces occupied the mouth of the Danube in July. The allied fleets passed the Straits in October. They entered the Black Sea in December. Throughout all this time there are only two passing references to the crisis in Bright's diary, one at the end of May, one in July. In October he addressed a conference of the Peace Society, but mainly on generalities with little reference to immediate events. Early in 1854, the crisis grew graver; on 27 March war was declared. Again Bright remained silent. On 15 March he wrote a letter to Lord Aberdeen, the prime minister, not for publication, arguing in favour of peace. His first speech was on 31 March, four days after the declaration of war. It was a speech to clear his conscience, not to change the course of policy. 'I am unwilling to lose this opportunity ... of clearing myself from any portion of the responsibility which attaches to those who support the policy which the Government has adopted.' At the end, he strikes the same note:

For myself, I do not trouble myself whether my conduct in Parliament is popular or not. I care only that it shall be wise and just as regards the permanent interests of my country, and I despise from the bottom of my heart the man who speaks a word in favour of this war, or of any war which he believes might have been avoided, merely because the press and a portion of the people urge the Government to enter into it.

Bright did not speak again on the war until 22 December 1854. This speech, too, was vindication, not advocacy – vindication this time more of Cobden, who had been attacked by Lord John Russell, than of himself. And there is the same note of clearing his conscience :

Let it not be said that I am alone in my condemnation of this war, and of this incapable and guilty Administration. And, even if I were alone, if mine were a solitary voice, raised amid the din of arms and the clamour of a venal press, I should have the consolation I have tonight – and which I trust will be mine to the last moment of my existence – the priceless consolation that no word of mine has tended to promote the squandering of my country's treasure or the spilling of one single drop of my country's blood.

In February 1855, negotiations for peace – abortive, as it turned out – were opened at Vienna. On 22 February, Bright made a short speech, appealing for an immediate armistice if the negotiations showed promise of success. Though this speech contains his most celebrated oratorical passage – the Angel of Death has been abroad throughout the land – it had a practical aim, and for once Bright addressed both Palmerston and Lord John Russell in conciliatory, friendly terms. Finally, when the negotiations at Vienna had failed, Bright spoke again on 7 June. He argued that the proposed peace-terms would have been satisfactory and that there was no purpose in continuing the war. But this time he did not merely protest or clear his conscience. He appealed to the House to revolt against Palmerston's government and against the bellicose press :

If every man in this House, who doubts the policy that is being pursued, would boldly say so in this House and out of it, it would not be in the power of the press to mislead the people as it has done for the last twelve months . . . We are the depositaries of the power and the guardians of the interests of a great nation and of an ancient monarchy. Why should we not fully measure our responsibility? Why should we not disregard the small-minded ambition that struggles for place? and why should we not, by a faithful, just, and earnest policy, restore, as I believe we may, tranquillity to Europe and prosperity to the country so dear to us?

Thus Bright spoke in all only four times on the war in a period of nearly two years. Only his first speech and his letter to Absalom Watkin stated his case against the war at length. Indeed we may say that his reputation as an opponent of the war was gained as much by silent and sustained disapproval as by his speeches. Before I discuss his criticism of the war, I should like to turn aside for a moment to consider why Bright was relatively so inactive – so much more silent, for example, than at the time of the American civil war a few years later. In part, he felt it hopeless to contend against the war-fever of the press. Cobden felt this even more strongly. He said in 1862:

I was so convinced of the utter uselessness of raising one's voice in opposition to war when it has once begun, that I made up my mind that so long as I was in political life, should a war again break out between England and a great Power, I would never open my mouth upon the subject from the time the first gun was fired until the peace was made.

This is a surprising tribute to the power of the press, the more surprising when one reflects that the total newspaper-reading public in England did not at that time number 100,000. Perhaps this is itself the explanation. In 1854 Bright sat for a middle-class constituency and thought only of his middle-class voters. His only public speech was an explanation to his constituents, not a general appeal. After 1858, when he sat for Birmingham, he addressed himself to working-class opinion, regardless either of the middle-class voters or the middle-class press. Indeed, it was the Crimean war which helped to set Bright on the democratic path. To adapt George

III's remark to William Pitt, it taught him to look elsewhere than the House of Commons, or even the electorate, for the will of the people.

Of course, this was not new to Bright. He was always more of a man of the people than Cobden. Cobden lived in Sussex, a failure as a businessman. Bright never moved from Rochdale, next door to his mill. Their paths diverged after the repeal of the Corn Laws. Free Trade had always been an international cause for Cobden – witness his triumphal tour of Europe in 1846 – and he went on to preach international arbitration and disarmament. Bright had been interested in the practical issue of cheap bread, and he turned from Free Trade to Parliamentary Reform – a course of which Cobden disapproved. This led Bright largely to ignore foreign affairs. It is no accident that Cobden spoke in the great Don Pacifico debate in 1850 and Bright did not – it was not his subject.

The early Radicals thought in terms of criticizing the established government, not of superseding it. Witness again Cobden's remark that he could have had a great career in the United States, but that it was useless for him to harbour ambition in aristocratic England. Bright and Cobden assumed that England was fated to endure aristocratic misrule for many years – Cobden supposed at least during his lifetime. Bright gradually moved to the more constructive position that aristocratic rule could be ended and democracy take its place. His last Crimean war speech contains a first statement of this new attitude. Yet, even now, it was the promise of a political leader of the right views from within the closed circle which gave him greater hope. This leader was Gladstone, after his resignation from Palmerston's government at the beginning of 1855. Here was the first hint of the alliance between Gladstone and Bright which triumphed in 1868 – an alliance in which Gladstone was the statesman and Bright the agitator.

Bright therefore learnt his way slowly in foreign affairs, beginning with a few radical prejudices and gradually examining the practical issues. Observe: I do not say Quaker prejudices. Though Bright spoke often – as anyone would – of the horrors and bloodshed of war, he never used pacifist arguments against it. Indeed, he was not a pacifist. He supported the forcible suppression of the Indian mutiny. He urged the North to continue the American civil war to decisive victory, when even Cobden favoured compromise. Bright doubted, I think, the relevance of Quakerism to public life. Dr Trevelyan remarks casually that Bright never spoke in Meeting, but draws no moral from it. Perhaps only someone of Quaker stock and upbringing can appreciate its significance. The Society of Friends was still 'quietist', concerned with the inner light, not with social duty, and, in addition, there was a distinction between 'ministers' and other members of the Society which has now almost disappeared. I do not say that Bright ever ceased to regard himself as a full member of the Society; but he thought that, by entering politics, he had made himself the humblest of members and, conversely, he kept Quakerism out of his politics. Or rather, though he kept out Quaker principles, he used Quaker methods. His speeches, for all their oratory, rely on fact and argument as much as on emotional appeal. As Bright said in answer to Palmerston: 'I am not afraid of discussing the war with the noble Lord on his own principles. I understand the Blue Books as well as he' – a claim that was fully justified.

Though Bright did not condemn war from pacificism, he certainly condemned it on grounds of economy. His Crimean war speeches all speak of the disturbance to trade and the increase of taxes. He has often been blamed for this. Tennyson wrote at the time of

> The broad-brimmed hawker of holy things,
> Whose ear is cramm'd with his cotton, and rings
> Even in dreams to the chink of his pence.

I should add, in fairness to Tennyson, that there is much

other internal evidence in 'Maud' to suggest that the hero, or narrator, of it was mad. Sir Llewellyn Woodward, who refers to 'the prosy and, at times, repellent religiosity of his letters and diaries', discredits Bright with the comic quotation : 'Our carpet trade grievously injured by war raising the price of tow.' Sir Llewellyn Woodward, I suspect, had heard that Bright was in the cotton trade and did not appreciate that John Bright and Bros. manufactured carpets, as they still do. What therefore more natural than that he should make a business note in his private diary? Bright showed during the American civil war that he could rise above arguments addressed to his economic interests or those of Lancashire. The story of Bright's commercialism, which brings together not only Tennyson and Sir Llewellyn Woodward but such strange companions as Palmerston and Karl Marx. springs largely – as Bright himself said – from the inability to answer his more serious arguments.

In any case, it is well to bear in mind the composition of the House of Commons, in which Bright delivered his speeches. Neither of the two great parties – the Conservatives under Disraeli and the Whigs led, if that is not too dignified a term, by Lord John Russell – had a majority. The balance was held by the Peelites – the remnant of those Conservatives who had followed Peel over Free Trade in 1846 – and the radicals. These last two had much in common so far as economic doctrine was concerned, despite their difference of social background. The Government of Lord Aberdeen, which began the Crimean war, was a coalition of Peelites and Whigs, with one radical member, Molesworth, and possessing radical support. Palmerston's Government, which took its place in 1855, was Whig and radical, the Peelites in uneasy and discredited neutrality. To whom then was Bright to appeal, if he was to achieve a practical effect at all? Not to the Conservatives. For, though they claimed to oppose Palmerston, Bright had an incurable distrust of Disraeli. Remember his reply when

Disraeli said to him after the 'Angel of Death' speech: 'I would give all I ever had to have made that speech you made just now.' 'Well, you might have made it if you had been honest.' He could not appeal to the Whigs. He regarded Russell and Palmerston as the principal authors of the war and directed his main arguments against the Whig doctrine of the Balance of Power. Besides, the Whigs had a long record of frivolity and incapacity in regard to finance.

Hence, his practical object was to persuade the Peelites and radicals to take advantage of their balancing position. They could bring the Whigs to heel if they wished to do so. His economic arguments were designed for the Peelites, as were his recollections of Peel himself. 'I recollect when Sir Robert Peel addressed the House on a dispute which threatened hostilities with the United States – I recollect the gravity of his countenance, the solemnity of his tone, his whole demeanour showing that he felt in his soul the responsibility that rested on him.' This appeal certainly had its effect on Gladstone, particularly after his resignation from office in February 1855. But Bright had to appeal especially to the radicals and Free Trade liberals – his former allies who had now abandoned their principles of economy for the sake of fighting a war of liberation against Russia. This is an essential point, one lost sight of in later years, when the Eastern Question came to be regarded as bound up with the route to India. The route to India had nothing to do with the Crimean war. The Danube, not the Suez Canal, was the only waterway involved. The Crimean war was fought much more against Russia than in favour of Turkey. And it was fought not only in the name of the Balance of Power. Russia was regarded as the tyrant of Europe, the main prop of 'the Holy Alliance', and English radicals thought that they were now getting their own back for the Russian intervention which had helped to defeat the revolutions of 1848. The veteran radical, Joseph Hume, who had moved a reduction in the army estimates every year since 1823, voted for the estimates in 1854. There could be no more striking evidence of the radical conversion.

The radical crusading spirit against Russia could be illustrated in a thousand ways. I will limit myself to one quotation from a correspondent of Cobden's:

This, then, is my creed. I look upon Russia as the personification of Despotism – the apostle of Legitimacy. In the present state of Poland and Hungary we see her work ... Such a power can be curbed only by war, and must be so curbed sooner or later, if Europe is to remain free ... If we believe that God wills the liberty and happiness of mankind, how can we doubt that we are doing God's work in fighting for liberty against aggression?

Perhaps I should add that this is a genuine quotation from a letter of November 1855, and is not taken from yesterday's newspaper. Bright's principal arguments were directed against this radical enthusiasm. Why was he not affected by it? It was, I think, a lesson learnt from Cobden. Cobden had always preached non-intervention in European affairs. What is more, he had always looked with a friendly eye on Russian expansion. In a pamphlet which he wrote as early as 1836, he asked: 'Can any one doubt that, if the Government of St Petersburg were transferred to the shores of the Bosphorus, a splendid and substantial European city would, in less than twenty years, spring up in the place of those huts which now constitute the capital of Turkey?' In this pamphlet Cobden even challenged the radical predilection for Poland. Russian rule, he wrote, 'has been followed by an increase in the amount of peace, wealth, liberty, civilization and happiness, enjoyed by the great mass of the people ... The Polish people, though far from prosperous, have enjoyed many benefits by their change of government.'

Bright had not always shared Cobden's view. As a young man, he wrote a poem in favour of Poland – a very bad poem

– which he once quoted with startling effect in a parliamentary speech. But he came in time to accept Cobden's belief that Free Trade would civilize every country, including Russia, and that political freedom would follow of itself. He wrote to Cobden in 1851, at the time of Kossuth's visit to England:

I shall go against any notion of *fighting* for Hungary or any other country... By perfecting our own institutions, by promoting the intelligence, morality and health of our own country, and by treating all other nations in a just and generous and courteous manner, we shall do more for humanity than by commissioning Palmerston to regenerate Hungary by fleets in the Black Sea and the Baltic.

He struck the same note in April 1854: 'they confound the blowing up of ships and the slaughter of thousands with the cause of freedom, as if there were any connection in matters wholly apart'. This was a clear doctrine of non-intervention, applicable to all wars of intervention anywhere at any time – applicable, for instance, as much to Italy as to the Balkans. But in regard to the Crimean war Bright did not really take a purely neutral attitude. Not only did he think that nothing good could be achieved by a Russian victory over Turkey. He dismissed all claims that the Ottoman Empire had reformed, or was capable of reform, and he referred to 'the natural solution' – 'which is, that the Mahometan power in Europe should eventually succumb to the growing power of the Christian population of the Turkish territories'. Observe that he does not refer to the national conflict between the Balkan peoples and their Ottoman rulers, and indeed he seems to have been unaware at this time that Turkey-in-Europe was inhabited by peoples of different, even conflicting, nationalities. He anticipated the establishment in Constantinople of 'a Christian state'. The Christian population would 'grow more rapidly in numbers, in industry, in wealth, in intelligence, and in political power'. Why did Bright believe this? He knew no more about Turkey than anyone else. No independent reporters had visited Turkey, and Bright took his information on conditions there from the Blue Books. His faith in the Balkan Christians rested solely on dogma – above all, on the dogma that they were more capable of absorbing the lessons of Free Trade. The dogma was well-founded. All the same, there is a striking contrast with the discussions on the Eastern Question later in the century – discussions which were based on reliable first-hand information and on awareness of the national issue.

Bright claimed to approach the Crimean war with detachment. In reality he came to it with his mind made up. First he was against the war; then he discovered the arguments to justify his opposition. But this is perhaps to anticipate what should be a conclusion. Let me turn to the arguments which he used. It will, I think, be convenient to put them into two categories, though Bright did not make this logical distinction: arguments against any war over the Eastern Question – perhaps even against any war at all – and arguments against this particular war, based on the Blue Books which recounted the diplomatic events of 1853. Incidentally, here is a practical reason why Bright only spoke so late in the day. The first Blue Book was published on 17 March 1854. Bright spoke against the war a fortnight later. He could not have made his case earlier. This speech gives Bright's main arguments against the war, and I shall analyse it in detail.

He begins, quite rightly, with the French demands of 1852 in favour of the Latin Church at Jerusalem. Then, he says, Russia 'required (and this I understand to be the real ground of the quarrel) that Turkey should define by treaty, or convention, or by a simple note, or memorandum, what was conceded, and what were the rights of Russia'. Turkey, he insists, was decaying, and Russia was bound to 'interfere, or have a strong interest, in the internal policy of the Ottoman Empire'. This Russian interference was, of course, the mission of Prince Menshikov to Constantinople. Here Bright made his first substantial point. On 5 May 1853, according to him, Lord Stratford de Redcliffe, British ambassador at Constantinople, insisted that the Turks should refuse the Russian demands. 'He urged upon the Turkish Government the necessity of resistance to any of the demands of Russia, promising the armed assistance of England, whatever consequences might ensue.' He makes the same point in the letter to Absalom Watkin.

But for the English minister at Constantinople and the Cabinet at home the dispute would have settled itself, and the last note of Prince Menshikoff would have been accepted . . . Lord Stratford de Redcliffe held private interviews with the Sultan, insisted on his rejection of all terms of accommodation with Russia, and promised him the armed assistance of England if war should arise.

Here then is the start of Bright's case. The Turks wanted to sign the Menshikov note; the French Government did not object; 'it was through the interference of Lord Stratford de Redcliffe – acting, I presume, in accordance with instructions from our Cabinet, and promising the intervention of the fleets – that the rejection of that note was secured'. On the basis of Bright's argument Stratford de Redcliffe has been branded with responsibility for the war from that day to this. But does our later knowledge confirm the accusation? I am afraid it does not. Firstly, there was never a secret interview of 5 May, and Bright himself subsequently dropped the story. Far from encouraging the Turks to resist, Stratford advised them to meet the Russian demands fully over the Holy Places; he took a different line only when Menshikov demanded the recognition of a Russian protectorate over all Orthodox Christians in the Ottoman Empire. The Turks would have resisted this claim with or without Stratford's advice – which was, in any case, directed to compromise, not rejection, and even now he gave them no promise at all of British support. Moreover,

Russia's demands were not as innocent as Bright made out. Menshikov wanted to make Russia supreme at Constantinople – 'to end the infernal dictatorship of this Redcliffe' and to put that of Russia in its place. The Russian claims were based on an interpretation of the treaty of Kutchuk Kainardji which the Russian experts themselves knew to be false, and in the following year the Tsar Nicholas I admitted that he had not realized what he was doing. 'His conduct in 1853', he said, 'would have been different but for the error into which he had been led.' The Russians were, in fact, demanding a protectorate over Turkey, and the Turks were bound to refuse, if they were to keep their independence at all. Of course, Great Britain could have washed her hands of Turkish independence, but this was not Bright's case at this stage. He claimed that the Russian demands were harmless. Stratford judged better.

At all events, Menshikov failed. Russia broke off relations with Turkey and, in July, occupied the Danubian principalities. Bright called this 'impolitic and immoral' in his letter to Absalom Watkin; he did not condemn it in his parliamentary speeches. The other Powers – England, France, Austria, and Prussia – then drew up in August 'the Vienna Note' which they offered as a settlement of the quarrel. It was accepted by the Russians in, says Bright, 'the most frank and unreserved manner'. The Turks had not been shown the Note beforehand. When it reached them, they saw at once the interpretation that Russia would place on it and refused it. This certainly reflected sadly on the diplomatic gifts of the negotiators at Vienna. But surely the question is – were the Turks right in their suspicions? Nesselrode, the Russian Chancellor, proved that they were. Early in September, he issued an interpretation of the Vienna Note, claiming that it gave to Russia the full protectorate over the Orthodox Christians allegedly stipulated in the treaty of Kutchuk Kainardji. What does Bright say to this? Merely, 'I very much doubt whether

Count Nesselrode placed any meaning upon the Note which it did not fairly warrant, and it is impossible to say whether he really differed at all from the actual intentions of the four Ambassadors at Vienna'. Again, 'this circular could make no real difference in the note itself'. Now this was being more Russian than the Russians. In October the tsar met Francis Joseph, Emperor of Austria, at Olomouc – the place which was then called Olmütz. He confessed that Nesselrode had made a 'forced interpretation' and now offered to withdraw it. In other words, the Russians had tried to cheat, and the Turks had caught them out. No one would deduce this from Bright's speech.

The meeting at Olomouc offered the one serious chance of avoiding war. Nicholas I was alarmed and in a conciliatory mood; he withdrew, for the time being, the demands that he had previously made. The British Government rejected his offer; they insisted that the Russian troops should be withdrawn from the principalities; and when Turkey declared war independently a couple of weeks later, they allowed themselves to be dragged into war on her side. Bright had a strong case here. He would have said to the Turks: 'If you persist in taking your own course, we cannot be involved in the difficulties to which it may give rise, but must leave you to take the consequences of your own acts.' But he weakens this case irremediably when he says a few sentences previously: 'It is impossible fairly to doubt the sincerity of the desire for peace manifested by the Emperor of Russia.' This is just what it was possible to doubt from the record of the previous months. Desire for peace perhaps; but equally a desire to get his own way at Constantinople even at the risk of war. Bright failed to allow for the suspicions which Russian policy had caused and for the Russian aggressiveness which the hesitation and muddle of British policy encouraged. Indeed, the war would have been avoided if Great Britain had followed the resolute line advocated by Palmerston and Russell – whom

Bright blamed for the war. The responsibility for the war lay with the pacific Lord Aberdeen, whom Bright admired, and Aberdeen later admitted it himself. Like King David, he refused to rebuild a church on his estates. 'But the word of the Lord came to me, saying, Thou hast shed blood abundantly and hast made great war: thou shalt not build an house unto my name.'

So much for Bright's criticism of the diplomatic background to the Crimean war. But his criticism did not stop at diplomatic detail. Indeed, this was not much more than a *tour de force* designed to show that he could meet ministers on their own ground. In reality, Bright did not accept this ground. He rejected the basic assumptions of British diplomacy. The major part of his speech of 31 March 1854 shows this. He turns from the Vienna Note and the Olomouc meeting to challenge the doctrine of the Balance of Power.

He has great fun quoting the opinions of the great Whigs – Burke, Fox and Lord Holland – against any idea of supporting Turkey; opinions that must have much embarrassed Lord John Russell, the last of the great Whigs, yet an enthusiastic supporter of the Crimean war. Bright continues: 'If this phrase of the "balance of power" is to be always an argument for war, the pretence for war will never be wanting, and peace can never be secure.' 'This whole notion of the "balance of power" is a mischievous delusion which has come down to us from past times; we ought to drive it from our minds, and to consider the solemn question of peace or war on more clear, more definite, and on far higher principles than any that are involved in the phrase the "balance of power".' This last sentence seems to promise that Bright will at any rate hint at an alternative foreign policy, but he does not do so. He merely goes on analysing the excuses for the Crimean war and demolishing them.

The integrity and independence of the Ottoman Empire? But Turkey cannot be independent with three foreign armies on her soil. If the government had wanted to preserve the independence of Turkey, they would have advised the Turks to accept either Menshikov's conditions or the Vienna Note. 'I will not insult you by asking whether, under such circumstances, that "integrity and independence" would not have been a thousand times more secure than it is at this hour?' This was exactly the argument – if you will forgive a contemporary allusion – with which Lord Halifax justified the desertion of Czechoslovakia in 1938: 'I have always felt that to fight a war for one, two, or three years to protect or re-create something that you knew you could not directly protect, and probably could never re-create, did not make sense.'

Next, what about curbing Russian aggression? Bright answers that it cannot be done. 'Russia will be always there – always powerful, always watchful, and actuated by the same motives of ambition, either of influence or of territory, which are supposed to have moved her in past times.' 'It is a delusion to suppose that you can dismember Russia – that you can blot her from the map of Europe – that you can take guarantees from her, as some seem to imagine, as easily as you take bail from an offender, who would otherwise go to prison for three months. England and France cannot do this with a stroke of the pen, and the sword will equally fail if the attempt be made.'

Finally, 'how are the interests of England involved in this question? ... It is not a question of sympathy with any other State ... It is not my duty to make this country the knight-errant of the human race, and to take upon herself the protection of the thousand millions of human beings who have been permitted by the Creator of all things to people this planet.' On the other hand, taxes have gone up, trade is injured, thousands of men are being killed. 'My doctrine would have been non-intervention in this case. The danger of the Russian power was a phantom; the necessity of permanently upholding the Mahometan rule in Europe is an absurdity ... The evils of non-intervention were remote and vague, and could neither be weighed nor described in any accurate terms. The good we can judge something of already, by estimating the cost of a contrary policy.' (These two sentences are from the letter to Absalom Watkin, but they fit in with the argument of Bright's speech.) Finally, Bright moves on to assert the general merits of non-intervention for this country 'where her interests were not directly and obviously assailed'. If we had adopted non-intervention for the last seventy years :

This country might have been a garden, every dwelling might have been of marble, and every person who treads its soil might have been sufficiently educated. We should indeed have had less of military glory. We might have had neither Trafalgar nor Waterloo; but we should have set the high example of a Christian nation, free in its institutions, courteous and just in its conduct towards all foreign States, and resting its policy on the unchangeable foundations of Christian morality.

Every orator must be forgiven something in his peroration.

The speech of 31 March 1854, which I have analysed at length, gives Bright's considered case against the Crimean war. The two speeches of 22 December 1854 and of 23 February 1855 do not add anything to that case. The one, as I said earlier, was a defence of Cobden; the other urged an armistice during the negotiations at Vienna. We can leave them aside when considering Bright's views. If we were considering his oratory, it would be a different matter; for they contain his most moving and also – a characteristic sometimes forgotten – his most humorous passages. The speech of 7 June 1855, however, raises some new points. In it Bright discusses not the causes of the war, but how it should end. I must turn aside to explain the diplomatic background. In the autumn of 1854 Austria – not herself a combatant, but wooed by the western allies – drafted 'Four Points' as reasonable terms of peace. These Four Points were accepted by England and France in the hope of drawing Austria into the war; then they were accepted by Russia in the better hope of keeping her out. The four Powers met in conference at Vienna in March and April 1855 in order to define the Four Points more closely and to turn them into practical terms. There was no difficulty about three of them. Russia was to give up her protectorate of the Danubian principalities; the freedom of navigation of the Danube was to be secured; and the Christian populations of the Ottoman Empire were to be put under a general European guarantee, instead of under that of Russia. Incidentally, these three Points were already an answer to the assertion that war accomplishes nothing. Russia would never have agreed to them without the Crimean war. I don't venture to determine whether they were worth a war, but that is a different question.

The dispute at Vienna came over Point III. This provided that the Straits Convention of 1841 should be revised 'in the interests of the Balance of Power'. In other words, Turkey was to be given some sort of security against Russia's naval preponderance in the Black Sea. Lord John Russell, the English representative, and Drouyn de Lhuys, the French representative, went to Vienna with instructions that they could agree to one of two things : either the Russian fleet in the Black Sea should be limited or the Black Sea should be neutralized altogether. Gorchakov, the Russian delegate at Vienna, refused to accept either. Buol, Austrian foreign minister, then came forward with another proposal : equipoise. The Russians could keep their existing fleet, but, if they increased it, the British and French could send ships into the Black Sea to balance the increase. Neither Russell nor Drouyn was authorized to agree to this scheme, but Drouyn was afraid of missing any chance of peace, and Russell was afraid of getting out of step with Drouyn. Both therefore accepted 'equipoise'. When they returned home, Napoleon III rejected the compromise and the British Government followed suit. The peace conference was abandoned, and the war was renewed. This was a bad, muddled piece of diplomacy. It is hardly surprising that Bright saw his chance and took it.

There is much the same pattern as in the earlier speech of 31 March 1854. He begins by meeting ministers on their own ground and attacking their incompetence; gradually he shifts his emphasis and moves over to more general principles. He asks what the war is about. It is not a war for Poland or for Hungary or for Italy. It is solely a war – and here he quotes ministers themselves – for the security of Turkey. Very well then, we want to reduce Russian preponderance. 'How is that preponderance to cease?' Bright looks first at the idea of neutralizing the Black Sea and dismisses it with vehemence. 'I conceive that was so monstrous a proposition, in the present condition of Europe, that I am surprised it should have been entertained for a moment by any sensible man.' He says much the same of limiting the Russian fleet. 'If any diplomatist from this country, under the same circumstances as Russia was placed in, had consented to terms such as the noble Lord had endeavoured to force upon Russia – I say, that if he entered the door of this House, he would be met by one universal shout of execration, and, as a public man, would be ruined for ever.' Bright has an alternative: the Straits should be opened to everybody:

Our fleets would visit the Black Sea in the course of the season, and the Russian Black Sea fleet, if it chose, would visit the Mediterranean. There would be no sort of pretence for wrangling about the Straits; and the balance of power – if I may use the term – between the fleets of Russia, France and England would be probably the best guarantee that could be offered for the security of Constantinople and Turkey, so far as they are in danger of aggression either from the Black Sea or the Mediterranean.

This is a surprising proposal. I say nothing of the fact that Russia would have rejected it emphatically, whatever Gorchakov might hint at Vienna. But Bright, in his eagerness to discredit imposing any terms on Russia – terms that certainly could only be imposed after her defeat – is reduced in practice to the crudest *realpolitik*. He says in effect: no treaty stipulations are of any value; the only effective course is to maintain a balance of power, a balance of actual force, by keeping a large fleet in the eastern Mediterranean. If Palmerston had said this, what an outcry Bright would have made; what assertions of Russian good faith; what cries, and justified cries, about the weight of taxes to maintain such a fleet. It has often been said that non-intervention and splendid isolation are luxuries dependent on naval supremacy; but Bright never came so near admitting it as in this passage. His judgement of fact, however, was not correct. Six months after he made this speech the Russians accepted the neutralization of the Black Sea, which he had dismissed as a monstrous proposition. It is true that they denounced it again fifteen years later when the diplomatic structure of Europe had changed fundamentally. Nevertheless Bright underrated what a Power will agree to when it has been defeated.

The rest of Bright's speech moves away from these diplomatic questions. He points to the folly of saying that Austria must be preserved and yet trying to draw her into a war that would exhaust her; he warns against the danger of relying on France as an ally; he denounces the idea of defending the liberties of Europe:

What a notion a man must have of the duties of the ... people living in these islands if he thinks ... that the sacred treasure of the bravery, resolution, and unfaltering courage of the people of England is to be squandered in a contest ... for the preservation of the independence of Germany, and of the integrity, civilization, and something else, of all Europe!

He quotes the things that Palmerston and Russell said against each other in the past. But his greatest emphasis is on the burden of taxation and the crippling effect which this will have in our competition with the United States.

Hon. Members may think this is nothing. They say it is a 'low' view of the case. But these things are the foundation of your national greatness, and of your national duration; and you may be following visionary phantoms in all parts of the world while your own country is becoming rotten within, and calamities may be in store for the monarchy and the nation of which now, it appears, you take no heed.

It may seem a little unfair to end the survey of Bright's speeches on this note, but it is the note on which he himself chose to end and, in the parliamentary circumstances of 1855, perhaps rightly. What are we to say, after this examination, of Bright's attitude towards the Crimean war? We are bound, I am sure, to admire the courage with which Bright expressed his views and still more the brilliance of his performance. If I had merely read to you one of his speeches, instead of trying to analyse them, you would certainly have been swept away and have been convinced, without further argument, that the Crimean war was all that Bright said – unnecessary, unjust, in short a crime. But do we feel the same if we escape from their spell? I have suggested, during the course of this lecture, that Bright was not always sound when he came to the details of diplomacy. It is difficult, when criticizing the Government of your own country, not to skate over the faults of other Governments, and Bright did not escape this danger. He was harsher towards Stratford de Redcliffe than to Prince Menshikov; professed more faith in the statements of Nesselrode than in those of Palmerston; gave the Russian, but not the British, Government the benefit of the doubt. There was certainly much muddle and confusion in the diplomacy of the Crimean war, but, to judge from Bright's speeches, you would imagine that it was all on the British side. This one-sidedness is almost bound to happen in parliamentary speeches. You may achieve some effect by attacking your own Government; you will achieve nothing by attacking foreign statesmen. In exactly the same way, Charles James Fox was often more charitable towards Bonaparte than towards William Pitt, and pacifists of the first world war, such as E D Morel, had more sympathy with German than with British imperialism.

One looks in vain in Bright's speeches for any satisfactory explanation of the causes of the Crimean war. He seems to suggest that it was due solely to newspaper agitation and to the irresponsibility of Palmerston and Russell. 'The country has been, I am afraid, the sport of their ancient rivalry; and I should be very sorry if it should be the victim of the policy which they have so long advocated.' Cobden was more cautious. He held that Russia, too, was 'much in the wrong' and therefore kept quiet, washing his hands, as it were, of both sides. Bright often implied that Russian expansion against Turkey was an unexceptionable, even a praiseworthy process. Not always. He said in his first speech: 'If I were a Russian, speaking in a Russian Parliament, I should denounce any aggression upon Turkey, as I now blame the policy of our own Government; and I greatly fear I should find myself in a minority, as I now find myself in a minority on this question.' But is not this justice a little more than even-handed? Does it not imply that to attack Turkey and to defend her are equally reprehensible and provocative? If Russian aggression, though deplorable, is inevitable, then is not resistance to this aggression equally inevitable? Or do we make allowances only one way? In the next eastern crisis of 1876–8 Gladstone took a clearer and more consistent line. He held that the destruction of the Turkish Empire in Europe was eminently desirable and therefore wished Russia to succeed, preferably in association with England. Though he opposed the actual course of British policy, he offered a positive alternative. Bright's attitude was one of aloof neutrality.

He was not clear about this himself. In a speech to the Peace Society, which he made on 13 October 1853 – before the Crimean war broke out – he attacked the idea of war 'for the miserable, decrepit, moribund Government which is now enthroned, but which cannot long last, in the city of Constantinople'. Surely the logical conclusion from this should have been to cooperate in the Concert of Europe, as Gladstone later advocated. But Bright always denied that he favoured the Russian cause, and in a later speech on foreign policy, which he made on 29 October 1858, preached high-minded isolation. This country should have 'adequate and scientific means of defence'.

But I shall repudiate and denounce the expenditure of every shilling, the engagement of every man, the employment of every ship which has no object but intermeddling in the affairs of other countries.

He refused to admit that an active foreign policy could ever be justified. 'This foreign policy, this regard for "the liberties of Europe", this care at one time for "the Protestant interest", this excessive love for the "balance of power", is neither more nor less than a gigantic system of out-door relief for the aristocracy of Great Britain.' All foreign policy was unnecessary. Instead 'we have the unchangeable and eternal principles of the moral law to guide us, and only so far as we walk by that guidance can we be permanently a great nation, or our people a happy people'.

When Bright said this, he had left Manchester and was already the representative of Birmingham. This was symbolic. Though he seemed discredited while the Crimean war was on, he triumphed afterwards. By 1858 he was back in the House of Commons, and his version of the Crimean war was already being accepted. English people usually think their wars a mistake when they are over and they thought this of the Crimean war sooner than usual. As a matter of fact, it achieved its purpose rather better than most wars. Russia's control of the Danube mouth, which was the largest issue in the war, was recovered only in 1945, and Turkey, whose demise has been so often foretold, possesses Constantinople and the Straits to this day. I do not venture to say whether these achievements are desirable. Bright, however, said that they were impossible. Most Englishmen soon came to agree with him. It is Bright's version of the Crimean war which has triumphed in popular opinion and in the history books. Bright had more success. Once it was agreed that the Crimean war had been a mistake, it was easy to draw the further conclusion that all wars were a mistake. The moral law which Bright invoked turned out to be the doctrine of the man who passed by on the other side. It is no accident that Bright, at the end of his life, had Joseph Chamberlain as his colleague in the representation of Birmingham. There was a continuity of ideas from Bright to Joseph Chamberlain and from Joseph Chamberlain to Neville. The Munich settlement of 1938 was implicit in Bright's opposition to the Crimean war. I am not sure whether this condemns Bright's attitude or justifies Munich.

12. *Palmerston*

This first appeared in a volume of essays on British Prime
Ministers (1954), published by Allan & Wingate with an
introduction by Duff Cooper. It is no longer true that the
brick fortifications behind Portsmouth are useful and
effective, if indeed they ever were.

Among the surprising careers of British prime ministers, none has contained more surprises than that of Lord Palmerston. For twenty years junior minister in a Tory government, he became the most successful of Whig foreign secretaries; though always a Conservative, he ended his life by presiding over the transition from Whiggism to Liberalism. He was the exponent of British strength, yet he was driven from office for truckling to a foreign despot; he preached the Balance of

Power, yet helped to inaugurate the policy of isolation and of British withdrawal from Europe. Irresponsible and flippant, he became the first hero of the serious middle-class electorate. He reached high office solely through an irregular family connection; he retained it through skilful use of the press – the only prime minister to become an accomplished leader-writer. Palmerston was not a member of one of the great Whig families or even connected with them. He was an Irish peer, moderately rich, who naturally entered politics to supplement his income. For a peer, he was an educated man. He went to Cambridge, which – even at the worst time – provided a solid grounding in mathematics, and he early absorbed the principles of political economy. Hence, he was not staggered, as Peel and Gladstone were, by the sudden impact of the Free Trade case; this had been a common-place of his thought for thirty years. Born in 1784, he entered the House of Commons at the age of twenty-three, without either strong convictions or defined party ties; simply a young man of the fashionable world who wanted a good appointment and – rarity enough – was qualified to hold one. Having a reasonable grasp of figures and of economics, he was offered his choice among the junior financial offices;[1] he chose that of secretary at war and retained it for twenty years. This was the equivalent of the present-day financial secretary to the War Office, a post strictly administrative and financial without a seat in the Cabinet. Though Palmerston ran his office competently, he

1. Spencer Perceval is said to have offered him the post of chancellor of the exchequer. Even if he did, this was not the important office that it has subsequently become. The first lord of the treasury himself conducted the financial affairs of the country, and – if he sat in the House of Commons – held also the office of chancellor. Spencer Perceval must have thought better of his proposal to Palmerston, for he adhered to the usual arrangement and was his own chancellor. Peel in 1841 was the first to sit on the Treasury bench, as first lord, with a chancellor beside him; Russell, in 1846, the first to leave financial business to a chancellor of the exchequer.

did not trouble much with politics and seemed to care only for life in society. Goodlooking and fickle, he established himself as 'Lord Cupid', a name which tells everything. But the years of obscurity were not wasted: he served a more prolonged apprenticeship in administration than any other prime minister has ever done and, when he came to sit in Whig Cabinets, was distinguished from his colleagues by his ability to run an office. It was this ability, not his policy or his personality, which finally made him prime minister in 1855.

Though Palmerston served a Tory ministry, it would be wrong to describe him as a Tory; he was simply a 'government man'. Nor was he a Canningite until late in the day. What brought him over to the Canningites was his support for Catholic emancipation. With his gaiety of spirit and his easygoing morals, he hated tyranny and oppression wherever they occurred. After twenty years of comfortable office, he left it for the sake of the Catholics, just as, at the end of his life, he threatened to resign as prime minister rather than relax the struggle against the slave trade. In 1828 Palmerston, out of office, found himself associated with Melbourne and Huskisson, the Canningite remnant who had broken with Wellington and were drifting over to the Whigs. There were also personal grounds for this tie. After a good many adventures, Palmerston had settled down with Lady Cowper, Melbourne's married sister. He lived with her more or less openly; had children by her; and married her in the late eighteen thirties after Lord Cowper's death. Melbourne was a more important man than Palmerston, more influential and better connected. When he joined the Whig Cabinet in 1830, he carried his illegitimate brother-in-law with him. Without the Melbourne connection, Palmerston would hardly have reached the Cabinet rank which started him on the path to the premiership, and Melbourne was to sustain him against the criticism of the orthodox Whigs at the end of the thirties. In the last resort, Palmerston owed his position as prime minister to the odd chance that the sister of one of his predecessors had become his mistress.

Palmerston was to make his name at the Foreign Office, but this was neither intended nor expected. Lord Grey, prime minister in 1830, had been foreign secretary in a remote era and meant to conduct foreign policy himself. All he wanted was a competent underling in the House of Commons. Lady Cowper was again of service. Princess Lieven, her closest friend, recommended Palmerston to Grey as presentable and well-mannered. For some time it was believed that Grey supplied the policy. Palmerston was held to be 'frivolous' and failed to establish a hold over the House of Commons. The peaceful solution of the Belgian question was primarily a triumph for Grey. When Melbourne became prime minister, Palmerston had things more his own way, and his conduct of British policy during the eastern crisis of 1839–41 was brilliant, perhaps the most perfect in the records of the Foreign Office. But it was a performance for experts. It did not make him popular with the general public, and it made him much disliked by many of the great Whigs, such as Holland and Durham. In 1841, when the Whig Government declined into collapse, Palmerston was still a relatively little-known figure. His frequent evocation of Canning, whose policy he neither understood nor followed, was an implied confession that he could not stand on his own feet.

The five years between 1841 and 1846, when Peel was in office with a Conservative Government, were decisive for Palmerston's future. The succession to Melbourne as Whig leader was open. Lord John Russell assumed that it would automatically be his as political representative of the greatest Whig family, and he thought he had done all that was necessary when he secured the allegiance of such Whig managers as 'Bear' Ellice. Palmerston could hardly play his family connection against Russell's, even if it had counted for anything. He therefore decided to play the British public. He built himself up deliberately as a public figure, established relations with the press and himself wrote leading articles in his forthright, unmistakable style. At the end of 1845, when Peel first resigned, the third Earl Grey made it a condition of his taking office under Russell that Palmerston should be excluded. The condition wrecked Russell's Cabinet-making. The episode was at once an unconscious recognition by the great Whigs that they had taken a cuckoo into the nest, and a sign that the cuckoo was now too strong to be ejected. Later, in 1846, Russell formed the last Whig Government of our history, and Palmerston went undisputed to the Foreign Office. This feeble Government had a record of failure broken only by Palmerston's dazzling display in foreign policy. His policy had its serious side and can be defended, as it were, on technical grounds, but there was a flamboyant touch as well – Palmerston was deliberately playing Russell off the centre of the stage. His triumph came in 1850 with the Don Pacifico debate, when he held his own against the greatest speakers of the age – Peel, Gladstone and Cobden – held his own and worsted them. The triumph was not one of oratory in the conventional sense. Palmerston was always a bad speaker full of 'hums' and 'haws', his voice trailing away before the end of the sentence, and the pause filled up by a flourish of his handkerchief. Rather it was a triumph of character. With his dyed whiskers and his red face, Palmerston exemplified British self-confidence and bounce.

Still, it needed the impact of war to finish the job for him. At the end of 1851 Russell finally got rid of Palmerston. Early in 1852 the Russell government fell in its turn. Then, at the end of the year, Russell and Palmerston found themselves together again in the coalition of Whigs and Peelites brought into being by Prince Albert and presided over by Aberdeen. Palmerston was relegated to the Home Office. He was rescued from it by the disasters of the Crimean war. Though he shared the common responsibility of the Cabinet, public opinion seized on him as the man of destiny, the man who would win the war. This was the moment of crisis in Palmerston's life and, for the historian, the most interesting point in his career. Again and again in modern history, Great Britain has drifted unprepared into war; then, after early failures, has discovered an inspired war-leader. How does public opinion make its choice? And what is it that Palmerston had in common with the elder Pitt, Lloyd George and Winston Churchill? It was not done merely by advertisement, though all four made skilful use of publicity. It was not even done by brilliant speeches in the House of Commons or outside. It turned rather on the impression of resolution and courage laid down in the House of Commons over a period of years. During a crisis the members of parliament broke away from the conventional pattern – whether of family connection or party organization – and acted according to their patriotic duty. Curiously enough, the popular choice has always been right: on all four occasions it hit on a leader who was not only more colourful or more dramatic than his peace-time predecessor but also more efficient technically.[2] This is puzzling. The general public or even the members of the House of Commons could hardly deduce from Palmerston's speeches that he was an administrator of the first quality who could challenge the Peelites on their own ground of efficient government without any of the high moral tone which they found necessary to accompany it.

The Government which Palmerston formed in 1855 was neither a party government nor a coalition; it was an association of individuals, united only to win the war. The old system of family connections was in decay; the new system of defined parties had hardly begun. The Conservatives were

2. On one occasion the public choice was flagrantly and persistently wrong. The younger Pitt, 'the pilot who weathered the storm', was not a good war leader; the nonentities who succeeded him did much better.

on the way to becoming a party in the modern sense; but they were doomed to perpetual minority so long as there was a middle-class electorate. Those acceptable as ministers were in confusion. The Peelites broke with Palmerston and disintegrated. When Russell bungled the conference at Vienna shortly afterwards, Whig solidarity also dissolved. Palmerston's personality was the only stable point in a fluid political system. It would be absurd to claim that his government was a war Cabinet of the highest order. Though it began the reform of the British military system, these reforms stopped half-way like the Crimean war itself. Opportunity had come to Palmerston too late in life: he was seventy-one when he became prime minister. More important, opportunity came at the wrong time: Great Britain could not be turned into a military nation only four years after the Exhibition of 1851. Still, in one way, Palmerston did better than his peers, those other great men who have saved their country. He not only won the war that he had been called on to win, he actually survived his success. The elder Pitt, Lloyd George, Churchill, were all ruined by victory. All three were ejected from office before the end of the war or shortly after it. Palmerston stayed safely in office and, even more remarkable, won a general election a year after the war was over.

The general election of 1857 is unique in our history: the only election ever conducted as a simple plebiscite in favour of an individual. Even the 'coupon' election of 1918 claimed to be more than a plebiscite for Lloyd George; even Disraeli and Gladstone offered a clash of policies as well as of personalities. In 1857 there was no issue before the electorate except whether Palmerston should be prime minister; and no one could pretend that Palmerston had any policy except to be himself. Of course, we know very little about the general election of 1857 (or for that matter about any other in the nineteenth century), and it may turn out on detailed examination that the result of it was really determined by less obvious factors. Still, there was in it, at the least, a plebiscitary element, as though even the British had to be in the fashion and had caught the taste from Louis Napoleon. In the same way, Neville Chamberlain in the nineteen thirties got as near the *Führerprinzip* as an Englishman could.

The political victory of 1857 was not the end of Palmerston's career. He had presided over, and in part caused, the end of the old political order; he was destined to inaugurate the new. His period of personal government lasted only a few months after the general election of 1857. The rather cantankerous patriotism which had sustained him against the Peelites and the pacifists turned on him when he tried, sensibly enough, to appease Louis Napoleon after the Orsini plot. Since no one could form a Government with majority support, the Conservatives – as in 1852 – formed a Government without one; this in turn was bound to be followed, again as in 1852, by a coalition. But the Government which Palmerston organized in June 1859 was a coalition of a different kind : not a coalition of groups which looked back to the past, but a coalition which anticipated the future. Had it not been for Palmerston himself – too individual, too full of personality to be fitted into a party-pattern – it would have been the first Liberal Government in our history. Everything that was important in it was Liberal – finance, administrative reform, its very composition : the first Government with unmistakable middle-class Free Traders as members. Palmerston would have included even Cobden, if he could have got him. It was Cobden who had scruples against tolerating the irresponsible survivor from an older world, and not the other way round. Of course, tolerance and good-nature had always been Palmerston's strong points, not virtues for which Radicals are usually distinguished.

Palmerston was too strong a character to be swamped by Liberalism even in old age. It was not so much that he resisted reforms; he himself had welcomed and often promoted the administrative reforms of the preceding thirty years. It was rather that he thought a Government had other tasks than to be always reforming: it should conduct a forceful foreign policy and strengthen the national defences. Palmerston is one of the few prime ministers who has literally left his mark on the face of the country: all those odd-looking brick fortifications behind Portsmouth are his doing – they are still useful and effective, which is more than can be said for Gladstonian finance. But Palmerston in his last ministry was fighting, and winning, the wrong battle. For nearly a hundred years – ever since Dunning's famous motion in 1780 – self-confident British aristocrats had aimed to reduce the powers of the Crown and to prevent its interference in the course of government and policy. Melbourne and Palmerston had had four blissful years on the accession of Queen Victoria when the Crown seemed on the point of becoming politically null. The process had been reversed by Prince Albert, and when Palmerston was at the Foreign Office between 1846 and 1851 he had to contend with ceaseless royal interference – the more galling for being justified by every historical precedent. The years of the Crimean war had been too serious to allow of constitutional squabbles, but these began again in 1859. Between 1859 and 1861 the Crown fought persistently the policy of Palmerston and of Russell, now foreign secretary; intrigued, as George III had intrigued, with members of the Cabinet behind the prime minister's back; dreamt of ejecting Palmerston as the Fox–North coalition had been ejected in 1784.

Then, in 1861, the Prince Consort suddenly died. Victoria was both unwilling and unable to carry on the contest; she became again and remained the political nonentity that she had been before her marriage. Palmerston had fulfilled the highest Whig ambition, though after the death of the Whig party: the Crown had been eliminated from politics. It turned out almost at once that the victory was of no use at all. The

Whigs had evoked public opinion against the Crown; Palmerston had played off public opinion against his Whig rivals. Now public opinion interfered more effectively than the Crown had ever done. Though Palmerston had been much harassed by the Crown when he was at the Foreign Office, he had always got his way in the end; and this was equally true of Palmerston and Russell in the severe disputes between 1859 and 1861. Despite the Prince Consort's Germanic enthusiasm for Austria, they managed to back up Italian unification from start to finish. Things were very different between 1862 and 1865. Russell, for instance, would have liked to recognize the southern states in the American civil war and go to war for the sake of Poland in 1863; Palmerston would have threatened war for the sake of Denmark in 1864. They were overruled by the majority of the Cabinet,[3] itself reflecting the opinion of the majority of members in the House of Commons, and they in their turn accurately voicing the opinion of the middle-class electorate. It is often said that Palmerston's foreign policy was a failure at the end of his life; it would be much truer to say that he was not allowed to have a foreign policy. Public opinion had pulled off the feat that was beyond the Prince Consort or even George III. Palmerston, the first – perhaps the only – prime minister to owe his success solely to public opinion, ended his life its prisoner.

Yet he was very near hitting on the method by which public opinion would be tamed. At the time of the general election of 1859, party organization meant nothing at all except perhaps among the Conservatives. Whig grandees put up money to fight a few constituencies, from a mixture of family and party motives; all the rest still depended on local initiative. By 1868 the Liberal Whips were handling a party fund, and were seeking subscriptions much more widely than at Brooks's. The transition took place when Palmerston was

3. Six members of the Cabinet out of fourteen favoured going to Denmark's aid in June 1864.

prime minister. He it must have been who decided to leave these matters to the Whips, and to keep the prime minister out of the financial side of the party-system; it may even have been Palmerston who first, though unwittingly, recommended men to honours in return for their contributions to the party chest. Gladstone found the system settled when he took over the leadership of the Liberal party in 1868. After all, it was the only way to run a party once the moneyed men pushed aside the members of the great families, and Palmerston no doubt acquiesced in it more easily since he had never belonged to these select Whig circles. Thus, without knowing it, he invented both the Liberal party and the modern party system, no mean achievement for an individualist adventurer.

This is the essential point about him, the secret of his failures as of his success. He was never dependent on connection or on party, and rather disliked both; he was self-made. Men have written many books about his foreign policy and will write more. Very little has been written, or ever will be, about his place in British political life, for it is an empty one. The British political system has no room for the rogue elephant. Though he may ruin others – as Palmerston ruined the Whigs or as Lloyd George wrecked the Liberal party sixty years afterwards – he will certainly ruin himself. He will be barren as prime minister; he will not create. Our system is admirably suited to represent interests and to voice general ideas; it does not like independent characters, except as an eccentric adornment. In war both interests and ideas are pushed aside; hence, as an exception to the rule, the great individuals then triumph. Once peace comes, their power is ended, even if they cling to office as Palmerston managed to do. The steady men of solid principle and mind are the ones who achieve effective success, but the adventurers are more fun. Palmerston was not the spokesman of a class, though he defended the Irish landowners towards the end of his life, and he did not voice any great principle or idea. He was simply an individual of strong personality – resolute, self-confident and with great powers of physical endurance. As foreign secretary he was always too independent of the prime minister and the Cabinet; as prime minister, though he stood loyally by his colleagues, he failed to dominate the Cabinet or even to lead it.

He was not an Irish peer and an Irish landowner for nothing. He had the Irish jauntiness which always wins English hearts. He could never rein in his irrepressible high spirits; even his best speeches have here and there a touch of flippancy. He would rather make a good joke than win a debate. He was not, as is sometimes alleged, a survivor from the eighteenth century. Rather he had 'Regency' written all over him – in his clothes, his morals, even in his way of talking and his metallic laugh. Nor did he 'represent' the electorate of the Reform Bill, if this means that he resembled the middle-class voter. The men of the time delighted in Palmerston just as Churchill is now admired by millions who would never vote for him, but their serious taste was for Peel and Gladstone – these were the truly 'representative men'. Palmerston was certainly the most entertaining of Queen Victoria's prime ministers. Though there have been greater prime ministers, there has been none more genial and, for that matter, none so good-looking.

13. Dizzy

New Statesman. The somewhat inadequate excuse for the essay was Tradition and Change, nine lectures delivered to a summer school at Oxford by leading Conservatives and published by the Conservative Central Office.

'I am their leader; I must follow them.' This, we suppose, is the essence of leadership in a democratic community. The members of a party, or the rank and file of a trade union, express their wishes, and it is the duty of the leader to translate these wishes, prejudices or ambitions into action. We interpret the past in the same spirit. History is no longer the record of the achievements of extraordinary men. Our historians accumulate the biographical details of a thousand forgotten figures, and the great men, if brought in at all. merely provide decorative symbols for the prevailing outlook. Napoleon becomes a shorthand sign for the profiteers of the French Revolution; Hitler for the German capitalists or for the German middle classes who have lost their savings; even that erratic genius Winston Churchill is made to appear somehow as 'old England'. Prime ministers were once little less than gods, shaping the destinies of the country by their individual genius. Now they are lay figures, their sole function to wear the appropriate period clothes. The two Pitts represent aggressive commercial imperialism; Palmerston a declining Whig aristocracy; Gladstone the Free Trade manufacturers. Lloyd George speaks for those who made money out of the first world war, and Baldwin for those who lost it.

Of course, there is some truth in this way of looking at things. A public man who cared only for outworn causes would no more command a following than a writer who used classical Latin in an age of vernacular literature would sell his books. Yet reality has a perverse way of going against the pattern that it ought to follow. The leader strays wildly from the class that he is supposed to symbolize and bears little resemblance to a composite picture of his followers. The millions of members of the Labour party, if superimposed one upon another, would never turn into a portrait of Ramsay MacDonald – or even of Clement Attlee. The shrewd operator of symbols could never divine that 'the gentlemen of England' were led by one who was unmistakably the son of a Lancashire millowner, or the Radical Nonconformists by a High Churchman of classical education, whose devotion to the traditional institutions of the country was dwarfed only by his absorption in the writings of the Early Fathers. Indeed, the greatest failures as leaders are those who best reflect their followers. Charles James Fox had Brooks's written all over him; Lord John Russell really belonged to a great Revolution family; and Neville Chamberlain had in fact been 'not a bad Lord Mayor of Birmingham in a lean year'.

Great political leaders are much more than symbols. They are individuals, capturing a cause for their own purpose and giving it an unexpected twist. This is tiresome for the historian, but – to adapt a phrase of Trotsky's – he who wants a quiet mind should choose some other study than that of history. Systems, patterns, faiths are an attempt to impose an artificial simplification on the infinite variety of the past. The historian remains sceptical of them all and can derive only malicious amusement from the efforts of present-day politicians to enlist their great predecessors in contemporary disputes. What would Oliver Cromwell have said about the nationalization of steel? He would have been even more tongue-tied than was usually the case with him. Benjamin Disraeli would hardly have expressed himself on Tradition and Change as did the nine Conservatives who evoked his shade at Oxford. Indeed he would not have chosen such a fatuous, banal subject. But, once landed with it, he would have said something provocative and no doubt wrongheaded. The Oxford lectures specialize in the balanced platitude – the conservatism which Disraeli defined as 'Tory men and Whig measures'. Highest award must go, of course, to Mr R A Butler, who described class privileges as '*the richness of developed differences*'. But the others qualify, too. Mr T E Utley, concealing the poverty of his thought by the incoherence of his style; Professor Hugh Sellon, ending his survey of foreign policy with the question, 'Are the old principles still a sufficient guide in the new world in which we live?' and answering plaintively, 'I do not know'; Mr Angus Maude voicing his confidence in 'the instincts of our people' – every lecture is excessively pleasurable and only 3d. each into the bargain.

Disraeli deserves to be lectured about. He was the oddest great man in our public life by a long chalk. Nothing connected him with the Tory party of the early nineteenth century – nothing, that is, except his calculation that its leadership would be easier to attain than that of the Whigs. He owned no land; he was not English in blood; he was lucky to be even a nominal member of the Anglican Church. In temperament he was even less conservative than in origin. He had a flighty mind which drifted from smart triviality to adolescent day-dreaming and back again. He held nothing sacred except perhaps some Hebrew phrases vaguely remembered. He despised the members of the aristocracy even more than he disliked the poor. He did not even enjoy power when he achieved it. It was not merely that, in his own phrase, 'it came too late'. Power was too practical an affair to interest him. He relished the trappings of power, not the reality – the drama of great debates, the high-sounding titles, his name echoing through history. Yet in appearance he was least conservative of all. Thick black ringlets, fancy waistcoats, powder and scent were not the marks of a gentleman or even of a politician and his affected voice – half-drawl, half-lisp – completed the foreign impression. Disraeli increased the obstacles in his path for the pleasure of overcoming them.

He was first and last a great actor, watching his own performance and that of others with ironic detachment. He cared for causes only as a means of combat. Having ousted Peel from the leadership of the Conservative party by defending the Corn Laws, he cheerfully proposed the next year that Protection should be dropped, and he did nothing to aid agriculture when the great depression hit it at the end of the eighteen seventies. He attacked Palmerston's irresponsible support of Turkey during the Crimean war, yet repeated this support even more irresponsibly twenty years later. He foresaw the independence of the wretched colonies – 'a millstone round our necks' – and welcomed this dissolution of the British Empire. A few years later he claimed a great stroke by making Queen Victoria Empress of India – the biggest piece of tushery even in his career. Sybil is supposed to contain a profound social analysis. In fact, it says no more than that the rich are very rich and the poor very poor – by no means a new discovery. His own social policy, when he came to power, turned out to be nothing more startling than municipal wash-houses. He took one step of real importance when he placed the trade unions above the law, but this was a matter of electoral calculation, not of social justice. His only genuine emotion in politics sprang from personal dislike – of Peel in his early career, of Gladstone even more strongly towards the end. What these two men had in common was a readiness to put their convictions above their ambition – the worst of offences in Disraeli's eyes.

In his novels Disraeli invented an interpretation of political history which is sometimes still taken seriously and was repeated in the twentieth century by our only anti-Semitic writer, Hilaire Belloc. This was the myth of the Venetian oligarchy which was supposed to have taken the Crown prisoner at the time of the Glorious Revolution and from which the Crown should rescue itself by an alliance with the people. This myth had no glimmer of truth. Though eighteenth-century England had indeed a rich and powerful aristocracy, the Crown was always the head of the executive and the ministers were its servants. The Whigs certainly talked of 'forcing the closet', but they never succeeded in doing so effectively until after the great Reform Bill and then only for a decade. The Crown was still of great weight in politics at the time of the Crimean war. By a wild irony, it was Disraeli himself who finally excluded the Crown from politics and turned it into a decorative figurehead. When he introduced household suffrage in 1867 in order to dish the Whigs, he made mass parties inevitable, and these could not be swayed, as the old aristocratic politicians had been, by personal loyalty to the Crown. Disraeli disguised this, perhaps even to himself, by the flattery which he gave to Queen Victoria, as to many other distinguished ladies, but this was play-acting, not politics.

The two-party system does not figure much in Disraeli's writings, but it was the real basis of his political life and his legacy to posterity. The Whigs had had a theory of party conflict, but they regarded this as a conflict between the party of the Crown and the party of the people, by which, of course, they meant themselves. Even when Peel recognized after the Reform Act that the Crown could not sustain a party of its own and therefore built up the Conservative party, he did not acknowledge any loyalty, as leader, to his own followers and said firmly in 1846: 'I am not under any obligation to any man or to any body of men.' This was his unforgivable sin in Disraeli's eyes. Disraeli hounded Peel out of the party leadership and seized the vacant place. He was the first politician to put loyalty to party above loyalty to country, and his example has been universally admired, though not always followed. Disraeli riveted on our political life the conception that politics consist entirely in two parties fighting for office. These two parties were to represent not programmes but interests. What interests Disraeli did not much mind. Sometimes he talked of the Conservative party as 'the landed interest'; sometimes he appealed to all who had 'a stake in the country'; in practice his party was an alliance between the City and the mob. None of this mattered. The important thing was the struggle for power – a tradition which the Conservative party has faithfully observed to this day. It is true also to Disraeli's tradition in not knowing what to do with power when it has got it. To catch the other side bathing and make off with their clothes is still its only resource.

One can understand how Disraeli achieved the leadership of the party by offering the prospect of unremitting combat. The field always prefers a huntsman who halloos them on. But Disraeli knew better tricks. His novels, his speeches, his casual remarks, all held out the promise of a mystery which he never revealed, which was not in fact there to reveal. He, not Napoleon III, was the true Sphinx without a secret. Or, rather, his secret was the absence of moral earnestness. A rarefied mountain-air becomes intolerable in time, and the holiday-maker is glad to escape to Monte Carlo. So it was with the Victorians. No age has been more high-minded, and the strain often became unendurable. Gladstone was the Victorian conscience; Disraeli the release from it.

14. Lord Salisbury

A talk given on the Third Programme of the BBC and then
published in The Listener. The Lord President of the
Council referred to was Herbert Morrison who described
another talk of mine on British foreign policy as 'anti-
British, anti-American and not particularly competent', a
rebuke echoed by R C K Ensor, the historian. When this
talk was given, the British Government had not yet
transferred the guardianship of anti-Communist Greece to
the United States.

Lord Salisbury was a consistent Tory. He never wavered in
his principles and never deserted them : in 1867 he risked his
political future rather than agree to the democratic Reform
Bill with which Derby and Disraeli hoped to 'dish the Whigs',
and twenty years later he took office as the uncompromising
opponent of Home Rule. He came of one of the few genuinely
Tory families – and one of the few, too, which went back
beyond the Glorious Revolution, a family which had never
joined in the hunt for honours under the Hanoverians. Two
great Cecils, William and Robert, served Elizabeth and James
I, then came an unbroken row of nonentities for more than
two hundred years. Here is the strange thing about Salisbury :
he was distinguished from his ancestors by his intellectual
gifts, which were very great; he had the political and religious
outlook of a slow-witted countryman. His own thinking was
ruthless – he spared nothing and nobody; the political creed
to which he held had been hammered out by generations of
Englishmen who distrusted thought in politics. He hated
society and social functions, he was impatient with hereditary
distinctions; the party which he led existed to preserve the

social order and valued hereditary claims. He arrived at his own conclusions by private thought, locked away in his study behind double doors, never consulting others until his mind was fully made up; yet he spoke with contempt of the study-made conclusions of political thinkers. His followers cared for the English countryside and country pursuits; he disliked horses and preferred the villa which he built at Dieppe to his historic house at Hatfield. The Tory party has been called the stupid party (and not unfairly, to be stupid and to be sensible are not far apart. The Progressive party, Radical and Socialist, is clever, but silly). Strange indeed : the most successful leader that the stupid party has had since the Reform Bill was an intellectual, supremely clever.

This contrast gives Salisbury's character a special fascination. Most prime ministers would not be interesting unless they had been prime ministers (and some are not interesting even then): most of their biographies are heavy going even for the historian – think of the dead-weight of Morley's Gladstone, or Monypenny and Buckle on Disraeli. Lady Gwendolen Cecil's life of her father is a work of art, a great biography which can be read for pleasure by someone with no interest in political history at all. Salisbury would have been a remarkable man even if he had never been prime minister or even if he had never gone into politics at all. He was a character as Dr Johnson was a character and on the same scale. Think of his monumental absent-mindedness which led him to greet his own son, encountered in the grounds of Hatfield House, as an important but unrecognized guest. Once at a breakfast party, sitting on his host's left, he asked in an undertone who was the distinguished man on the host's right. It was Mr W H Smith, Salisbury's chancellor of the exchequer, who had sat at Salisbury's side in Cabinet for years. Equally delightful was his scientific enthusiasm, which led him to put glaring and erratic electric light into Hatfield House; it worked from the river and sank to a dull red when the stream was low. Hatfield was also wired for a primitive telephone, with a sort of loud-speaker attachment, by means of which Salisbury could boom into every room : 'Hey diddle diddle, the cat and the fiddle; the cow jumped over the moon.'

He was a first-rate writer. His letters and dispatches are still, after half a century, a delight to read – no one could say the same of Peel or even of Gladstone. His political journalism is as fresh now as when it was written. His essay on the Polish question, for instance, written in 1863, is the most sensible thing ever written on Poland and Russia; it was heavily drawn on by Eden during the debate in the House of Commons which followed the Yalta Agreement of 1945. Eden jibbed however at the conclusion that the best one can hope for Poland is that she should enjoy a limited autonomy under Russian protection. He was a master of the telling phrase. 'Backing the wrong horse' – the policy of propping up Turkey instead of cooperating with Russia in the Near East. 'Splendid isolation' – not, as is often supposed, a description of his policy, but a reminder that only a Power whose vital interests are not involved can examine a problem in an 'emotional and philanthropic spirit'. Some of his most telling phrases had a jaunty air which would have brought the wrath of Mr Ensor and the Lord President of the Council down on me if I had used them. Thus he described the Cape-to-Cairo railway as 'a curious idea which has lately become prevalent', and the conflict of the Great Powers in China as 'a sort of diplomatic cracker that has produced a great many detonations, but I think the smoke of it has now floated into the distance'. When the Russians occupied Port Arthur in 1898 he wrote that the British public would demand 'some territorial or cartographic consolation in China. It will not be useful, and it will be expensive; but as a matter of pure sentiment, we shall have to do it.' Once, defending an agreement which assigned to France a large part of the Sahara, he said : 'This is what agriculturists would call very "light" land' – not a tact-ful way of recommending the agreement to French public opinion.

All these dazzling phrases are about foreign affairs, and foreign policy was his consuming interest. He first stepped into the front rank in politics in 1878; he became foreign secretary in place of Lord Derby and got British foreign policy out of the mess into which it had been landed by the conflict between the pacifism of Derby and the erratic, unpredictable bellicosity of Disraeli. Sitting in the House of Lords – he was the last prime minister to sit in the Lords and I don't suppose we shall have another, the peerage is not likely to produce a man of Salisbury's genius in centuries – he had few parlia-mentary cares and, except for a few months in 1886 and again for a few months at the end of his life, he combined the jobs of prime minister and foreign secretary. He was very much the senior, too, in his Cabinets. He could conduct foreign policy virtually uncontrolled – not checked by a prime minister, not interfered with much by the Cabinet and re-mote even from questions in the House of Commons. Add to this that Rosebery, the Liberal foreign secretary in the short break between Salisbury's governments, was virtually im-posed on Gladstone by the Queen, at Salisbury's prompting, and that Rosebery was Salisbury's obedient pupil. As a result, Salisbury had fifteen years, from 1885 to 1900, of directing foreign policy, a record in our history; moreover, it was really a policy he directed. He was fond of saying that a British foreign secretary could have no policy. In his own words 'British policy is to drift lazily downstream, occasionally putting out a boat-hook to avoid a collision.' But this apparent planlessness was really a device to keep his hands free and to conceal his plans from foreigners. There is nothing in the history of our foreign policy to compare with the prolonged and patient way in which Salisbury solved the difficulties of the British position in Egypt, isolating Egypt first from one country and then another, and finally staging the open challenge to France at Fashoda in 1898. Indeed, I would say that Salisbury laid down the lines on which British foreign policy was to develop for many years after his death: he saw that so long as we were quarrelling with France and Russia all over the world – in Egypt, in Persia, in the Far East – we were dependent on German favour, and he was determined to escape this favour. Therefore, slowly and persistently, he prepared the way for the Anglo-French entente, which matured in 1904, and the Anglo-Russian entente, which matured in 1907. At the very basis of his thoughts was the fact that has been brought home to us by two great wars: if England and Russia, the two Great Powers on the edge of Europe, fall out, they will have Europe, in the shape of Germany, on their backs. That is why Salisbury, greatest of our foreign secretaries, was the greatest advocate of Anglo-Russian cooperation.

In comparison with these great world affairs, Salisbury had less interest in the humdrum tasks of a prime minister. He was too outspoken to be a good manager of men and could never have been a successful leader of the House of Commons. But, to his surprise, he found that he could compete with Gladstone as a public speaker at mass meetings: like many intellectuals, an impersonal mass audience drew him out where a few dozen individuals did not. He spoke in the fine Victorian way without notes, sometimes pausing for as much as thirty seconds between sentences; the effect was ponderous, absolutely sincere, like the strokes of a great hammer. But, with this sincerity and greatness of character, what had he to say? Very little. The only question on which he felt strongly was the defence of the Established Church. This marks him off from other Victorian prime ministers: most of them were lukewarm in religion. Gladstone, on the other hand, was so devout that he desired to disestablish the Church so that it could develop the virtue of apostolic poverty. Apart from this,

Salisbury excelled at exposing the follies of others, but had little to advocate himself. Though a good landlord in private life, he had no social philosophy : he accepted private enterprise and Free Trade like any Liberal. When Disraeli urged that the Conservatives ought to take the lead in social reform, Salisbury complained that Disraeli was 'featherbrained'.

The truth is that this great man, so free from illusions, had one great illusion : fear of democracy and belief in the virtue of resisting for resisting's sake. During the American civil war, when he was, of couse, strongly on the side of the slave-owning South, his mind was so agitated that he took to sleep-walking, and one night his wife saw him rise from his bed and stand at the open window, warding off an imaginary attack; the forces of democracy were trying to break into Hatfield House. He spoke all his life as though democracy was a sort of germ people catch, much as people now talk of Communism as a germ that will get into the Western world unless we keep the Greek window closed. Instead of the process of compromise between parties which has been the normal pattern of our political life, he wanted to make a sharp division between them and have a fight. The issue he found to fight on was Irish Home Rule. Gladstone had hoped that the Conservatives would carry Home Rule as Peel had carried Free Trade. Instead Salisbury – it was his decision that mattered – made it the matter of political conflict for a generation. In one sense it did the trick : it gave the Conservatives almost twenty years of office. But at a high price. It left the Irish question to be settled later at a terrible cost in bitterness and bloodshed. It taught the Conservatives to value violence and pugnacity as a policy and so led them to the follies of defending the House of Lords in 1910 and to the worse-than-folly of the Ulster rebellion in 1914. What is more, it made Salisbury himself the prisoner of all the violent men prepared to resist Home Rule, the prisoner of Joseph Chamberlain and of the unscrupulous Imperialists, the prisoner even of Cecil Rhodes.

Salisbury had begun as the leader of devout country gentle-men with centuries of honest tradition behind them. He ended as the leader of the Unionists, the party of the City and high finance. He took the lead in the partition in Africa in order to end the slave trade; this was not the motive of his party-backers in the Chartered Companies. His last great act was to lead this country into the Boer war. Undoubtedly he hoped to establish the British ideal of racial equality in South Africa. The Boer war made the gold and diamonds secure for the city companies; it has not, so far, benefited the South African natives. And here, I think, we have got to the secret of his strange personality, of the contrast between his private charitableness and the bitterness of his public expression: he loved the joy of battle, but found no worthy cause for which to fight. He fought for victory; he expected defeat. His two great ancestors had founded the greatness of the British Empire; Salisbury heard from afar the notes which announced its end. When Salisbury resigned in 1902, old England too passed from the stage of history.

15. Prelude to Fashoda: The Question of the Upper Nile, 1894–5

English Historical Review. This academic exercise was stimulated by the publication of the relevant volume of French diplomatic documents and the opening of the Foreign Office papers to the end of 1902. The essay contains my only discovery of something previously unknown: the Anglo-Congolese agreement of 12 April 1894, soon to be superseded by a similar agreement on 12 May 1894.

1

The Anglo-Congolese treaty of 12 May 1894 and its aftermath have often been discussed by historians;[1] its origins have not been made clear, and the negotiations that followed have remained obscure – the accounts of them have been based on casual (and inaccurate) references by Hanotaux and Harcourt. These obscurities can be removed with the aid of the French documents[2] and of the Foreign Office archives.

In the eighteen nineties Africa dwarfed all other questions in British diplomacy. Previously it had been rare to separate a topic from the general 'diplomatic' correspondence, and these independent files had been short-lived. Egypt, as a subdivision of Turkey, was the first to acquire a permanent separation for obvious reasons. In 1893 the old 'Slave Trade' file (F.O. 84) was closed and 'Africa' became a separate heading in the correspondence with France, Germany and Belgium; these

1. W L Langer, The Diplomacy of Imperialism (New York, 1935), i, chs. iv and ix.
2. Documents Diplomatiques Français (1871–1914), Ier série, tome xi (1947). Cited henceforth as D.D.F.

'Africa' files bulked larger than the general 'diplomatic' files in size and importance.[3] For instance, the French 'diplomatic' files for the period when Kimberley was foreign secretary (March 1894 to June 1895) contain trivialities except for a few conversations on Armenian affairs in the autumn of 1894 and on Far Eastern affairs early in 1895. The only memorable remark is a minute by Kimberley which reads : 'It will be a misfortune if M. Delcassé becomes colonial minister.'[4]

Africa was important to the Foreign Office in another way. Starting with Egypt, and then proceeding to a bewildering accumulation of protectorates and chartered companies, the Foreign Office was acquiring an empire of its own, which it conducted without reference to the Colonial Office. The Foreign Office staffed and administered this unofficial empire, drew its boundaries, and devised its legal codes, as though the British had no previous experience of imperial affairs, and negotiated with the Colonial Office as with a foreign power. The lord of this African empire was Sir Percy Anderson, the African expert at the Foreign Office.

After the death of Gordon in 1885, the British postponed, though they did not renounce, the recovery of the Sudan, and their diplomacy aimed at excluding others. This had been achieved in the case of Germany by the agreement of 1 July 1890, and in the case of Italy in 1891. The Anglo-German agreement contained a recognition of 'the British sphere of influence', specifically defined on east and west and extending northward 'to the confines of Egypt'. Since this agreement was public and was not at the time disputed by any Power, the British later claimed it as 'an international instrument', giving

3. These files were closed at the end of 1898 for interesting reasons which are irrelevant here. As well there was a special 'Africa' class (F.O. 2) which contained the correspondence with the various commissioners and consuls-general.

4. Minute by Kimberley on Phipps to Kimberley, no. 117, 18 March 1894, F.O. 27/3171.

authority to their 'sphere'. In 1890 the British were thinking solely of the danger to the Sudan from the east and supposed that, by means of the agreement with Germany and Italy, they had done the trick. Early in 1894 it became obvious that both France and Leopold II, as sovereign of the Congo Free State, were threatening to break into the Nile from the west. The British had tried to bar the way against a French advance by an agreement with Germany in November 1893, which would have allowed the Germans to advance up to the Nile watershed, but the Germans dodged this dubious attraction by an agreement with the French, initialled on 4 February 1894, and confirmed on 15 March. Leopold II was in an even stronger position. He had an agreement of 1890, made with Sir William Mackinnon, chairman of the British East Africa Company, which permitted him to enter the valley of the upper Nile, and he claimed (though without justification) that this agreement had been approved by Lord Salisbury. However, Leopold was not happy about this title and had already thrown out a suggestion in 1892 that he might renounce it if the British Government would instead give him a lease of the same territories.[5]

In 1892 no reply had been made. In 1894, through the thick African haze, the British saw both Belgian and French expeditions on the Nile. The Belgian expedition was a fact: it was supposed to be at Lado, though Eetvelde, the king's Congo agent, revealed, when the negotiations had been successfully concluded, that it had only reached Wadelai.[6] The French expedition was a vaguer, and more alarming, affair. The British did not, of course, know of the grandiose decision made by President Carnot on 3 May 1893 : 'We must *occupy* Fashoda';[7] but the purport of the Franco–German

5. Monson to Salisbury, no. 63, 7 July 1892, F.O. 10/577.

6. Anderson, Note on the Belgian negotiations, 13 April 1894, F.O. 10/625.

7. Monteil to Lebon (under-secretary for Colonies), 7 March 1894,

negotiation was clear,[8] and the Belgians did their best to make the British flesh creep with stories of French preparations.[9] Lugard, home on leave to advise on these questions, was sent over to Paris to have a friendly chat with Monteil, the leading French advocate of advance to the Nile, and returned on 10 March 1894 with the news: 'Monteil means to march on Lado or Fashoda with an exceptionally well-organized expedition.'[10]

The final impulse to negotiations with Leopold was the impending declaration of a protectorate over Uganda, which was made on 12 April: the main purpose of this was to secure the route to the upper Nile, and therefore it was urgent both to avoid a conflict with the Congolese forces and to bar the way against the French. Leopold, on his side, recognized that he could not afford to quarrel with both the French and the British. He was already in dispute with the French over the Franco-Congolese frontier on the Ubanghi and hoped to get British backing here, if he met British wishes on the Nile. Moreover, he had – or so he supposed – the advantage over the French in a 'standstill' agreement on the Ubanghi, made on 20 March to allow of negotiations; this made it impossible for the French to move towards the Nile, while the Congolese forces could reach it without passing through the territory covered by the standstill agreement.

On 5 March 1894, Rennell Rodd, one of the 'Africans' in

D.D.F., no. 65. Unlike the Foreign Office, the French department of foreign affairs never developed an independent 'empire'; indeed, it was often in the dark as to French colonial plans.

8. Anderson minuted on 13 February 1894 (on Plunkett to Rosebery, no. 18, 11 February 1894, F.O. 10/614): 'It is certainly probable that when the negotiations with Germany are concluded Captain Monteil will push towards the Nile.'

9. They succeeded. Anderson minuted Plunkett to Kimberley, no. 35, 31 March 1894, F.O. 10/614: 'The presence of the French in force seems to be beyond doubt.' At this time Monteil was still in Paris.

10. Lugard memorandum, 10 March 1894, F.O. 83/1310.

the Foreign Office, was instructed to go to Brussels. He was to demand, as a preliminary, 'an unreserved abandonment' of the Mackinnon agreement. This, it was pointed out, should not be difficult,

> as the retirement of the East African Company from the interior precludes for ever the possibility of its being able to occupy and then to cede the Nile watershed, and as Lord Salisbury has distinctly denied that he gave the sanction attributed to him by misunderstanding, to the abandonment by Great Britain of any portion of her sphere.

Rodd was then to ask for a recognition by the Congo Free State of the British sphere of influence (as defined in the Anglo-German agreement of 1890) and for the transfer to Great Britain of all treaties made or to be made in this territory by officers of the Free State. In return Leopold was to be offered a lease (terminable on his death) of the left bank of the Nile as far north as Fashoda; this territory was to include the Bahr el Ghazal, which lay between the Nile valley and the nearest French post.[11] Both lessor and lessee would declare that they did not ignore the contingent claim of Turkey. Finally, as an afterthought, Anderson added the condition of 'a concession to powers of telegraphic communication in the State territories between the British spheres'.[12]

Rodd was unable to see Leopold II, who had developed a convenient illness. He submitted his proposals through Eetvelde, Congo minister of the interior, and the king's factotum for Congo affairs.[13] On 17 March Leopold transmitted

11. The territory was that subsequently defined in the treaty, except that its northern limit was fixed at the 8th parallel. This was supposed to include Fashoda; the Intelligence Department of the War Office subsequently pointed out that Fashoda was to the north of this line, which was then advanced to parallel 10. (Note on the Belgian negotiations by Anderson, 13 April 1894, F.O. 10/625.)

12. Rosebery to Rodd, 5 March 1894, secret, F.O. 10/625.

13. Leopold conducted these negotiations with great secrecy. He told his Belgian ministers nothing; and even de Grelle Rogier, who

counter-proposals, demanding a lease which should terminate 'only if Belgium became a republic or if the Congo passed to other hands'. Eetvelde hinted that these demands were 'trying it on'; at the same time he made it clear that, if the British did not settle, it would be easy for Leopold to agree with the French. Rodd reported:

M. de Eetvelde was constant in his assurances that it was the King's desire to anticipate this [French] movement by an occupation effected under agreement with us, that the Congo State had nothing but enemies in France &c., but the fact must not be lost sight of that if France, having become 'plus aimable', should suddenly recognize the claims of the King on the Nile, the way would be open for an agreement for mutual support in the Nile basin as against us.[14]

Anderson rejected Leopold's proposal. It was the ultimate intention of British policy to turn the Belgians out of the valley of the Nile when British forces arrived there; besides, Leopold's scheme would involve Great Britain in the internal affairs of Belgium, if ever there were a movement against the monarchy. Anderson therefore suggested 'a lease for a fixed term, renewable by consent, to be made personally to the King and his descendants, terminable by notice'; Rodd, who had gone on to Paris, should return to Brussels, and negotiate a compromise.[15] Rosebery, who had just become prime minister,

---

was in charge of the foreign affairs of the Congo State, was unaware on 20 April that the agreement with Great Britain had been signed on 12 April. He said to Plunkett: 'One of the greatest difficulties arose from the jealousy of England shown by the French delegates, who seemed to imagine that the Congolese government is somehow in league with the English, or has some arrangement with them. You know very well that is not the case.' Punkett shrugged his shoulders and, saying 'I wish it were the case', left the room. (Plunkett to Kimberley, no. 49, 21 April 1894. F.O. 10/614.)

14. Rodd to Anderson, 17 March 1894, private; Report by Rodd, 19 March 1894, secret, F.O. 10/625.

15. Minute by Anderson, 25 March 1894, F.O. 10/625.

thought it 'essential' to proceed without delay. The question of Uganda and, from it, of the upper Nile had dominated his tenure of the Foreign Office; it had led to endless disputes in the Cabinet, and it is reasonable to suppose that he was anxious to see both questions settled while still in close touch with the Foreign Office. He therefore directed that 'the King's man' should be invited to London to settle the final details.[16] On 28 March, Kimberley, Rosebery's successor as foreign secretary, broke the news of the negotiations to Harcourt, chancellor of the Exchequer,[17] in terms which clearly implied that agreement was in sight; indeed, since Harcourt had always been the principal opponent of the Foreign Office in these questions, it would have been pointless to inform him before the matter was ripe for the Cabinet.

Eetvelde therefore came to London on 9 April without any further negotiations through Rodd. He proposed an accept-able compromise. The left bank of the Nile as far north as Fashoda and as far west as longitude 30° east should be leased to Leopold for his lifetime only; the larger area of the Bahr el Ghazal, outside the Nile valley (i.e. between 25° and 30° east), should be leased to the king and his successors. This suited both parties. Leopold got what he regarded as the most valuable territory more or less for good; the British got security that the Nile valley would revert to them within a few years and yet established a permanent buffer against the French. Further, in exchange for the permanent lease of a corridor from Congo territory to the Nile, Eetvelde agreed to lease to the British a similar corridor across Congolese terri-tory from north to south (this was a last-minute addition by Anderson to his earlier request for a telegraph concession).[18]

16. Minute by Rosebery, 27 March 1894, F.O. 10/625.

17. Kimberley to Harcourt, 28 March 1894, A G Gardiner, Life of Sir William Harcourt (1923), ii, 313.

18. These geographical details will be made clear by reference to the map in Langer, Diplomacy of Imperialism, i, 133.

The agreement was signed by Eetvelde and Kimberley on 12 April;[19] it was to be kept secret for three months. Leopold thought that he had secured British backing against the French. The British thought that they had put Leopold as a barrier between France and the upper Nile—and an effective barrier, since there was talk of six, or sometimes eight, 'Krupp guns'. Besides, by accumulating recognitions of the British 'sphere of influence' from everyone except the French, the British hoped to argue that in some curious implicit way the French, too, had been committed to it.[20]

The French also were anxious to settle with Leopold II in order to prevent an agreement with the British such as had already been secretly made. A French delegation led by Hanotaux, then African expert at the French foreign ministry, came to Brussels on 16 April. Hanotaux offered a favourable settlement of the Ubanghi frontier, on condition that France secured 'son chemin libre' to the valley of the Nile. Leopold could not make this bargain, and negotiations were broken off on 23 April.[21] Leopold now became alarmed. The French would have 'a plausible cause of complaint', when they discovered that he had made an agreement with Great

19. Kimberley to Plunkett, no. 23, 9 April; no. 24D, 12 April 1894, F.O. 10/613. Though Harcourt makes an obscure reference to agreement having been reached on 12 April the signature of a valid agreement then was unknown until the opening of the archives. Both British and Belgians had later good grounds for concealment.

20. Note on the Belgian negotiations by Anderson, 13 April 1894, F.O. 10/625. At the conclusion Eetvelde said: 'the French have always referred to the Anglo-German agreement as an instrument with which they have no concern. They may contrive to neglect it, but it will be difficult, even for French Chauvinists, after the publication of its recognition by the Congo State, to send an armed expedition to the Nile ... We have two weapons to oppose to them, our garrisons, and prior occupation.' Anderson added: 'Whatever may be the efficiency of the former, there is no doubt that, unless the Mahdists bar the way, we, or they, should have enough to secure the latter.'

21. Plunkett to Kimberley, no. 52, 24 April; no, 55, 27 April 1894, F.O. 10/614. There is no record of these negotiations in D.D.F.

Britain 'shutting France out from the valley of the Upper Nile', four days before Hanotaux arrived in Brussels.[22] The British refused to delay publication; indeed they were anxious to accelerate it, for the same reason which made Leopold anxious to put it off. Nor would they cancel the agreement which had been duly signed.[23] They offered to substitute a more general agreement by which Leopold would recognize the British sphere and would admit that he must withdraw from it when given notice to do so. By this he would have had all the disadvantages of the original agreement and less security.[24] The British finally consented to alter the date of the agreement so that it should seem to have been made after Hanotaux's visit to Brussels, and a new agreement, virtually in the same terms as that of 12 April, was signed in Brussels by Eetvelde and Plunkett, the British minister, on 12 May. Leopold had to pay for this concession by consenting to the publication of the agreement when the British parliament met on 21 May.[25]

22. Plunkett to Kimberley, no. 51, 24 April 1894, F.O. 10/614.

23. According to Harcourt (Gardiner, *Harcourt*, ii, 315), Anderson was sent to Brussels on 23 April, after a row in the British cabinet, 'to see if the king of the Belgians will give it [the treaty] up'. There is no trace of this in the F.O. correspondence: indeed the Foreign Office was holding Leopold to the treaty against his will. Probably it is one of the many instances of keeping Harcourt at bay. Moreover, there is fairly decisive proof that Anderson never went to Brussels. Eetvelde, when signing the revised treaty on 12 May, deleted a reference to a conversation with Anderson, 'since he could only have seen him in London (between 9 and 12 April) and the attention of France must not be called to this visit'. (Plunkett to Kimberley, no. 68, 12 May 1894, F.O. 10/615.)

24. Rosebery to Queen Victoria, 4 May 1894. *Letters of Queen Victoria*, 3rd series, ii, 396. Kimberley to Plunkett, telegram, no. 2, 5 May 1894. F.O. 10/618.

25. Plunkett to Kimberley, no. 68, 12 May 1894, F.O. 10/615. The date of publication was determined solely by the meeting of parliament. There is therefore no foundation for the surmise (Langer, *Diplomacy of Imperialism*, i, 134) that publication was designed to

It is convenient to summarize here the principal provisions of the Anglo-Congolese agreement, and especially the clauses which gave rise to subsequent dispute. In the preamble, Leopold, as sovereign of the Congo Free State, recognized the British 'sphere of influence' in the Nile valley, as defined in the Anglo-German agreement of 1890. In exchange for this the Free State received, by Article I, a 'rectification' of frontier towards the Nile valley (though not actually reaching it) which, in fact, amounted to a considerable concession of territory. Article II then leased to Leopold all the sphere on the left bank of the Nile which he had just recognized. The lease was in two parts: the Bahr el Ghazal and also a corridor to the Nile 25 kilometres wide to Leopold and his successors; the left bank of the Nile as far west as longitude 30° east to Leopold during his life. This article, by fixing the northern limit to the lease at latitude 10° north, obliquely gave to the British 'sphere' the northern definition which had been lacking in the Anglo-German agreement. Article III gave the British the lease of a similar corridor 25 kilometres wide across the Congo Free State from north to south. Article IV laid down that Leopold could not acquire sovereign rights in the leased territory.[26] By an exchange of letters both parties de-

---

coincide with the ministerial crisis in France. This could not have been foreseen on 12 May.

26. This article was the only one substantially amended from the agreement of 12 April. The amendment was designed to conceal the fact that, before the signing of the agreement, Leopold had already acquired (dubious) sovereign rights by treaty with native chiefs, since it could be argued that these had been acquired by him as ruler of the Congo Free State and therefore could not be renounced without allowing the French to exercise the right of pre-emption to Free State titles, which they had been granted in 1884. The original Article II had provided that the leased territories should use the British flag with a white star in the middle. The agreement of 12 May substituted 'a special flag', and one of equivocal significance was designed though never used. Plunkett to Kimberley, telegram, no. 2, 9 May 1894, F.O. 10/618.

clared that they did not ignore 'the claims of Egypt and Turkey'. It is difficult to imagine a stranger transaction. A, in return for recognizing B's disputed title, at once receives from B the grant of part, and the lease of the rest, of the property. Yet, at the same time as B (by Article I) is making a final cession to A, both declare that they do not ignore the rights of third parties – and indeed subsequently assert these rights as against others.

2

The French Government do not seem to have had any suspicion of the agreement between Great Britain and the Congo Free State.[27] They realized that the British and the Belgians would attempt to race them to the upper Nile, and they were confident that they would win this race – rightly, as it turned out, for Marchand was first at Fashoda. They were therefore anxious to keep the question of the upper Nile on the practical basis of a race in Africa and away from the field of diplomacy. The Anglo-Congolese treaty threatened this plan, and Casimir-Périer, who was just leaving office, protested against it in Brussels and London[28] as soon as it was published. Hanotaux, his successor, though an African specialist in the foreign ministry, was less of a colonial enthusiast than Delcassé; he gladly accepted the description that 'he had always acted as a drag-chain on M. Delcassé'.[29] In later years, when Hanotaux's

27. There is no hint of pre-publication knowledge in D.D.F. On 30 August (Plunkett to Kimberley, no. 225, F.O. 10/617) Lambermont, of the Belgian Foreign Office, alleged that Hanotaux was aware that the agreement of 12 May was not the original one, and that he had treated the Congolese delegates harshly because of this. Again, there is no hint of this in D.D.F., and Lambermont was probably cadging for British sympathy.

28. Casimir-Périer to Bourée, 26 May 1894, D.D.F., no. 109; Decrais to Kimberley, 28 May 1894, D.D.F., no. 113.

29. Phipps to Dufferin, enclosed in Dufferin to Kimberley, no. 148, 6 June 1894, F.O. 27/3185.

policy seemed to have led to Fashoda and Delcassé's to the Entente Cordiale, reputations were reversed, and even Hanotaux presented himself as a colonial enthusiast whose legacy had been squandered by Delcassé. The contrast between them, in either period, was overdrawn. Both desired a settlement with England; both desired it on colonial terms profitable to France. At all times the colonial minister thought primarily of colonial details, and the foreign minister (whether Hanotaux or Delcassé) primarily of the entente. Both men, as foreign ministers, knew that the entente would not be accepted by French public opinion unless the colonial terms were tolerable; hence they sometimes seemed to the British to be driving a hard bargain. Their ultimate objective, a general settlement, did not alter.

Hanotaux understood both the broad issues and the points of detail raised by the Anglo-Congolese Treaty.[30] He was alone in this. Lord Dufferin, the British ambassador, was a former Viceroy of India, a *grand seigneur* who knew nothing of African trivialities; besides, he was annoyed that his arrival in Paris had not led to an immediate improvement in French feeling towards England and was hostile to the French as a

30. Hanotaux, a future Academician, kept full and well-written accounts of his conversations: this was rare for a French foreign minister. As a witness, however, he had the faults of a good writer: he would put things too sharply and exaggerated his own successes. On the other hand, when challenged, he would modify his original version without complaint – again the quality of a good writer. Thus in his Note to the British Government of 6 August 1894 (D.D.F., no. 209) he claimed: 'Lord Dufferin had admitted that most of the observations made to him are well-founded.' When Dufferin objected to this, Hanotaux withdrew and claimed only that Dufferin had described the French thesis as 'debatable'. Again, he fathered on to Phipps the 'self-denying' arrangement which was the highwater mark of negotiations in October; when challenged by Phipps, he admitted that they had devised it together, and that Phipps had merely given it precise form so as to submit it to London. (Phipps to Kimberley, no. 266, 9 October 1894, F.O. 27/3187.

result.[31] Phipps, the British minister under Dufferin, was well-grounded in African frontier questions, which he had often discussed earlier with Hanotaux; his frank reporting of the French case made the Foreign Office write him off as too French in sympathy. In England, Kimberley had only just entered the Foreign Office. He was garrulous and elderly and had had no experience of foreign affairs for twenty-five years. Though always running over with conciliation and goodwill towards France in conversation, he was dominated by Rosebery, and followed Rosebery's violent promptings without demur.[32] Anderson, who determined African policy, worked directly with Rosebery and often informed Kimberley only when a decision had been made. Anderson had no interest in general policy or in French goodwill. For him the friendship of France was of no account in comparison with any scrap of African territory, and he thwarted Phipps's efforts at conciliation with an equipment of even greater knowledge of detail. It is, of course, the duty of the permanent officials to be stiff on every detail; both British and French diplomats tried to drive as hard a bargain as possible during the successful negotiations ten years later. But there was then also the will to agree in the last resort. The disputes between England and France could never be ended merely by contesting every issue as it arose. New disputes would arise endlessly unless there were the desire for a general settlement. The British at this earlier period had no such desire. The French could never lose sight of Europe as the British had done. This held them back all along from war; it did not yet lead them to make concessions for the sake of British friendship.

31. Dufferin, too, was a distinguished writer, and therefore, like Hanotaux, an unreliable witness.

32. Rosebery recommended Kimberley as foreign secretary to the queen thus: 'Lord Rosebery thought it would do quite well, as he spoke French, and had been the under-secretary under Lord Clarendon.' (The Queen's Journal, 5 March 1894. Letters of Queen Victoria, 3rd series, ii, 376.)

Hanotaux lost no time. He called on Dufferin on 1 June and warned him that the Anglo-Congolese treaty would ruin relations with France. Dufferin knew nothing about it : Hanotaux, he said, 'had surprised him in a complete ignorance of African affairs',[33] and he asked Hanotaux : 'What are we to do now? The convention is made ... How are we to get out of the difficulty without putting the British government in a most false position?' Hanotaux could only suggest that the convention should be withdrawn or at any rate 'held in suspense'.[34] Dufferin appealed to Kimberley in a private letter. On 5 June Kimberley, with the authorization of the Cabinet, agreed to discuss the French objections to the treaty and offered to enter 'into a general review of all African questions pending between the two governments for the purpose of such an adjustment as would place the relations of the two countries in that continent on a more satisfactory footing'; Egypt was to be excluded from the discussion as 'un trop gros morceau'.[35] Dufferin was able to pass this offer on to Hanotaux on 6 June;[36] as a result Hanotaux, speaking in the Chamber on 7 June, adopted a conciliatory, though firm, attitude and met Dufferin for a friendly discussion two or three days later.[37] At this meeting Dufferin tried to make out that the treaty had been made to avoid a conflict with the Belgians, 'without thinking of the effect it would have in France'. He

33. So he told Revoil on 3 June, D.D.F., no. 126.

34. Note by Hanotaux, 2 June 1894, D.D.F., no. 123. Dufferin made no official report of this interview, though he wrote privately to Kimberley. This private correspondence is not available (if it exists).

35. Kimberley to Dufferin, no. 187A, 5 June 1894, F.O. 27/3171. Decrais to Hanotaux, telegram, 5 June 1894, D.D.F., no. 129.

36. Dufferin to Hanotaux, 6 June 1894, D.D.F., no. 133.

37. Hanotaux in his account (D.D.F., no. 139, 11 June 1894) makes Dufferin speak of 'your speech of yesterday', i.e. 7 June. This is impossible, since Hanotaux replied to Dufferin's letter of 6 June only on 9 June (D.D.F., no. 136). Dufferin reported only on 13 June (to Kimberley, nos. 162 and 163, F.O. 27/3185) without mentioning the date of the meeting. 10 June seems the most likely date.

added, 'It is not likely that there was much chance of the arrangements consigned to the Anglo-German agreement being cancelled or essentially modified.' Hanotaux answered, 'That treaty does not exist in our eyes ... We cannot admit this new diplomatic system, which consists in claiming territories, either by arrangements between Powers who have no right, or by simple declarations in parliament ... Our rights in this part of the basin of the Nile are as serious as those of England.' Dufferin went away with the impression that 'The real desire of the French is to prevent us from establishing ourselves ... in the Bahr el Ghazal and in the valley of the Nile, and perhaps to anticipate us in the occupation of these districts.'

The issue had been clearly stated. The British had, as they thought, a satisfactory treaty with the Congo Free State and did not mean to retreat from it. They therefore did not take up Hanotaux's offer of friendly discussion and waited for him to formulate detailed objections, the discussion of which could be dragged out indefinitely. Besides, the British Government had their hands full with the German objections to Article III, by which Congolese territory adjacent to German East Africa had been leased to the British. Here the new material does not essentially modify the existing account. The German move was principally an attempt to blackmail the British into renewing their support of Austria-Hungary and Italy in the Mediterranean; it had perhaps a secondary motive of improving German relations with France. It did not achieve either of these aims. It put Rosebery in a bad temper with the Germans and with the Triple Alliance generally.[38] The French (contrary to German belief) were not taken in and never counted

38. Kimberley, in his muddled way, went on treating the Germans as allies and immediately after giving way to them over Article III, consulted Hatzfeldt, the German ambassador, as to how he should deal with the French. Kimberley to Malet, telegram, no. 93, 18 June 1894, F.O. 64/1335.

on German backing in their dispute with England; moreover, they took care to document the German failure to support them after first promising to do so. The French made sceptical inquiries whether, in view of this newly displayed friendship, the Germans would support them in the Egyptian question;[39] this was the only price at which a Franco-German entente could have been established. The Germans did not respond to this suggestion and the French went on their way alone. The Franco-German cooperation is, in fact, a myth, based only on a tendentious selection of documents in the Grosse Politik.

The French foresaw that the British would meet the German objections and that the Germans would then profess themselves satisfied. The British, alarmed enough in any case, were urged by Leopold II to give in to Germany. On 22 June Leopold and the British signed an agreement abrogating Article III of the agreement of 12 May. The British thus renounced their lease of a corridor across the Free State without demanding from Leopold any lessening of the advantages which he had gained and of which the corridor was supposed to be part of the price. The British surrender to the Germans strengthened the French position. The withdrawal of Article III provided a precedent for the withdrawal of other articles. Moreover, the alarm of Leopold II at German pressure showed his weakness. His Belgian ministers were furious at the dangers in which his greed for African territory threatened to involve Belgium;[40] the British Government refused to promise him support.[41] In fact the British, far from acquiring in Leopold a buffer against France, had undertaken a liability; now they would not accept this liability. The object of the

39. Herbette to Hanotaux, 17 June 1894, D.D.F., no. 154; 20 August 1894, D.D.F., no. 223.

40. Plunkett to Kimberley, nos. 142 and 143, 23 June 1894, F.O. 10/616.

41. Plunkett to Kimberley, no. 114, 10 June 1894, F.O. 10/616; Kimberley to Plunkett, no. 61, 13 June, 1894, F.O. 10/613; Harcourt to Kimberley, 12 June 1894, Gardiner, Harcourt, ii, 317.

Anglo-Congolese treaty was to avoid an Anglo-French dispute; if this dispute was to take place, the British might as well defend their own claims rather than those of Leopold. Hanotaux, at any rate, recognized that the weakest link was in Brussels, and on 22 June he proposed, or rather demanded, negotiations with Leopold II.[42]

Nevertheless, Hanotaux would have preferred to follow the way of conciliation with Great Britain[43] and made repeated attempts to do so. On 18 June he asked Dufferin if he had received any reply from London; Dufferin had received nothing. Hanotaux then decided to appeal to the supposedly friendly disposition of Kimberley. On 19 June he instructed Decrais, ambassador in London, to raise in detail the question of Article II (the clause leasing territory to the Free State).[44] However, on 20 June Dufferin, though still without instructions, came to discuss Article II, and Decrais was therefore told not to raise the question with Kimberley.[45] Dufferin was probably playing at diplomacy on his own. Since the dispute with Germany was not yet technically settled, he wanted to keep Hanotaux in a good temper. He listened, without objection, to Hanotaux's proposal that Leopold II should renounce Article II, as he had already renounced Article III, and himself suggested that Article II might be 'suspended'. What they wanted, he said, was some plan 'under which the principle

42. Hanotaux to Bourée, telegram, 22 June 1894, D.D.F., no. 170.

43. On 14 June Hanotaux told Phipps (to Anderson, private, F.O. 27/3185) that he was unwilling to put his objections on paper 'as he could not be so "large" in writing or show such elasticity as he had shown in conversation with "un ambassadeur courtois" '. This was an excuse with some sincerity in it.

44. Hanotaux to Decrais, telegram, 19 June 1894, D.D.F., no. 160.

45. Hanotaux to Decrais, telegram, 20 June 1894, D.D.F., no. 165; Decrais, in fact, saw Kimberley, though he did not report the interview. All he got from Kimberley was that there must be 'an exchange of views, in order that we might understand exactly the French objections, and what means there were of meeting and satisfying them'. Kimberley to Dufferin, no. 216, 21 June 1894, F.O. 27/3182.

for which he [Hanotaux] contended might be maintained, at the same time that the practical object which we had in view ... might be arrived at'. Since Dufferin had repeatedly assured Hanotaux that this practical object was to avoid a conflict with the Belgians, a solution seemed possible – unfortunately Dufferin was being disingenuous.[46]

Hanotaux also threw out the suggestion, during the conversation of 20 June, of a Conference of the Powers who had created the Congo Free State. This sounded imposing; in reality it was an empty threat. Though France had a good legal case, she could not count on the backing of any Great Power in the Egyptian question, let alone in the question of the upper Nile. This was so obvious in the case of Austria-Hungary and Italy that France had not even asked their opinion. Germany had been appeased by the British, and on 25 June Marschall, the secretary of state, went on holiday so as to avoid further reminders of the approach he had made to France.[47] Russia was no better. On 1 June Hanotaux had invoked the Franco-Russian alliance in an appeal for Russian encouragement and support.[48] After three weeks of evasion a single sentence was extracted from Giers: 'the Emperor entirely approves the point of view of the Government of the Republic'.[49] No action, not even an expression of opinion in London, followed, and the question of the upper Nile continued to revolve between Hanotaux and Dufferin.

They met again on 29 June for an acrimonious discussion. The British surrender to Germany on 22 June had increased the tension between England and France. The British Government were unwilling to discredit themselves further by concessions to France, and Dufferin must have known of Rose-

46. Note by Hanotaux, 20 June 1894, D.D.F., no. 163; Dufferin to Kimberley, no. 169, 21 June 1894, F.O. 27/3185.
47. Herbette to Hanotaux, telegram, 26 June 1894, D.D.F., no. 175.
48. Hanotaux to Montebello, telegram, 1 June 1894, D.D.F., no. 122.
49. Montebello to Hanotaux, telegram, 21 June 1894, D.D.F., no. 169.

bery's mounting irritation. Hanotaux, on his side, was being urged by the colonial ministry to abandon conciliation and to launch Monteil on the race for the upper Nile. Moreover, he knew that Leopold was beginning to yield to French pressure; England would lose the trick in any case, and it was hardly worth while for France to make great concessions. Thus both men were on edge, embarrassed by the combativeness of those behind them, vaguely desirous of agreement, yet with no clear idea what they were discussing. The words 'ultimatum' and 'menace' were exchanged.[50] Hanotaux demanded the uncondi-

50. The 'ultimatum' made such an impression on Hanotaux that he referred to it years later in his book, *Fachoda*, p. 76. It is true that he ascribes it to the first meeting after his speech. This is a pardonable error, and his memory was never reliable (he later ascribed the Phipps–Hanotaux agreement of 9 October to January 1895). He goes on to allege that Dufferin spoke of an ultimatum which he had in the pocket of his frockcoat. This is nonsense. Dufferin had no instructions of any kind, let alone an ultimatum. Hanotaux does not mention a British ultimatum in his note made at the time. According to this, though Dufferin used the word, it was to describe the French demand for the withdrawal of Article II. 'It is an *ultimatum* which you are presenting to us. That cannot be called *negotiating*.' Dufferin does not mention this exchange: no doubt he knew that an account of it would have infuriated Rosebery and made him unyielding. On the other hand, Dufferin, at a later stage of the conversation, described Hanotaux's threat to launch Monteil on the upper Nile as 'a menace'. Hanotaux replied: 'Oh! for heaven's sake do not let it have that character.' Hanotaux, in his turn, does not record this exchange, and for equally obvious reasons: the challenge would have strengthened the impatience of the colonial ministry. In fact, each saw the possibility of a conflict and tried to avoid it.

There is a further curious point. In warning Monteil off the upper Nile, Dufferin used strong language (even invoking his Indian associations). He said: 'It was better that I should at once inform him [Hanotaux] that if M. Monteil attempted to act the part of a second Mizon [a French explorer who had caused a conflict in West Africa] in the Nile valley it would simply mean war between the two countries; and that it would be a terrible thing if we were going to revive in Africa the miserable combats which had deluged India with French and English blood in the middle of the last century.' At

tional withdrawal of Article II; Dufferin refused and denied the right of France to a voice in the upper Nile. Deadlock was reached. Dufferin took his stick and walked towards the door. Hanotaux saved the situation. France, he said, was demanding only the withdrawal of Article II of the Anglo-Congolese

some time after the arrival of this dispatch in London, this passage was deleted and a less offensive passage substituted: 'On this I thought it as well to refer to the great risks which might ensue if an energetic officer, reflecting perhaps the strong views of that Colonial party whose extravagance M. Hanotaux admitted it was necessary to curb, were to start on a strong military expedition unfettered by definite instructions. In the middle of the last century India had been the scene of disastrous conflicts between British and French troops during a period when their respective mother countries were at peace. Were anything of a similar kind to occur in Africa ... the consequences might be very serious, for the deliberate and unprovoked irruption of French troops into a territory over which our jurisdiction had been proclaimed in an international instrument such as the Anglo-German Convention would naturally exasperate public opinion at home and produce a situation fraught with danger to the peaceable relations of the two countries.' The original passage is scored at the side with three large exclamation marks in red pencil. Kimberley used red ink, Rosebery (after he became prime minister) ordinary pencil. Harcourt, to whom this dispatch is marked as having been sent, sometimes ticked dispatches with red pencil, but this marking does not appear to be his. The revised version, in two copies, is on paper and in typescript similar to the original; this proves nothing, as the same paper was used by the F.O. and the embassies, and typescript at this period (when few typewriters were in use) is uniform – at least I am unable to distinguish one from another. One of these copies is headed in Anderson's writing: 'Substitute for passage "On this I said it was better &c".' The original passage had then been deleted and the new passage written in (on the margins, the foot and the reverse) in the handwriting of one of the F.O. clerks.

It is impossible to disentangle what occurred. Presumably Kimberley (or perhaps Harcourt) took alarm at the original passage – no doubt with a Blue Book in mind. Then, either Dufferin was asked to provide an alternative version or Anderson drafted one, and subsequently obtained Dufferin's approval. It is strange that no minute, recording the transaction – or hinting at it – was bound up with the correspondence.

treaty; she was not at present discussing the Anglo-German agreement of 1890, which recognized the upper Nile as a British sphere of influence. The implication of this involved statement was clear : if the claims of Leopold II were dropped, France would be prepared to negotiate about the upper Nile and to leave it to the British – at a price. Both men saw an opening, though the frequent mention of Monteil's name was a reminder that the way of conciliation would not remain open indefinitely.[51]

Still, the opening was not very great. Dufferin, no doubt, thought the agreement with Leopold II a great blunder. For that very reason, he did not want to be the person responsible for withdrawing it – and no one in London would take this responsibility. Besides, the Foreign Office wanted to know what sort of price the French would claim for recognizing the British sphere. This was the object of a further meeting between Hanotaux and Dufferin on 4 July. Dufferin said, 'If France objected, was it not for France, in view of the friendly spirit in which we had entered upon the discussion, to suggest some way out of the difficulty?' Hanotaux replied that he must first have some evidence that Great Britain really wished for a settlement;[52] this evidence would be the withdrawal of Article II.

Kimberley now took a hand. On 11 July he had a rambling discussion with Decrais, in which he touched on every disputed topic except the Anglo-Congolese treaty.[53] He was no doubt hinting that Great Britain would be reasonably conciliatory elsewhere if France would give up all interest in the upper Nile. Hanotaux was not moved. He at once instructed Decrais that a general African settlement could not be dis-

51. Dufferin to Kimberley, no. 173A, 30 June 1894, F.O. 27/3185; note by Hanotaux, 29 June 1894, D.D.F., no. 178.

52. Dufferin to Kimberley, no. 178, 5 July 1894, F.O. 27/3186; note by Hanotaux, 4 July 1894, D.D.F., no. 184.

53. Decrais to Hanotaux, 12 July 1894, D.D.F., no. 190.

cussed until the treaty of 12 May was out of the way.[54] In a private letter he revealed more of his thought: France could get rid of the objectionable treaty in other ways than by agreement with England (and did so shortly afterwards); the only advantage of doing it by agreement was the general improvement of relations that would follow.[55] In other words, Hanotaux was groping towards the Entente Cordiale; the British were thinking solely of the upper Nile. At this time, neither side made any serious move towards the other. The British would have been quite willing to be on good terms with the French, if they could have all they asked in Africa; the French thought that the British ought to sacrifice some of their African ambitions for the sake of good relations. Of the British observers, Phipps believed that Hanotaux was genuine in his desire for a general settlement; Dufferin had little hope of a concrete outcome. Phipps knew more of feeling inside France, and he grasped what appears to be the key to Hanotaux's policy – though he genuinely desired a reconciliation with England, he had first to achieve a striking success over her for the sake of French public opinion. Hanotaux never extricated himself, or the negotiations, from this dilemma; he posed the problem of the entente, but found no solution.

On 17 July Kimberley weakened a little. He agreed that the Anglo-Congolese treaty should be discussed before any general discussion of African questions; only he insisted that the French objections should be formulated in writing and he 'reserved full liberty of action when he saw the French objections'.[56] This was a defeat for Hanotaux: once he formulated objections in writing, he would have to insist on them instead of leaving the way open for some impossible demonstration of goodwill. At this moment, he made his only concrete gesture

54. Hanotaux to Decrais, 15 July 1894, D.D.F., no. 194.

55. Hanotaux to Decrais, private, 15 July 1894, D.D.F., no. 194.

56. Decrais to Hanotaux, telegram, 17 July 1894, D.D.F., no. 196; Kimberley to Dufferin, no. 260, 17 July 1894, F.O. 27/3183.

of conciliation. On 13 July Monteil, on the point of departing for Africa, received strict instructions from both Delcassé and Hanotaux that he was never to send 'a force or even a man into the basin of the Nile'.[57] This short-lived restriction was the only effort ever made by either side to avoid a conflict.

Hanotaux now despaired of persuading the British to give up Article II. The alternative was to bring pressure to bear on Leopold II, and he, though independent as sovereign of the Free State, was already giving way before the indignation of his Belgian ministers. They regarded the Free State as embarrassment enough, and had no wish to add to its territories, let alone to quarrel with France. On 16 July Leopold agreed to send negotiators to Paris.[58] He still hoped to get British backing. Dufferin, however, was recalled to London, ostensibly to advise on the pending discussions between England and France (which were, in fact, not pending), actually to be beyond the reach of the Free State representatives.[59] On 8 August Leopold appealed directly for British support.[60] Rosebery wished to show fight – or rather wished to compel Leopold to show fight. He therefore replied, 'the King must adhere to his position that no alteration can be made in the provisions of the Anglo-Congolese African agreement without the privity and consent of Great Britain'.[61] A few days later, however, he was overruled by the Cabinet,[62] and Leopold was told:

57. Delcassé to Monteil (with minute by Hanotaux), 13 July 1894, D.D.F., no. 191.

58. Leopold to Hanotaux, private, 16 July 1894, D.D.F., no. 195.

59. Leopold complained much of Dufferin's absence. Plunkett to Kimberley, no. 201, 11 August 1894, F.O. 10/617.

60. Plunkett to Kimberley, telegram, no. 33, 8 August 1894, F.O. 10/618.

61. Sanderson to Plunkett, telegram, secret, 8 August 1894, F.O. 10/618. The telegram was sent on Rosebery's instructions, during Kimberley's absence at Windsor. It was made official (no. 41) the following day.

62. Harcourt (Gardiner, *Life*, ii, 320) speaks of a Cabinet on 11

Her Majesty's Government do not feel called upon to oppose the King's desire to sign the Arrangement with the French Government as they have not taken part in the negotiations which have been pending between France and the Independent Sovereign of the Congo and cannot insist on the Congo Government occupying territory leased to them under the Agreement of the 12th of May.[63]

On 14 August Hanotaux signed an arrangement with the Congolese representatives.[64] The Free State received a favourable settlement of the Ubanghi frontier; in return it promised 'to renounce all occupation and not to exercise in future any political action of any sort' west of longitude 30° or north of latitude 5° 30'. This effectively removed the barrier between France and the upper Nile. On the other hand, the French allowed the Free State to take up that part of the lease which did not interfere with French plans (the left bank of the Nile as far north as Lado). They thus deserted their objection of principle that, since the Egyptian title to these territories was still valid, the British had no right to lease them. Their practical aim was, however, achieved: the main purpose of the Anglo-Congolese treaty had been defeated. Yet in the end this French success turned to the advantage of England: Leopold at Fashoda would have been much more difficult to dislodge than Marchand, since he would have possessed a title which the British, at least, could not dispute. As it was, Leopold held on to the left bank of the Nile as far north as Lado, which the

August. He also speaks of the king's being given 'leave to accept'; this is, for a lawyer, a curiously slipshod way of describing the British response which, as Rosebery insisted, was negative – they did not oppose the king's desire, which is a weaker matter than giving him leave. Rosebery (Letters of Queen Victoria, 3rd series, ii, 419) dates the Cabinet at 13 August; he also gives a correct report of its proceedings.

63. Kimberley to Plunkett, telegram, no. 45, 13 August 1894, F.O. 10/618; Plunkett to Kimberley, no. 201, 13 August 1894, F.O. 10/617.

64. D.D.F., no. 217.

French had allowed him to retain, until his death in 1908. Still, as the result of French diplomacy, Leopold (who remained bound by the rest of the treaty of 12 May) had recognized the British sphere of influence, and received only a fraction of the price on which he had always insisted.

3

The affair of the Anglo-Congolese treaty was over; the question of the upper Nile remained. The abortive Article II had made it acute for the first time. Before the discussions of June the British could pretend to be ignorant of the French objections and could claim that their 'sphere of influence' had received international recognition. Now they knew that there must be either negotiation or conflict, and the divided Liberal Cabinet was not a reliable body with which to start a conflict. On the other hand, the British Government had no urgent need for French friendship and negotiated suspiciously, in a grudging spirit. The topics discussed in September and October resembled those settled in the agreement of 8 April 1904; what was lacking was the cordiality.

On 8 August Hanotaux had lodged with the British Government a statement of the French objection to Article II of the treaty;[65] this was no more than a precaution against a possible Blue Book. On 11 August he made a more conciliatory approach to Phipps. He said, 'there is no question of the French advancing to the Bahr el Ghazal', and added : 'Do you imagine that two such nations as England and France contemplate for one moment going to war on account of Sierra Leone, or any other corner of Africa?' This was indeed the weakness of the French position; the statement was, and remained, true of France – it did not remain true of England.

65. D.D.F., no. 209. The Foreign Office prepared, but did not use, an answer to the French arguments. Kimberley to Dufferin, no. 300, 14 August 1894, F.O. 27/3183.

Hanotaux repeated the offer at which he had hinted before: he might recognize the British sphere of influence as 'part of a comprehensive settlement'.[66] The British Government, having been defeated over the Anglo-Congolese treaty, decided to explore this offer, and Dufferin returned to Paris on 14 August with the British terms. The British asked for the recognition of their sphere of influence; in return they would promise that 'the rights of Egypt shall only be in suspense, until the Egyptian government shall be in a position to re-occupy the territories in question'. Further, the British Government would then settle all other African questions 'in a spirit of conciliation'.[67] This proposal was made to Hanotaux on 16 August. It seemed to him unequal: France was presented with a *demand* to recognize the British sphere and would receive, in return, only a vague promise of conciliation. However, he agreed to put the offer before the French council of ministers, when it met on 30 August,[68] and the council evidently authorized him to proceed. Dufferin meanwhile had gone on holiday, and the negotiations were conducted with Phipps, the British minister. Phipps was no doubt better qualified in African detail; at the same time, this arrangement left the British Government freer to repudiate any concession that he might make.

Phipps and Hanotaux negotiated throughout September.[69]

66. Phipps to Kimberley, nos. 202 and 203, 11 August 1894, F.O. 27/3186.

67. The instructions were put in the unofficial form of a private memorandum by Dufferin, 'confirming a conversation with Lord Kimberley', 14 August 1894, F.O. 27/3183. The instructions also contained the suggestion that Great Britain might ask for recognition of her 'sphere' in exchange for recognizing the Franco-Congolese treaty of 14 August. This idea seemed preposterous even to Dufferin, and he did not put it to Hanotaux.

68. Dufferin to Kimberley, no. 209, 16 August 1894, F.O. 27/3186. Note by Hanotaux, 17 August 1894, D.D.F., no. 218.

69. Hanotaux only records a meeting on 5 September 1894, D.D.F., no. 234. Phipps records this (telegram, no. 38, F.O. 27/3188, and to

On the various points in West Africa agreement was reached without difficulty. A separate bargain was struck on each point, and Phipps observed honestly to Anderson that in none of them was there the special 'concession' which France had been promised;[70] no doubt Anderson thought it 'concession' enough to agree with the French at all. Hanotaux complained : 'he could not see . . . any concession, any bait, offered to France at all in proportion with what had been granted to the other Powers'.[71] Still, he declared repeatedly that he would recognize the Anglo-German convention of 1890 (which defined the British sphere) when the British 'bid high enough'. Here a more serious objection arose. They had agreed not to raise the Egyptian question, and the Anglo-German convention itself defined the British sphere as extending 'to the confines of Egypt'. Hanotaux, too, would recognize the British sphere so long as it did not involve recognizing British authority over Egyptian territory. What, then, were the 'confines of Egypt'? It was impossible for the British to answer this question, though the answer was simple. Where territory formerly Egyptian was accessible to the British, Egyptian rights had lapsed; where it was accessible to others (whether France or Italy) Egyptian rights were still valid. Phipps had never been told what was the British sphere, for which he was supposed to be contending; he made a guess and, assuming that it was defined in the Anglo-Congolese treaty, replied that the British sphere extended to latitude 10° north, that is, to Fashoda. It was held in London that a sphere extending as far

Kimberley, no. 223, F.O. 27/3186), and also further meetings on 12 September (telegram, no. 42, F.O. 27/3188, and to Kimberley, no. 223, 13 September, F.O. 27/3186), and on 22 September (telegram, no. 44, F.O. 27/3188, and to Kimberley, no. 247, F.O. 27/3186).

70. Phipps to Anderson, private, 14 September 1894, F.O. 27/3186.

71. The Foreign Office devised an answer (Kimberley to Phipps, no. 330, 14 September 1894, F.O. 27/3183), seeking to prove that Germany and Italy had been paid nothing. This was so much in contradiction with the facts that Kimberley cancelled most of the draft.

north as Fashoda would effectively bar the way against France; Phipps was therefore told that he had guessed correctly.[72]

For Hanotaux the answer was both irrelevant and provocative. Though the British had regarded themselves as free to lease this area to Leopold, they had also asserted in it as against France 'the rights of Great Britain, of Egypt, and the Porte'. He was therefore being asked 'to trench on the Egyptian question'. He had asked to be told the southern limit of Egypt, not the northern limit of the British sphere, and this the British would not tell him. On 30 September he himself attempted a practical definition. The Franco-Congolese arrangement of 14 August, by allowing the Belgians to advance as far north as Lado, had implicitly acknowledged that the rights of Egypt on the west bank ended at latitude 5° 30′ N. Hanotaux now offered to recognize the British sphere on the east bank to the same northern limit. Since the Belgians were already excluded from the rest of the British 'sphere' by the promise made to the French on 14 August, the alleged immediate object of British policy would be attained. Further, to avoid an Anglo-French conflict, he proposed 'a self-denying ordinance'; France would promise for the moment not to pass the Nile–Congo watershed; England would not advance beyond her present posts in Uganda and Unyoro. Once Egypt could take action, there would be a new agreement between

72. The British never discriminated clearly between their sphere and the rights of Egypt; they certainly did not regard them as excluding each other. Fashoda was named as the northern limit of the British sphere simply because it was believed that the French could not reach the Nile farther north, if they recognized the British sphere of influence; but there was never any intention of admitting a 'no man's land' between the confines of Egypt and the British sphere. The entire Nile valley was regarded by the British as being included in one or the other, though they were sometimes doubtful which a particular place was in. They certainly never admitted that Egyptian rights ended at Khartoum. The elaborate speculations of Langer (Diplomacy of Imperialism, i, 260–62) therefore fall to the ground.

the two Governments.[73] Phipps was delighted. He put the proposal into diplomatic form[74] and, after securing Hanotaux's approval of this on 5 October,[75] telegraphed to Anderson on 6 October:

Surely my dispatch of yesterday offers, if not a solution, an indication. Is there not something anomalous in asking for the recognition as a British sphere of a territory admittedly accruing to Egypt. Would it not intrench dangerously on the Egyptian Question proper which I hear privately the greedy Colonials wish to disturb? We might try define and restrict French sphere.[76]

Moreover, with that human failing of not hearing the unwelcome, Phipps ignored Hanotaux's limitation 'for the moment': he assumed, in complete honesty, that France had agreed to recognize the British sphere, and transmitted the offer in this form to the British Government. Admittedly, the British would be barred from entering the Nile valley without French permission. But if, as Phipps had been told, the British object was to prevent by diplomacy a French expedition to the Nile which they had no means of stopping otherwise, that object had been attained. With each inquiry from London, Phipps became increasingly emphatic. On 11 October he telegraphed: France would declare 'the territory east of the

73. Note by Hanotaux, 29 September 1894, D.D.F., no. 237. Phipps to Kimberley, no. 225, 29 September 1894; to Anderson, private, 30 September 1894, F.O. 27/3186. There is also a retrospective account of the negotiations in Hanotaux to d'Estournelles de Constant, 28 October 1894, D.D.F., no. 257.

74. This enabled Hanotaux to father the idea on Phipps; later, on 10 October, he admitted that he had originated it.

75. Note by Hanotaux, 7 October 1894, D.D.F., no. 249. The footnote in D.D.F. errs in referring to the conversation of 29 September; that of 5 October (not described in D.D.F.) is meant. Phipps to Kimberley, telegram, no. 49, 5 October 1894, F.O. 27/3188; no. 263, 5 October 1894, F.O. 27/3187.

76. Phipps to Anderson, private telegram, 5 October 1894, F.O. 27/3188.

Congo as absolutely outside the sphere of French influence',[77] and in a further telegram of the same date: 'there was certainly no question of any such counter-declaration from us'.[78] Of course he did not conceal that there was a condition: 'we declaring that we will not advance into that Egyptian territory from the south without previous understanding with France'. This condition he treated as temporary; 'by negotiations this difficulty may be surmounted'.[79]

Thus Phipps supposed that he had succeeded. On 9 October he transmitted the draft entente agreement to London for approval.[80] The Foreign Office was not impressed with Phipps's achievement. Intoxicated with the victory of forcing

77. Phipps to Kimberley, telegram, no. 55, 11 October 1894, F.O. 27/3188.

78. Phipps to Kimberley, telegram, no. 56, 11 October 1894. F.O. 27/3188.

79. Phipps to Anderson, private, 15 October 1894. F.O. 27/3187. 'Hanotaux seems to be ready ... to agree that the Nile valley is without the French sphere of influence and not to demand from us a declaration that it is "without" ours. They declare that they respect Egyptian rights and pretend they only wish us to do the same.'

80. D.D.F., no. 243, 245, 246; Phipps to Kimberley, no. 266, 9 October 1894, F.O. 27/3187. The agreement covered nine points: compensation for French missionaries in Uganda; frontier settlement at Sierra Leone; conflicts between British and French forces at Waïma and N'Compabo; frontier settlement west of the Niger; interpretation of certain points in the Anglo-French convention of 1890; the Mizon expedition; commercial agreement between certain adjacent colonies; the hinterland of Ashanti; and, finally, the upper Nile. Agreement, more or less acceptable even to Anderson, was reached on all points except the last; when this fell through, only the frontier settlement at Sierra Leone was saved. This agreement has been the subject of much speculation; date and contents were unknown until the opening of the archives. Even Hanotaux was bewildered and ascribed it later to December 1894. The agreement was a formal draft accepted by Hanotaux and Phipps, except for the final point of the upper Nile. Phipps recognized that it was useless to formulate this until the British Government gave its consent in principle; instead this consent was refused.

the protectorate over Uganda on a reluctant Cabinet, Rosebery and Anderson dreamt of marching from Uganda to
Fashoda and were unwilling to agree to even a temporary
suspension of this advance. Rosebery drafted a contemptuous
telegram of rejection to Phipps on 10 October:

> On the face of it, it appears to be an attempt to debar us from
> entering on our sphere on condition that the French do not enter
> it. This seems a somewhat one-sided arrangement considering that
> our sphere is recognized by three out of the four Great African
> Powers.[81]

Anderson noted: 'I fear Phipps has been much too sanguine',
and Kimberley echoed him loyally: 'much what I expected'.[82]
Two days later Anderson produced a more detailed criticism:

> In the watershed of the Nile Great Britain and France are placed
> on the same footing. The question of its administration is kept
> open for future negotiation. Our present claim is to be extin-
> guished. There is no recognition of any part of our sphere. The
> Anglo-Congolese Agreement is torn up ... We are offered nothing
> beyond the partial abandonment of extravagant pretensions which
> we are well able to resist.[83]

Still, in Anderson's words, 'to keep France entirely off the
Nile would be a triumph for British diplomacy and might
justify a surrender elsewhere'. He did not attempt to suggest
what this surrender might be. Instead he devised an alternative proposal, by which Great Britain would get her hands
on the upper Nile, under cover of Egyptian authority:

81. Kimberley to Phipps, telegram, no. 60, 10 October 1894, F.O.
27/3188, draft by Rosebery.

82. Minutes on Hanotaux to Phipps, 10 October 1894 (D.D.F., no.
245), F.O. 27/3187.

83. This comes towards the end of comments on the Phipps–
Hanotaux agreement which seems to have been written on 12 October
and were printed for circulation to the Cabinet on 16 October 1894,
F.O. 27/3209.

France admits her sphere is bounded by the Congo–Nile watershed.

Great Britain gives assurance that it is not her intention directly to govern or to administer that part of the Nile watershed, mentioned in the Anglo-Congolese Agreement, which lies to the north of the 5° 30′ parallel.

Anderson added: 'This would leave us a free hand to the east of the Nile and would involve an indirect recognition of our sphere by the reference to the Agreement with the King.'[84]

Anderson thought that Hanotaux would agree to this only if he were treated roughly. 'M. Hanotaux would require to be hard pressed to concede it and hitherto Phipps has not pressed him at all. A different tone would have to be used in the negotiations from Phipps' apologetic, almost supplicatory, language'. Kimberley once more agreed: 'It seems to me that Phipps has got to the length of his tether and that it is necessary for Lord Dufferin to take up the matter.'[85] Phipps was therefore told on 12 October that he was not to see Hanotaux again.[86] Hanotaux meanwhile was being hard pressed, though not in the direction that Anderson desired. On 15 October he was warned that the colonial ministry did not accept the self-denying proposal, and a few days later Delcassé told him that the French expeditions on the Ubanghi could race the British to the Nile.[87] Hanotaux needed an early reply from the British in order to fight his battle with Delcassé in the council of ministers, and he appealed to Phipps on more than one occasion.[88] Phipps could only tell him that he had been instructed to suspend negotiations.

84. Anderson first devised this formula as a minute on Phipps's telegram, no. 56. Its final form appears in the comments mentioned in the previous note.

85. Minutes by Anderson, 9 October, and by Kimberley, 10 October 1894. F.O. 27/3209.

86. Anderson to Phipps, telegram, 12 October 1894, F.O. 27/3188.

87. Note by Hanotaux, 30 October 1894, D.D.F., no. 260.

88. Phipps to Kimberley, telegram, no. 57, 18 October 1894, F.O.

Dufferin returned to Paris at the end of October; he had had to cut short his holiday, and was in a bad temper. When he met Hanotaux on 31 October, he tried threats, as Anderson had recommended : the British Government, he said, would not agree to the settlement of West African affairs unless France adhered to the Anglo-German convention of 1890. Hanotaux replied that France was willing to do this, once the British defined 'the confines of Egypt'. Discussion was back at its starting-point.[89] Anderson, late in the day, now attempted a definition of 'the confines of Egypt'. These, he wrote on 2 November, were laid down in the Hatti-Sherif of 1841; very conveniently, their southern limit was parallel $10°$ N., and thus 'with a little adjustment', Fashoda was in the British sphere. As to the equatorial provinces, these were unknown in 1841. They were 'temporarily occupied and then abandoned by Egypt', but 'we recognize the contingency of the resumption of these abandoned rights'.[90] In other words, the rights of Egypt, though ineffective against the British 'sphere', could still be invoked against anyone else. This definition was passed on to Dufferin on 3 November. Dufferin was further told that the British Government would not accept the mutual self-denying proposal : 'it would amount practically to the abandonment by them of a large portion of the British sphere which has been formally recognized by Germany and Italy and recently by the Congo Free State'. A last formula was produced more futile than its predecessors :

In case, however, the French Government display an insurmountable reluctance to formally recognize our sphere but should

27/3188 : no. 280, 24 October 1894, F.O. 27/3187. Hanotaux mentions a meeting on 20 October; he probably meant the meeting of 18 October. Hanotaux to d'Estournelles de Constant, 29 October 1894, D.D.F., no. 258.

89. Note by Hanotaux, 1 November 1894, D.D.F., no. 263. Dufferin to Kimberley, telegram, no. 58, 31 October 1894, F.O. 27/3188.

90. Memorandum by Anderson, 2 November 1894, F.O. 27/3257.

161

be disposed to give an assurance that they would not advance beyond the watershed of the Nile we on our side might take act of such an assurance and thus arrive at a practical settlement.

Dufferin was to insist that there could be no agreement on other African questions without a recognition of the British sphere. At the same time he was not to press Hanotaux, 'as the result might be that he would be led to make declarations, denying our right to the sphere instead of leaving the matter, as he appears at present inclined to do so, open for possible negotiations at some future time'.[91]

Dufferin and Hanotaux had a final, decisive interview on 7 November. Dufferin was by now in a better temper and perhaps even a little ashamed at having to break off negotiations. At any rate, he agreed that the frontier settlement at Sierra Leone should be salvaged from the general wreck. On the Nile, however, deadlock had been reached. Dufferin asked for recognition of the Anglo-Congolese treaty of 12 May. Hanotaux quoted against it the Franco-Congolese convention of 14 August and observed that the Congo State had consulted England before signing this. Dufferin, at sea as ever, asked Hanotaux if he could see a solution to the Sudanese conflict. Hanotaux replied that 'the proposition of provisional mutual disinterestedness or desistence' was all that occurred to him. This was rejected by Dufferin : 'Phipps had advanced too far, and the views that he had expressed were not at all those of the London Cabinet.' Dufferin then demanded that Hanotaux should take an engagement in the name of France 'not to extend our sphere of influence beyond the basin of the Congo'. Hanotaux refused. There was no more to be said.[92]

Ten days later the French council of ministers decided to suspend negotiations regarding the upper Nile and the colonial ministry was instructed to ensure that France should

91. Kimberley to Dufferin, no. 390, 3 November 1894, F.O. 27/3183.

92. Note by Hanotaux, 7 November 1894, D.D.F., no. 272; Dufferin to Kimberley, no. 293, 7 November 1894, F.O. 27/3187.

occupy as much as possible of these territories ahead of Colville, who was preparing to advance from Uganda. Delcassé claimed that Liotard, the explorer who had taken the place of Monteil, could be on the Nile within a year.[93]

4

Diplomacy had ceased; the race to the Nile had begun. Each side was a little frightened by what it had started. Hanotaux still hankered after negotiations, and in December sent Courcel, the best French diplomat of his day, as ambassador to London. Kimberley, sandwiched between Anderson and Rosebery, had not been allowed much say in the previous negotiations and was perhaps glad to do a little diplomacy on his own. On 18 December Kimberley and Courcel ranged once more over the question of the upper Nile. Kimberley inquired whether it would help things if Great Britain declared the contested territory to be Egyptian – this might even be a sign that England and France were drawing nearer on the Egyptian question. Courcel did not care for this idea : it would not do to settle the first chapter of the Egyptian question unless they were willing to go on to the second. He took up Kimberley's suggested promise 'not to annex any part of this territory' and asked whether he would promise not to occupy it. Kimberley answered : 'No, for that would in effect be to relinquish the sphere altogether to which we could not consent.' Courcel then suggested a British promise not to enter the disputed territory for a given length of time, say for ten years. This also was too much for Kimberley, but he added, in his weak way, 'I don't think we shall be led to enter the territory concerned for a long time. We have quite enough to do in Unyoro.'[94]

93. Note by Hanotaux, undated [17 November 1894], D.D.F., no. 285.

94. Courcel to Hanotaux, 19 December 1894, D.D.F., no. 319; Kimberley to Dufferin, no. 434A, 18 December 1894. F.O. 27/3183. Kimberley, not surprisingly, did not record this last remark.

Agreement was still out of sight.

Kimberley, during the conversation of 18 December, mumbled the usual warning against any French attempt to enter the upper Nile. The warning was delivered in a friendly tone, and he added: 'Do not even say that I have told you that we do not want you to enter the disputed territory; these are things that are not said to a friendly Great Power.' Kimberley had reckoned without Rosebery. The distracted Liberal Cabinet was moving towards its fall, and Rosebery, always nervous and irritable, wished to explode against someone. At the end of March 1895, he exploded against the French. There had been further disputes with the French on the Niger; there was no recent or reliable information regarding any French expedition towards the Nile – and in truth the French plans had fallen through. The only spur to action was a report from the Intelligence Department of the War Office, made on 6 March: the department had just come across a German map of the Sudan, showing the effects of the Franco-Congolese agreement of 14 August 1894, and their penetrating military minds deduced from this that the French route to the Nile was still open.[95] No other background for the 'Grey declaration' is to be found in the Foreign Office papers. However, for whatever reason, Kimberley was pushed into action by Rosebery on 28 March. Simulating an unusual indignation, he complained to Courcel about French encroachments on the Niger and added a general reference to difficulties with France elsewhere. Courcel, though he caught the word 'Siam', seems to have missed the Nile altogether.[96]

The same evening Grey, the under-secretary for foreign affairs, spoke in the House of Commons on the Foreign Office

95. Intelligence Department to Foreign Office, 6 March 1895, F.O. 27/3257.

96. Kimberley to Dufferin, nos. 111 and 111A, 28 March 1895, F.O. 27/3229; Courcel to Hanotaux, telegrams, 28 March 1895, D.D.F., nos. 412 and 413.

vote. He disclaimed knowledge of any French expedition to the upper Nile, and said, in a famous phrase, that any such expedition would be 'an unfriendly act'.[97] This was no more than had been said repeatedly to the French in private, and similar warnings would have appeared in the promised Blue Book on the Anglo-Congolese treaty if it had ever been published.[98] Only in that case the warnings would have been accompanied by the French answer. As it was, the Grey declaration – lacking any justification of a specific French act – was surely a way of trying to get by public statement what the British Government had failed to get by diplomacy, a legacy to the succeeding government that was visibly in the offing. It would have been sharp practice for the French to send an expedition to the upper Nile while negotiations were proceeding, if, in fact, they had been; it was equally sharp practice for the British Government to bring the issue into the open without warning to the French.

Courcel at once lodged a written protest with Kimberley;[99] he followed this up in person on 1 April. Kimberley, on whom no doubt the Grey declaration had been sprung unawares,[100]

97. The F.O. papers contain the drafts of Grey's answers to questions. The Grey declaration, however, was made in the course of debate, not as an answer to a question, and no draft has been preserved.

98. Grey intended to promise papers 'if pressed' when he was questioned about the Franco-Congolese agreement on 16 August 1894. But no demand was made (F.O. 10/625). The government announced a Blue Book on 23 August 1894, but never proceeded with it – a unique case.

99. Courcel to Hanotaux (with enclosures), 29 March 1894, D.D.F., no. 419.

100. Grey's own version, according to which he was told by Kimberley to use strong language about the Niger and accidentally transferred the strong language to the Nile (Twenty Five Years, i, 18), has been rejected by more than one historian. Langer, Diplomacy of Imperialism, i, 265; Temperley and Penson, Foundations of British Foreign Policy, p. 501.

reverted to his most apologetic mood. Grey, he said, was 'a simple Under-Secretary', whose declaration had less weight than if it had been made by the foreign secretary or the prime minister; he had merely repeated the British thesis or 'claim', and France was free to reject this thesis – 'the question therefore remained open to debate', and the only object of Grey's declaration was to prevent a French occupation while the debate was proceeding. Further, the British Government had no intention of taking any action at present (this was true – hence their hostility to French action): 'We shall not have the intention of attacking the Sudan for a long time, nor even of entering the regions which you dispute to our sphere of influence; we are not now planning to go into the Bahr el Ghazal.' Finally he said that even if the Sudan were recovered, it would be occupied by Egyptian troops and administration, and would be associated with 'the destiny of Egypt itself'.[101]

Hanotaux certainly did not wish to respond to Grey's challenge. He had written sharply on 29 March : 'I cannot admit that points which are the subject of diplomatic dispute shall be declared *indisputable* in the British parliament.'[102] Kimberley's apology gave him, however, a way of escape; Kimberley himself had said : 'the question remains open to debate', and this was all that Hanotaux claimed when he spoke in the French senate on 5 April. In the end, he declared, 'two great nations will know how to find formulas which will reconcile their interests and satisfy their common aspirations towards civilization and progress'. Kimberley praised Hano-

101. Kimberley to Dufferin, no, 112A, 1 April 1895, F.O. 27/3229. Courcel to Hanotaux, telegram, 2 April 1895; 2 April 1895, D.D.F., nos. 423 and 429. Kimberley's account is naturally less apologetic, but Courcel read him the telegram to Hanotaux (Courcel to Hanotaux, 3 April 1895, D.D.F., no. 430), and he confirmed it except (i) he would not bind himself for the future so far as the Bahr el Ghazal was concerned; (ii) he had not meant to imply that British troops would not cooperate with Egyptian troops in reconquering the Sudan.

102. Hanotaux to Courcel, private, 29 March 1894, D.D.F., no. 416.

taux's conciliatory tone to Courcel the following day. In an excess of conciliation he now proposed something like the standstill agreement which the British Government had rejected when Hanotaux had proposed it the previous autumn – 'a tacit agreement implying a *modus vivendi* acceptable to the two countries and excluding any unilateral act which could prejudice the rights or claims of one or the other'. Courcel did not respond to this suggestion. At the end of the conversation Kimberley remarked that Grey's declaration was merely a reply to Hanotaux's speech of 7 June of the previous year and that 'he quite agreed with us not to attach any importance in diplomatic negotiations, to parliamentary declarations'.[103] Kimberley at any rate had done his feeble best to erase the effects of the Grey declaration.

However, it was not only Kimberley who had second thoughts. By now the dream of conquering the Sudan from Uganda had proved unworkable, and it had become obvious that the Sudan could only be entered from the north. The British were thus belatedly willing to leave the Nile alone south of Fashoda if the French would do the same. On 6 May Anderson minuted that Rosebery wished to renew negotiations with the French about the 'projet de désistement'. Anderson produced a new formula: 'the two Powers recognize that they cannot make acquisitions in, or infringe upon the Provinces of Darfur and Kordofan ...[104] They agree that they will not make acquisitions in, nor infringe upon, the territory' adjoining these provinces (i.e. the territory as defined in the lease which Leopold had not been allowed to take up). By this arrangement Great Britain, acting in the name of Egypt, would have had exclusive control of the Nile as far south as Fashoda; beyond that would have been a no man's land, which both France and Great Britain would be pledged

103. Courcel to Hanotaux, telegram, 6 April 1895, D.D.F., no. 435.
104. These provinces were included within the Hatti-Sherif of 1841, and were therefore indisputably Egyptian.

not to enter, while all other neighbours would have recognized it as a British sphere of influence.[105] On 10 May Kimberley timidly sounded Courcel along these lines. Courcel rejected 'the connection which it was sought to establish between our occupation of Egypt and the sphere of influence which we claimed on the Upper Nile'.[106] The conversation ended; it was the last that took place during the tenure of the Liberal Government.

The objection which ended the negotiations had overshadowed them from the beginning: it was impossible to separate the upper Nile from the Egyptian question. At the start, the British had tried to draw a line between their sphere of interest and the rights of Egypt; this line could never be found, and the 'Grey declaration' completed the entanglement of British and Egyptian rights. For Leopold II the upper Nile was, no doubt, valuable in itself; for the French it was a means with which to 'trench upon the Egyptian question'. The French were not concerned to establish themselves in the valley of the Nile or even to eject the British from Egypt. The Egyptian question was for them a matter of internal politics – to find some compromise which would reconcile French public opinion to the loss of Egypt and so enable good relations between England and France to be restored. In 1898 the British 'solved' the question of the upper Nile: by superior force, not argument, they compelled the French at last to recognize their 'sphere of influence'. Though this deprived France of a bargaining counter, it did not settle the Egyptian question. The question of Egypt could not be solved by force; it could be solved only by compensation and goodwill. In 1894 Hanotaux alone had the goodwill, and even in his case it lacked urgency; at any rate he made no serious effort to formulate the price at which France would accept British primacy in Egypt. At most, he sought to postpone Fashoda,

105. Memorandum by Anderson, 6 May 1895, F.O. 27/3257.
106. Kimberley to Dufferin, no. 151, 10 May 1895, F.O. 27/3229.

not to avoid it. It needed the decay of Morocco and a shift in the balance of the Great Powers to bring Great Britain and France together.

16. *Economic Imperialism*

New Statesman. These reflections on J A Hobson's
Imperialism (1902) came fifty years after the original
publication of the book.

Ideas live longer than men, and the writer who can attach his name to an idea is safe for immortality. Darwin will live as long as Evolution, Marx be forgotten only when there are no class-struggles. In the same way, no survey of the international history of the twentieth century can be complete without the name of J A Hobson. He it was who found an economic motive for Imperialism. Lenin took over Hobson's explanation, which thus became the basis for Communist foreign policy to the present day. Non-Marxists were equally convinced, and contemporary history has been written largely in the light of Hobson's discovery. This discovery was an off-shoot from his general doctrine of under-consumption. The capitalists cannot spend their share of the national production. Saving makes their predicament worse. They demand openings for investment outside their saturated national market, and they find these openings in the undeveloped parts of the world. This is Imperialism. In Hobson's words, 'the modern foreign policy of Great Britain has been primarily a struggle for profitable markets of investment' – and what applied to Great Britain was equally true of France or Germany. Brailsford put it a few years later in a sharper way :

Working men may proceed to slay each other in order to decide whether it shall be French or German financiers who shall export the surplus capital (saved from their own wages bill) destined to subdue and exploit the peasants of Morocco.

This idea is now so embedded in our thought that we cannot imagine a time when it did not exist. Yet the earlier Radical opponents of Imperialism knew nothing of it. They supposed that Imperialism sprang from a primitive greed for territory or a lust for conquest. The more sophisticated held that it was designed to provide jobs for the younger sons of the governing classes (a theory which James Mill invented and himself practised and which Hobson did not discard). Marx had no theory of Imperialism. In classical Marxist theory, the state exists solely to oppress the working classes – to silence their grievances, destroy their trade unions and force them ever nearer to the point of absolute starvation. Marx jeered at the 'night-watchman' theory of the state, but the only difference in his conception was that it stayed awake in the day-time. Hobson added a true Marxist refinement. Marx had demonstrated that the capitalist, however benevolent personally, was condemned by economic law to rob the worker at the point of production. Similarly Hobson showed that the capitalist, however pacific, must seek foreign investment and therefore be driven into imperialist rivalry with the capitalists of other states. Previously Marxists had condemned capitalism as being pacific and particularly for preventing the great war of liberation against Russia. Now all wars became 'capitalistic', and war the inevitable outcome of the capitalist system. It is not surprising that, when the first world war had broken out, Lenin seized on Hobson's 'bourgeois-pacifist' theory and made it the cornerstone of his neo-Marxism. Like most prophets, he boasted of his foresight only when his visions had become facts.

Hobson wrote his book immediately after the partition of Africa and when the experiences of the Boer war were fresh in everyone's mind. For him, Imperialism was mainly the acquisition of tropical lands, and what he foresaw next was the partition, or perhaps the joint exploitation, of China. In the spring of 1914 Brailsford applied similar doctrines to a wider field. The War of Steel and Gold (1914) is a more brilliant book than Hobson's, written with a more trenchant pen and with a deeper knowledge of international affairs. Though less remembered now, it had probably a stronger influence on its own generation, and American historians between the wars, in particular, could hardly have got on without it. Our own thought is still unconsciously shaped by it. Brailsford speaks more to our condition. The aggressive, self-confident Imperialism of the Boer war seems remote to us; the competition of great armaments is ever-present in our lives.

Both writers wrote with Radical passion. The first sensation in re-reading them is to cry out: 'Would that we had such writers nowadays!' Take Hobson's peroration:

Imperialism is a depraved choice of national life, imposed by self-seeking interests which appeal to the lusts of quantitative acquisition and of forceful domination surviving in a nation from early centuries of animal struggle for existence ... It is the besetting sin of all successful States, and its penalty is unalterable in the order of nature.

Or Brailsford's:

Let a people once perceive for what purposes its patriotism is prostituted, and its resources misused, and the end is already in sight. When that illumination comes to the masses of the three Western Powers, the fears which fill their barracks and stoke their furnaces will have lost the power to drive. A clear-sighted generation will scan the horizon and find no enemy. It will drop its armour, and walk the world's highways safe.

These are heavyweights of political combat. The intellectual diet of the mid twentieth century cannot nourish such stamina. But we must stay the flood of our admiration with some doubting questions. Was the Hobsonian–Leninist analysis of international capitalism a true picture either then or now? Has the struggle for overseas investments ever been the mainspring of international politics?

The export of capital was certainly a striking feature of British economic life in the fifty years before 1914. But its greatest periods were before and after the time of ostensible Imperialism. What is more, there was little correspondence between the areas of capitalist investment and political annexation. Hobson cheats on this, and Lenin after him. They show, in one table, that there has been a great increase in British investments overseas; in another that there has been a great increase in the territory of the British Empire. Therefore, they say, the one caused the other. But did it? Might not both have been independent products of British confidence and strength? If openings for investment were the motive of British Imperialism, we should surely find evidence for this in the speeches of British imperialists, or, if not in their public statements, at any rate in their private letters and opinions. We don't. They talked, no doubt quite mistakenly, about securing new markets and, even more mistakenly, about new openings for emigration; they regarded investment as a casual instrument. Their measuring-stick was Power, not Profit. When they disputed over tropical African territory or scrambled for railway concessions in China, their aim was to strengthen their respective empires, not to benefit the financiers of the City. Hobson showed that Imperialism did not pay the nation. With longer experience, we can even say that it does not pay the investors. But the proof, even if convincing, would not have deterred the advocates of Imperialism. They were thinking in different terms.

The economic analysis breaks down in almost every case which has been examined in detail. Morocco has often been treated as a classical case of finance-imperialism, by Brailsford himself and in more detail by E D Morel. In fact, the French financiers were forced to invest in Morocco, much against their will, in order to prepare the way for French political control. They knew they would lose their money, and they did. But Morocco became a French protectorate. Again, Brailsford made much play with the British investment in Egypt, which Cromer had promoted. But Cromer promoted these investments in order to strengthen British political control, and not the other way round. The British held on to Egypt for the sake of their empire; they did not hold their empire for the sake of Egypt. Even the Boer war was not purely a war for financial gain. British policy in South Africa would have been exactly the same if there had been no gold-mines. The only difference is that, without the profits from the dynamite-monopoly, the Boers would have been unable to put up much resistance. Rhodes was a great scoundrel in Radical eyes, and quite rightly. But not for the reasons that they supposed. Rhodes wanted wealth for the power that it brought, not for its own sake. Hence he understood the realities of politics better than they did.

Those who explained Imperialism in terms of economics were rationalists themselves and therefore sought a rational explanation for the behaviour of others. If capitalists and politicians were as rational as Hobson and Brailsford, this is how they would behave. And of course a minority did. They took their profits, agreed with their enemy in the way and died quietly in their beds. But they did not set the pattern of events. It is disturbing that, while Hobson and Brailsford were so penetrating about the present, they were wrong about the future. Hobson ignored Europe altogether – rightly, since he was discussing colonial affairs. He expected the international capitalists to join in the exploitation of China and even to recruit Chinese armies with which to hold down the workers of Europe. Brailsford looked to Europe only to reject it. He wrote – this in March 1914 : 'the dangers which forced our ancestors into European coalitions and Continental wars have gone never to return'. And again, 'it is as certain as anything in politics can be, that the frontiers of our modern national states are finally drawn. My own belief is that there will be no more wars among the six Great Powers.' Even if there were a war, 'it is hard to believe that .. German Socialists would show any ardour in shooting down French workmen. The spirit which marched through Sedan to Paris could not be revived in our generation.' It may be unfair to judge any writer in the light of what came after. Yet men with far less of Brailsford's knowledge and intellectual equipment foresaw the conflict of 1914, and even the shape that it would take. The true vision of the future was with Robert Blatchford, when he wrote his pamphlet, Germany and England, for The Daily Mail.

This is a sad confession. Hobson and Brailsford are our sort. We think like them, judge like them, admire their style and their moral values. We should be ashamed to write like Blatchford, though he was in fact the greatest popular journalist since Cobbett. Yet he was right, and they were wrong. Their virtues were their undoing. They expected reason to triumph. He knew that men love Power above all else. This, not Imperialism, is the besetting sin. Lenin knew it also. Hence, though a rationalist by origin, he turned himself into a wielder of power. Thanks to him, there is nothing to choose between Rhodes and a Soviet commissar. Nothing except this : the capitalist may be sometimes corrupted and softened by his wealth; the Soviet dictators have nothing to wear them down. If the evils which Hobson and Brailsford discovered in capitalism had been in fact the greatest of public vices, we should now be living in an easier world. It is the high-minded and inspired, the missionaries not the capitalists, who cause most of the trouble. Worst of all are the men of Power who are missionaries as well.

17. The Jameson Raid

Manchester Guardian. A review of The Jameson Raid by
Jean van der Poel (1951).

The Jameson Raid of 29 December 1895 is one of the most
controversial episodes in recent British history. Was Joseph
Chamberlain implicated in it? For many years it was thought
that the answer might be found in the 'missing' telegrams,
exchanged between Cecil Rhodes and his London agents,
which were produced before the Select Committee of Inquiry.
Garvin published extracts from these in the third volume of
his Life of Chamberlain and argued that while Chamberlain
knew that a revolution against Boer rule was being prepared
at Johannesburg (a revolution which never came off) he did
not know that Rhodes and Jameson were gathering a force
outside the Transvaal to go to the aid of the rising. This,
though damning enough, was still inconclusive and it was
supposed that a final verdict could never be reached. A South
African scholar has now opened a new source. Sir Graham
Bower, imperial secretary to Robinson, the high commissioner, was the 'fall-guy' of the Jameson affair. His official
superiors persuaded him to admit his own complicity but to
deny that of Robinson or of Chamberlain. He had his career
ruined as a reward. Though he loyally kept silence until
death, he left his papers and a full record for future historians.
They are decisive: the mud sticks to Chamberlain and to
others besides.

The idea of engineering a rising in Johannesburg was devised by Rhodes in the days of the Liberal Government. It was
approved by Rosebery, and Sir Hercules Robinson, a share-

holder and director of Rhodes's concerns, was appointed high commissioner in the belief that he would be clay in Rhodes's hands. Bower was sent out with him to keep the technical side of things in order. When Chamberlain took over the Colonial Office in July 1895, Rhodes was in high hopes. It was the essence of his plan that a force should be stationed outside the Transvaal, ready to make a dash for Johannesburg, and territory in Bechuanaland Protectorate had to be handed over to Rhodes's company in order to make this possible. This is the key-point: if Robinson and Chamberlain knew why Rhodes wanted this land, they condoned and encouraged the raid.

It is now clear that they both knew. Robinson said to Bower after a talk with Rhodes: 'The less you and I have to do with those damned conspiracies of Rhodes and Chamberlain the better. I know nothing about them.' But, adds Bower, 'he ordered me to allow the troops to come down to Pitsani' (the jumping-off ground for the raid). As to Chamberlain, he wrote to Robinson on 2 October asking for his views on a rising at Johannesburg, 'with or without assistance from outside'.

In December 1895 the conspirators at Johannesburg began to falter. Fairfield, assistant under secretary at the Colonial Office, told Bower later 'he had written to Mr Chamberlain at Birmingham suggesting that the revolution be damped down. Chamberlain had replied telling him to hurry it up on account of the Venezuela dispute [with the United States]. He had therefore instructed Lord Grey and Maguire accordingly and they had telegraphed in the sense I have given.' Bower saw Rhodes show this telegram to Robinson on 20 December. It has been alleged by Garvin and others that the telegrams urging Rhodes to hurry came only from Rutherford Harris, his shady man-of-affairs, and that they were designed to blackmail Chamberlain. This will not do for Earl Grey and Maguire, a fellow of All Souls. Chamberlain later intended to put the blame on Fairfield, who wrote to Bower that 'he was to be the scapegoat of the Colonial Office and was to be disavowed'; he would be required 'to conform his evidence to that of the others'. Fairfield, however, died suddenly before he could have the pleasure of perjuring himself for the sake of Joseph Chamberlain. Rhodes, at any rate, had no doubts. When Bower expostulated, Rhodes replied, 'Then you are disloyal to your chief, Chamberlain, who is hurrying me up.'

Of course part of Chamberlain's defence is technically true. He did not know that there would be a raid without a revolution. But no one knew this, neither Rhodes nor Jameson himself. The latter decided on it spontaneously when the revolution in Johannesburg 'fizzled out'. But that there was to be a raid as well as a revolution was planned by Rhodes, authorized by Chamberlain, and known to Robinson. The raid did immeasurable harm in South Africa. More than any other single event it caused the Boer war, and it left an estrangement between Boer and Briton which is not yet removed. The authors of the Jameson Raid were those two builders of Empire Cecil Rhodes and Joseph Chamberlain.

Why did this not come out at the time? Far from Rhodes blackmailing Chamberlain, it was Chamberlain who blackmailed Rhodes. He threatened to take away the charter of the British South Africa Company if the telegrams came out, and Rhodes paid the price of silence. According to Bower the attorney-general thought that the only telegram that 'could not be explained away' was the Grey–Maguire message. It was not produced at the inquiry, nor has it been published by Garvin. Bower would not 'fling all the mud at Rhodes and Jameson'. Therefore he was instructed to confess that he had known of the preparations for the raid but had not told either Robinson or the Colonial Office. Rhodes said to him : 'If you branch off and divulge this correspondence old Robinson will be carried into the box in his bandages like the dying Chatham and will give you the lie. He will be backed by Chamberlain, and at the day of judgement those two old men will shake hands and say they did the right thing.'

Why did the Liberals on the Select Committee swallow this suppression? Miss van der Poel suggests that they knew that Rosebery had been involved in the original plans for a rising and were afraid to discredit their former leader. This seems unlikely. It appears from Harcourt's 'Life' that they were content to have secured a unanimous condemnation of Rhodes. No doubt they did not realize the weight of evidence against Chamberlain or appreciate how he had behaved. For, in fact, Chamberlain stood in exactly the same relation to Rhodes and Jameson as Hitler stood to Henlein and the Sudeten Germans in 1938. Perhaps it was this which made Neville Chamberlain listen so sympathetically to Hitler's tales of innocence. They were no worse than those which Joseph Chamberlain had dished up to the Committee of Inquiry.

18. *The Man in the Cloth Cap*

Manchester Guardian. Written to mark the fortieth anniversary of Hardie's death. If I had been more patient and waited a year it could have marked the hundredth anniversary of his birth. NATO, mentioned in the last paragraph, was a military alliance designed to protect western Europe from the supposed danger of Communism. There are reports that it still exists.

A visitor to the House of Commons in 1892 would have seen an assemblage of great figures. Gladstone was prime minister, preparing for his last battle over Home Rule; his memories going back beyond Palmerston, beyond the repeal of the Corn Laws to the political world before the great Reform Bill. Harcourt, John Morley, Joseph Chamberlain were on the front benches; Haldane and Grey were showing their first distinction. A shrewd observer could have spotted four future prime ministers: Balfour, Campbell-Bannerman, Asquith, Lloyd George. Even the shrewdest would have spared a glance at the member for West Ham (South) only as the sensation of a day: the man in a cloth cap, whose supporters brought him down to Westminster in a two-horse brake with a trumpeter on the box. It seemed a vulgar demonstration. But the trumpet sounded the note of doom both for the Liberal party and for old privileged England.

The man in the cap was Keir Hardie, and though he then stood alone, the only 'unwhipped' member of the House, he was to do more for the shaping of the future than all the giants who surrounded him. The Labour party and the Welfare State were both his children. He made the political and social order in which we now live. No doubt some such outcome would have happened in any case, but not quite as or when it did.

Keir Hardie was that rare character, a truly independent workingman. Independence was the key-word of his career. 'I know what I believe to be the right thing, and I go and do it.' He lost his job as a miner for taking the lead against the mineowner. He founded the Independent Labour Party, and he was the principal agent in creating independent Labour representation in Parliament. Yet he was equally insistent in demanding freedom from his own colleagues. He ran his own paper, took his own line on the public platform. He wanted the Labour party to be a federal body, 'leaving each organization free to maintain and propagate its own theory in its own way', and he refused to be tied by instructions from a party conference. His political outlook stemmed neither from Marx nor from Methodism, but from Robert Burns. 'I owe more to Robert Burns than to any man dead or alive.'

Hardie's socialism has been called emotional. Certainly he hated poverty and oppression. He was more moved on 23

June 1894 by the death of 260 miners in a colliery disaster than by the birth of a royal baby. He was not ashamed to point the contrast between the luxury of the wealthy classes and the death of children by starvation. But this was a statement of fact, not a rhetorical flourish. Fundamentally Hardie started from the simple proposition that the only rational form of society was one which recognized 'the divine spark' in every man.

Faith in humanity gave Keir Hardie his power. He was not a great orator; what moved his audiences was 'the homely, essentially human tone'. His writing had a soggy romantic flavour which made it much inferior to Blatchford's. But he had a burning faith that carried all before it. Hardie believed unquestioningly in the virtue of the working class and he believed that this virtue would lead to a Socialist order. The Labour party has always been torn between immediate social reforms and the ideal community of the future. Hardie saw no conflict of loyalties. They were two different aspects of 'the Cause', and it is this union for the Cause which maintains the Labour party to the present day.

Not that Hardie ever put material benefits first. Though he repudiated the class war, no man was more class-conscious or, rather, class-confident. He had no interest in going up in the world. 'Emancipation' meant for him that privilege should cease, not that the children of working-class families should have a share in these privileges. Bernard Shaw once called Hardie 'the damnedest natural aristocrat in the House of Commons'. In fact, Hardie was something beyond Shaw's comprehension: a natural democrat. Towards the end of his life he told the ILP: 'Nature never intended me to be a leader. I find myself happier among the rank and file.'

Hardie assumed that every Socialist must be a Radical. This belief gave him strength; it also, perhaps, led him to misjudge the future of the Labour party. He never thought of himself as one of 'His Majesty's Opposition'. Rather he regarded all institutions, including parliament, as 'quaint without being impressive'. Parliament was important to him as the instrument of democracy, not as the emblem of historic continuity. He wore his cloth cap without affectation. Later he dressed more as an artist, with a long cloak and flowing cravat. But it is inconceivable that he would ever have worn the robes of a Knight of the Garter. In 1908 he criticized Edward VII's visit to the tsar at Reval. The king retaliated by striking him off the list of guests at a royal garden party. The stroke miscarried. Keir Hardie had never attended a garden party and at first did not know he had been excluded. When the news reached him, he said: 'If I am fit to represent the working classes of Merthyr, I am fit to attend the garden party at Windsor' and all the Labour MPs boycotted the garden party until the exclusion was lifted.

In his first stretch in Parliament, between 1892 and 1895, Keir Hardie stuck exclusively to social affairs and never opened his mouth on imperial or foreign questions. The Boer war ended his silence. He became an extreme pro-Boer, desiring not compromise but a Boer victory, and he dreamt of a great Radical party on an anti-imperialist basis. He even offered to put himself under the leadership of the individualist John Morley. Hardie's fraternity did not stop with the people of England. It embraced all the peoples in the world. He gave great offence by sympathizing with the national movement in India, and he advised the nationalists of Egypt in their first, stumbling steps.

After 1906, when he had some forty Labour colleagues in parliament, he increasingly left social reform to others and preached international conciliation. He became a great figure in the Socialist International and was largely responsible for its resolution on the general strike against war. The German Socialists regarded this as a pious gesture; Hardie took it seriously. The outbreak of war broke his heart. What shattered him was not so much the war in itself as that the working class went along with it. He said after a rowdy meeting in Merthyr, his constituency: 'I understand what Christ suffered in Gethsemane as well as any man living.'

He died on 26 September 1915. On his death the political truce was broken, and Merthyr returned a bellicose trade unionist in his place. Now, too, any Labour party members eager to fight for NATO must be relieved that Keir Hardie lies a-mouldering in his grave. Perhaps his soul goes marching on.

19. *The Boer War*

Manchester Guardian. Written for the fiftieth anniversary
of the outbreak of the Boer war or, as it is now called, the
Anglo-Boer war.

On 11 October 1899 the Boer ultimatum expired and Boer forces crossed the frontier into Natal. The Boers hoped to overrun all South Africa before British forces arrived; more remotely, they had hoped for the intervention of European Powers. The British, on their side, had expected the Boers to give way without a struggle; at worst, in Milner's words, 'an apology for a fight' would be necessary. 'A slap in the face' would do the business. Though Boer hopes were disappointed, British hopes were disappointed also. The war dragged on for three years, and by the end the eclipse of Boer independence was of less importance than the deflation of British Imperialism. In fact, the Boer war had a more decisive effect on British politics than on Imperial history. It brought first the culmination and then the end of an arrogant, boastful epoch, in which British public opinion seemed to have abandoned principles for power – the political equivalent of that *fin de siècle* spirit in art and literature which produced decadence and Oscar Wilde.

The Boer war caused a bitterness in British politics without parallel since the great Reform Bill and never equalled since except in 1914 during the Ulster rebellion (and perhaps, briefly, at the time of Munich). 'Pro-Boer' was a more opprobrious epithet than ever 'pro-German' became in either German war. No minister during these later world conflicts openly regretted the escape of an opponent from physical violence or even death as Chamberlain regretted Lloyd George's escape from Birmingham Town Hall. His comment was : 'What is everyone's business is nobody's business.'

This bitterness had many causes. Every dispute in which Chamberlain was involved was conducted in a savage, scurrilous way (on both sides); the Boer war gave the cheap press its first chance to display its quality; most of all, the war had the bitterness of a family quarrel – not merely a quarrel within the Empire but a quarrel in England between politicians of the same party origin. Imperialism and anti-Imperialism were both advocated by men of Liberal background. Even Disraeli had been originally a Radical; Milner, Chamberlain, and their associates had all started as Liberals; and Milner's friends were still mostly Liberals – it was Grey, Haldane, and Asquith whom he visited when he came to England. In the same way Rosebery, not Salisbury, had been the most Imperialist of prime ministers. Old Toryism, with its roots in the countryside, had little sympathy with the aggressive and optimistic spirit of Imperialism. In August 1899 Salisbury passed this verdict on the coming war : 'We have to act upon a moral field prepared for us by Milner and his Jingo supporters. And therefore I see before us the necessity for considerable military effort – and all for people whom we despise and for territory which will bring no profit and no power to England.'

Salisbury was dragged into war by Chamberlain; and Chamberlain was dragged into war by Milner. Certainly

Chamberlain wanted to establish British supremacy in South Africa; this he had hoped to do gradually, by persuasion and the passage of time. But Chamberlain was fatally compromized by his association with the Jameson Raid, the greatest blunder in his career. The Raid ruined the chance of the Boer moderates and made it certain that Milner would have to deal with Kruger and his associates, men as violent and as obstinate as himself. Milner was a great administrator, but no statesman and no diplomatist. He hated inefficiency and delay; most of all, he hated compromise. With German dogmatism he wrote on 16 August 1899: 'They will collapse if we don't weaken, or rather if we go on steadily turning the screw.' Milner had a great vision of a British South Africa, which would escape dependence on the goldmines by wise economic planning and by raising the standard of life of the native population: he destroyed this vision by his impatience with the Boers. After the Jameson Raid the Boer war was probably inevitable, but it was Milner who determined that it should come when it did and in the way it did.

Milner made a mistake not uncommon among civilian politicians: he supposed that the soldiers would conduct the war as competently as he had brought it about. The early disasters could be repaired; what could never be repaired was the prestige of Imperialism, on which Milner and Chamberlain had staked their political existence. Even worse than the blow to prestige was the damage to England's moral position on the continent of Europe. No war has been so unanimously condemned by enlightened European opinion. Even forty years afterwards, every European, though few Englishmen, recognized the taunt in the Nazi 'concentration camps', which deliberately parodied in name and nature the British 'methods of barbarism'. Yet it will not do for the later historian to react against this by idealizing the Boers, as the pro-Boers did at the time. Though the Boers fought to preserve their independence they were even more concerned to preserve other, and less admirable, things: their policy of racial exclusion; their share of gold profits; and their tyranny over the natives.

Fifty years afterwards, it is clear that victory has gone to the worst elements on both sides. Milner got his war without achieving his vision; the Boers lost their independence without being won for progress and civilization; soon the British citizen in South Africa will be again an *uitlander*, as he was before the Boer war. The mining houses and the most narrow-minded Boers, Johannesburg and Pretoria, have joined hands to oppress and exploit the native peoples who are the overwhelming majority of the population and Smuts, the last General of the Boer war, lived to accuse the prime minister of South Africa of using 'the methods of Fascism'. If Milner could see the results of victory, or Campbell-Bannerman the results of Boer self-government, would either have reason to be proud of his handiwork?

The pro-Boers were wrong about the Boers; they were right about the war. The great underlying issue at stake was not whether the Boers stood for a moral cause but whether the British Empire stood for one. Milner and Chamberlain had appealed from principles to power; the pro-Boers re-asserted the claims of principle, and four years after the end of the war this despised minority received at the polls the greatest majority that any party had won since the Reform Act. Many men fought bravely in the Boer war, but none acted more bravely or served his country better than the politician who declared in the St James's Hall on 15 September 1899:

You may make thousands of women widows and thousands of children fatherless. It will be wrong. You may add a new province to your Empire. It will still be wrong. You may give greater buoyancy to the South African stock and share market. You may

185

create South African booms. You may send the price of Mr.
Rhodes's Chartereds up to a point beyond the dreams of avarice.
Yes, even then it will be wrong.

The outbreak of the Boer war were better passed over in
silence, were it not for the occasion it gives for reprinting
Morley's words.

20. *'Joe' at his Zenith*

Manchester Guardian. A review of The Life of Joseph
Chamberlain, vol. IV, by Julian Amery (1951). Chamberlain
actually received two further volumes, published by Julian
Amery in 1969.

We have had to wait a long time for the Life of Joseph Chamberlain. The late J L Garvin gave up after publishing three
volumes which carried the story to the end of 1900. Mr Julian
Amery is to complete the task in the present and a subsequent volume. 'Joe' will receive five volumes where Mr Gladstone had to be content with three and most prime ministers
with two or even one. Though Chamberlain's political importance does not justify this excessive length it was inevitable
once Garvin was given the job; he was incapable of writing
concisely, and the three volumes were composed in the
oracular style of his famous Observer articles. Mr Amery was
bound to follow the Garvin pattern of treatment, though
not, fortunately, the Garvin style. The best that can be said
of his book is this: since someone had to wield Garvin's bow,
Mr Amery is to be congratulated on having done it successfully.

The present volume runs only from the end of 1900 until
the spring of 1903, when Chamberlain returned from his visit
to South Africa. He was overworked and getting old; as a
result, the revelations in this volume are fewer and less inter-

esting than previously. For instance, in spite of a valiant attempt by Mr Amery to build up Chamberlain as 'the chief author of the revolution in British foreign policy', there is nothing of importance on foreign affairs; the bulk of the story is taken from German documents long published. There is one document of interest: a memorandum of 10 September 1900 naïvely proposing to play off Germany against Russia in the Far East:

Both in China and elsewhere it is our interest that Germany should throw herself across the path of Russia ... the clash of German and Russian interests, whether in China or Asia Minor, would be a guarantee for our safety.

The other curiosity is the comment of Paul Cambon when he learnt that Chamberlain had become the advocate of friendship with France:

It must not be forgotten that Mr. Chamberlain has no political principles. He lives in the present and changes his opinions with incredible ease; he is not in the least embarrassed by his own statements and contradicts himself with extraordinary ease. He has a very accurate sense of what public opinion wants and follows its fluctuations while having the air of guiding them – hence his popularity.

Mr Amery calls this judgement 'myopic'.

The two principal themes of the volume are South Africa and the origins of Tariff Reform. South Africa bulks the larger, though here again there is not much to add, especially to the material published from the Milner Papers. It is clear that Chamberlain meant ultimately to give self-government to the Boers, equally clear that he meant to humiliate them first. There is an account here of the lamentable scene when he met the Boer generals who had come to Europe to seek help for their women and children:

A launch swept them out to Nigeria [the Colonial Secretary's ship]. There, on the deck, they came face to face, for the first time, with Chamberlain. The Colonial Secretary, immaculately dressed as ever, was accompanied by Roberts and the colonial dignitaries assembled for the Coronation. Behind him the battle fleet of Britain stretched out in four grey lines to the horizon. Amid the pageantry of Empire, the generals seemed awkward in their crumpled country clothes. For all their valour and cunning they were only simple farmers seeing the world for the first time.

This is how German historians used to write of Bismarck, but one of the Boer generals was called Botha. Would it have increased their faith in Chamberlain if they had known that Milner, his chosen pro-consul to whom he gave 'a Roman welcome', was writing in 1902:

What I have seen of the working of 'responsible government' in South Africa makes it wholly impossible for me to labour for its extension with any sort of zeal;

or that Chamberlain himself, who had once denounced the population of Johannesburg as 'devoted to money-making and their own interests', should write after his visit there:

The population of this city . . . is keen, intelligent, and responsive, with an inclination to be too impatient and critical but still at the bottom intensely loyal and Imperialist.

In fact, Chamberlain, once a social reformer, even – as Mr Amery calls him – a revolutionary, had energy without principle and became the willing prisoner of the most energetic men of his time, the great capitalist magnates, whether in London or Johannesburg. He thought of the Empire as power or as an undeveloped estate, not as a moral cause, and he said, with profound misjudgement: 'The days are for great Empires and not for little States.'

This led him to Imperial Preference and so, ultimately, to Tariff Reform. Mr Amery has been able to use the unpublished minutes of the Colonial Conference of 1902, and these show how Chamberlain's plans for Imperial Federation and for military unity broke on colonial resistance. The great colonies, Canada in particular, wished to be equal nations, not daughters of the Mother Country, and Chamberlain, without sentiment himself, could not conceive of a Commonwealth held together by sentiment alone. Imperial Preference seemed to be the answer and it suited Canada's needs.

But there were also motives of domestic politics. As Mr Amery shows in the most interesting part of his book, Imperial Preference was taken up by Chamberlain in order to put new life into the dying party of Liberal Unionism. This had been essentially the party of the industrial middle class, which needed a separate organization so long as the Tory party was 'a predominantly landed interest'. But now the Tory party, too, had become a party of business men; they could promote their interests there without paying the price of social reform, on which Chamberlain had previously insisted. Hence, as Mr Amery points out, Chamberlain had to drop his advocacy of old-age pensions if he was to keep his followers. The one thing which discriminated the Liberal Unionists from the Tories was their Nonconformity, and here the Education Bill of 1902 was decisive. Chamberlain supported the Bill so as to have his hands free for South Africa, and he rammed it down the throats of his Nonconformist followers. Also, in part, he wanted to pay the Nonconformists out for having supported Gladstone. He said to a leading Nonconformist Liberal:

Had the Nonconformists supported me, they would have had Disestablishment long ago. Now they have got nothing. When Mr. Gladstone suddenly sprang his Irish policy upon the country after consulting Morley, it was not so much to satisfy Ireland that he did so as to prevent me placing the Disestablishment of the Church of England in the forefront of the Liberal programme, as Mr. Gladstone knew and feared I meant to do.

Since Chamberlain could no longer use a sectarian appeal for his party, he sought something else, and believed that

189

Imperial Preference would do the trick. In the words of Lord George Hamilton, 'If we had had no Education Bill of 1902, we should have had no Tariff Reform in 1903.' The move was not designed only to salvage the Liberal Unionist party; it was designed ultimately to oust Balfour from the leadership of a great party of Imperial Union. As it was, Chamberlain only managed to destroy the Unionist party, as he had earlier destroyed the old Liberal party. Like all men who split their party, he was a failure, slightly above the level of Ramsay MacDonald, a great deal below that of Lloyd George.

21. The Chief

New Statesman. A review of Northcliffe by Reginald Pound and Geoffrey Harmsworth (1959). Beaverbrook said of the book: 'It weighs too much.'

On 15 July 1921 Lord Northcliffe inspected the editorial staffs at Carmelite House. He snapped at a sub-editor: 'What was the best story in this morning's Daily Mail?' The sub-editor quoted: 'Viscount Northcliffe is leaving tomorrow on a world tour and will be away from England for several months.' There was a shocked silence. Northcliffe looked stern. Then he turned to his secretary: 'See that man gets a hundred-pound bonus.' Nearly everything about Northcliffe can be deduced from this story. There is the boundless arrogance, tied up with the zest for news; the nature which swung from bullying to generosity. But look a little closer. Whose leg was being pulled in the last resort – Northcliffe's or the sub's? Perhaps even ours? Many writers have had a shot at Northcliffe. They have depicted him as everything from the supreme newspaper-genius to the corrupter of English journalism. His career has been explained over and over again in terms of power. Power over the public through his newspapers; power over that great symbol of respectability, The Times; power in the straight political sense – either as a maker of Governments or aspiring to be prime minister himself. Reading his earlier biographers, following the narrative in The History of the Times, accepting the trenchant sentences of Lord Beaverbrook, it was difficult to resist the impression that he was an early sketch for Adolf Hitler.

What contemporaries think of a man is, of course, highly relevant in judging him, but it is also useful to know what he thought of himself. In the biography by Reginald Pound and Geoffrey Harmsworth, Northcliffe is displayed from within for the first time. The result comes near to an autobiography, composed by snipping out innumerable sentences from his letters and piecing them together. This is a crushing book, with a powerful impact appropriate to its subject. It is heavy to hold, and there are nearly 900 pages to read. The reader can get through it with enjoyment only if he shares Northcliffe's own assumption that every scrap of information about himself is of intense importance, and the assumption must extend to the entire Harmsworth family. H G Wells, who originally suggested the book, wanted to have it called The Harmsworth Adventure. It would have been even more appropriate to call it The Harmsworth Saga. The narrative runs with the elaboration and distractions of an ancient legend. It seems incredible that many of the things in it really happened, and within recent memory. Not that the book contains anything sensational. On the contrary it knocks on the head many previous revelations confidently made or casually implied. For instance, it challenges convincingly the statement in The History of The Times that Northcliffe bought his peerage. All probability is the other way : Balfour, the prime minister, wished to reward Northcliffe for his assistance to Conservative newspapers in the provinces.

All the same, the book establishes one major fact about

Northcliffe, the decisive fact in his life. It is not new. Others have seen it, but could not bring themselves to believe that it was the only fact about Northcliffe which counted. Hence they had to call in power or money or even wickedness as the explanation of his career. The plain fact is that Northcliffe was a newsman first, last and all the time. He loved news and information. He loved making newspapers succeed, and he made them succeed by making them better newspapers, more crammed with information easily absorbed than any newspapers had been before. Success brought him money, and this he enjoyed spending on himself and, with erratic generosity, on others. It also brought him power – both of a political and non-political kind. This too he used, though he enjoyed it less. He tried to make English people eat standard bread and wear The Daily Mail hat. He promoted flights across the Channel and across the Atlantic. He advocated policies of a simple patriotic kind. But essentially this wielding of power was a nuisance to him, a distraction from the real business of getting out tomorrow's paper.

Take, for instance, the story of Northcliffe's relations with The Times. We have all been fascinated by the narrative presented in The History of The Times; how Northcliffe bought control and how he then set out to destroy every barrier against his autocratic will. First the 'Old Gang' had to go; then Dawson was driven out; finally Steed was sacked, and Northcliffe meant to run the paper himself as Editor-Proprietor. It is all very dramatic, and quite wrong. Naturally members of The Times staff think it the most important paper in the world. Northcliffe did not; he always rated The Daily Mail as more important and a better paper, which it was. He did not want power over The Times. In his boyish sentimental way, he regarded The Times as a national institution, and he wanted to save it, much as he contributed lavishly to the restoration of Westminster Abbey. He did not fight with the 'Old Gang' over power. He fought with them and got them out, because they were incapable of producing an efficient newspaper. He quarrelled with Dawson over policy. He believed that Dawson was too much in the pocket of the prime minister and that he was pro-German. 'I liked Dawson very much. I had nothing against him except that he is just naturally pro-German. He can't help it.' Later events confirmed Northcliffe's opinion. As to Steed, though he was a forceful writer and a brilliant correspondent, he was not a good editor. He committed dangerous indiscretions, one of which (his rash talk in New York) brought undeserved discredit on Northcliffe. Maybe Northcliffe would have done better not to touch The Times. But what he did, as The History admits, was to put the paper on its feet financially and journalistically. This cost him much money and more worry; it brought him no advantage.

There is also an instructive story here in regard to Northcliffe's political activities. It has to do with the fall of the Asquith coalition in December 1916. On Sunday, 3 December, Asquith and Lloyd George reached an acceptable compromise – Lloyd George to head the war committee, Asquith to remain as nominal prime minister. On Monday, 4 December, The Times came out with a fierce leader against Asquith. He used this as an excuse to break with Lloyd George; dissolved his Government; and provoked a fight which he lost. Asquith alleged that Lloyd George had inspired The Times leader. Lloyd George denied it. It is now known that Dawson wrote the leader quite independently after a visit to Cliveden – inspired perhaps by Carson, certainly not by Lloyd George. But Northcliffe had seen Lloyd George on 3 December. Surely they must have conspired against Asquith? Both men denied it; they even hinted that they had not actually conversed. What was their guilty secret? It is now out and is funny, though not at all guilty. Lloyd George was insuring against failure. Being a poor man, he wanted a contract to write political articles for The Daily Mail and American papers.

Northcliffe negotiated the contract. By 6 December Lloyd George was prime minister. Naturally he did not wish to confess that he had envisaged failure, still less that he had proposed to write for The Daily Mail. Nor did Northcliffe wish to confess that he had missed a catch. Hence on 8 December, 'Lord Northcliffe sees no advantage in any interview between him and the Prime Minister at this juncture.'

Of course Northcliffe had political views and expressed them strongly. He threw all his weight into winning the war just as he did into making The Daily Mail a success. He did his best to drive Kitchener from the War Office over the shell shortage, even though he had backed the appointment in the first place. He made a tremendous contribution to Anglo-American friendship by his visit to the United States in 1917. He probably helped to destroy Austria-Hungary by his conduct of enemy propaganda. Those who denounced Northcliffe's political line really disliked his attitude towards Germany. It all depends on the point of view. The reporting of Germany in The Daily Mail before 1914 was, in fact, more accurate than that in the highminded Liberal press. For that matter, his insistence on reparations, however mistaken economically, was more straightforward than that of the politicians who had preached hatred of Germany and were now buttering her up for use against Russia. 'They will beat you yet, those Junkers' disturbed tender consciences. It proved to be true.

The real dislike of Northcliffe did not spring from politics. It sprang from resentment against his journalistic success. He was accused of playing down to popular taste, of giving people what they wanted. This was untrue. He set his face sternly against vulgarity or sensationalism. He did not allow 'rupture' or 'constipation' in an advertisement. He complained : '*Merry and Bright*, No. 3. The front page is occupied by a fat man and an over-developed young woman ... On page 6 there is a man holding a revolver.' What Northcliffe did was to give people papers which they were eager to buy, better papers in every class than those offered before. His technical innovations were two. First, he exploited the paragraph – the short, quickfire presentation which makes modern newspapers readable, the greatest advance in communication since the abandonment of Latin for English. Second, he provided accurate information of every kind. He himself read every number of each of his papers. He spotted mistakes in the advertising columns – a WANTED appearing under FOR SALE. He told his reporters to find out whether the queues outside Maypole Dairy shops were a 'crude form of advertising'. Either he was reading newsprint or asking questions. No wonder that he had little aptitude for private life. For good or ill, he remained a zestful, overgrown schoolboy, his exaggerated affection for 'the Mother' now as embarrassing as Peter Pan. He liked to be called The Chief; and *Chief* appeared invariably as the signature of his letters. This is supposed to be an importation of 'chief editor' from the United States. Was there not in it also a touch of Red Indian glamour? Northcliffe liked war-paint and bloodcurdling howls. But he also made English newspapers the best in the world, and he established the freedom of the press on the only firm foundation – the great principle that freedom must be paid for like everything else and that newspapers have a right to exist only if they can meet their bills.

22. *The Anglo-Russian Entente*

Manchester Guardian. Written for the fiftieth anniversary of the Anglo-Russian entente.

The Anglo-Russian entente was formally concluded on 31 August 1907. Unlike the Entente Cordiale with France, it has vanished into the mists of history. Yet, for good or ill, it ranks high among the significant events of the century. Its making and its ten years of existence changed the face of the world. The Anglo-French entente, though sentimentally admirable, was no more than a renewal of good relations which had been temporarily interrupted by rivalry in the Nile valley. The entente with Russia was a revolution. Great Britain and Russia had never been on close terms before, at any rate not since the end of the Napoleonic wars. Usually, indeed, they had been on bad terms – at war in the Crimea, and on the brink of war over Pendjeh in 1885. Continental statesmen, especially German, based their plans on the expected clash between the elephant and the whale. Instead the two countries composed their differences, cooperated diplomatically, and finally, to their mutual surprise, found themselves partners in a great European war.

The agreement of 31 August was modest in form. The two Powers merely promised to keep their hands off the buffer states of Central Asia. Afghanistan and Tibet were to be left alone. Even in regard to Persia, which is often described as 'partitioned', the bargain was negative. The British were to keep out of the north, the Russians out of the south; the centre lay neutral between them. Sir Edward Grey boasted that, unlike some earlier agreements, this contained no secret clauses. He spoke the truth, yet there were understandings unwritten but binding.

The Russians received a hint that they would get concessions at the Straits if they behaved well for a few years. As a matter of fact they had to wait until 1915 before they secured the promise of Constantinople, and then they proved unable to cash the cheque. More broadly, the two countries were committed to diplomatic cooperation. The Triple Entente came into existence, though both Grey and Izvolski tried to avoid using the phrase. Neither side liked its implications. The British had no wish to support Russia's ambitions in the Balkans (so far as she had any); the Russians managed, more successfully, to keep clear of the naval dispute between England and Germany. All the same, the consequences were inescapable. Germany could no longer exploit her policy of 'the free hand', once England and Russia were on good terms. Henceforward the Germans aimed to disrupt the Triple Entente and when they failed flung themselves in exasperation against it.

The Anglo-Russian entente was a business deal, not a matter of sentiment. In England it was unpopular as no diplomatic step has been except the policy of 'appeasement'. Most Conservatives swallowed it cynically as strengthening the balance against Germany. Liberal ministers – Grey and Morley, for example – excused it on the ground that otherwise large forces would have to be provided for the defence of India. The Radical rank and file abhorred the friendship with an autocratic Power, the more so when Russia's only democratic Duma had been recently dissolved. In 1908 the Labour party protested, with some Radical support, against Edward VII's visit to the tsar at Reval; and their renewed protests kept the tsar confined to Cowes when he wished to visit England the following year. The betrayal of Persia made them yet more indignant. English Radicals believed that Persia could maintain her own independence of Russia if she received some British backing, and they were probably right. It was additionally tiresome that, whatever the professions of the Russian ministers at St Petersburg – and they were perhaps sincere – the representative at Tehran went cheerfully on encroaching as he had done for years. Persia caused Grey more trouble than any other question in foreign affairs. Exasperation with Russian behaviour made him threaten to resign and to make way for a pro-German foreign secretary – a step that would have been welcome to the Liberal majority in the House.

At the outset the Radical critics complained that Persia had been sacrificed to 'that foul idol, the Balance of Power'; it had been the price for Russian backing against Germany. Later they turned the accusation the other way round and made out that the peace of Europe was being endangered for the sake of Imperialist gains in Persia and elsewhere. These charges were too simple. The entente was a bargain of mutual advantage, and, if this weakened Germany's position, Great Powers cannot be expected to bicker merely to please some third party.

The real British commitment was to France, not to Russia, but undoubtedly Great Britain had to be somewhat complaisant towards Russia in order to ensure that France could count firmly on her eastern ally. The British government decided, rightly or wrongly, not to tolerate a German hegemony of the Continent. Once having decided this, they had to go along with Russia in the last resort. In peacetime Russia benefited more than Great Britain from the entente. When war came it was the other way round. It was the Russian army which ensured that there should be a Western front in the first world war and which, moreover, ensured that the Germans could never put their whole weight on that front until too late.

In Russia, too, the policy of the entente was not without its critics, though occupying almost exactly reverse positions from those in England. The Russian liberals wanted to turn towards Europe and away from Asia. Therefore they welcomed the compromise over imperial interests and, still more, friendship with the Western Powers. The realists of the extreme Right deplored being involved in European affairs, and, paradoxically, Lenin shared their view. Lenin and Witte both regarded the entente as the root of all evil. Both wanted the European Powers to destroy themselves in a great war, while Russia developed the riches of her Asiatic empire.

The first Russian revolution of March 1917 would have marked the triumph of the entente, if it had been a triumph for anything. The Bolshevik revolution ended the entente and led logically not only to the peace of Brest-Litovsk but to the Nazi–Soviet pact. The Anglo-Russian entente has been forgotten by both partners. Yet, oddly enough, it has been more successful than the Anglo-French entente as a practical arrangement. England is no longer paramount in Egypt, nor France in Morocco. But the buffer states of Asia survive. Tibet is safe from Russia or the British Empire. Afghanistan is still neutral and independent. Most remarkable of all, Persia still defies Imperialist encroachment from every quarter with supreme self-confidence.

23. 'We Want Eight, and We Won't Wait'

Manchester Guardian. Written to mark the fiftieth
anniversary of the great controversy over naval building
in March 1909. The German naval archives have now been
returned to Germany but the secrets of German
anticipation have not yet been adequately revealed.

Armament programmes have often been the subject of controversy in British politics from the 'French panic' of 1860 to nuclear weapons at the present day. No controversy has been fiercer than that over naval building in March 1909. The phrase then coined still rings down the avenues of time. 'We want eight, and we won't wait.' The Liberal party, with its great majority, was deeply divided on this question; the Cabinet itself threatened to disintegrate. The Unionists saw their chance to reverse the electoral defeat of 1906. They exploited popular passion and believed office to be again within their grasp.

The origin of the crisis lay in 1906 when Sir John Fisher, first sea lord, introduced the Dreadnought, the first all-big-gun ship. The Dreadnought made all existing navies out of date; it was more powerful than three of its immediate predecessors put together. For the time being the Dreadnought increased British superiority and upset all other programmes; the Germans did not lay down a single battleship for nearly two years. But the superiority, though greater, rested on a narrower margin. In March 1909 the British had forty-three pre-Dreadnought battleships as against twenty-two German. They had two of Dreadnought type completed and three battle-cruisers; the Germans had none. But the Germans had fourteen ships projected; the British only seven. The gap between the two navies might close ominously when the Germans began to build.

Here was the second and more dangerous point. It had always been assumed that Great Britain, as the greatest industrial Power, could build more ships than any other Power and could build them faster. Even if another country stole a march on the British, they could catch up before the danger point was reached. Gladstone had said it in 1894: 'Our means of construction are overwhelming ... Our methods of construction are far more rapid.' Goschen, Unionist first lord, repeated this confidence in 1898. Ten years later it was ceasing to be true in the opinion of many experts. Germany, too, was now an industrial Power of the first rank. Though still inferior in the number of her shipyards, she was equal, if not ahead, in the armament factories producing the guns, gun-mountings, turrets and armourplate which a battleship needed. The Germans could, if they put themselves to it, build up to the British programme and, what was more, with their industrial efficiency, they could build as fast, if not faster.

It was the duty of the expert advisers to tell the Government how British supremacy could be maintained. By 1909 they had reached the conclusion that the yardstick should no longer be German ships, built or projected, but German capacity. This opened the door to fantastic calculations. The needs of the German army were ignored, all budgetary considerations disregarded. The only question was: how many battleships can the Germans have if they concentrate on this and nothing else? According to the published programme, the Germans would have ten battleships completed in the spring of 1911. Asquith, the Prime Minister, striking a moderate note, held that they would have thirteen or at most seventeen. Balfour, leader of the Opposition, excelled in these speculative subtleties; according to him, the Germans would have at least twenty-one battleships in 1911, but more probably twenty-five.

In face of these imagined perils the Board of Admiralty wished to increase the British building programme for 1909 from four battleships to six, and to maintain this rate for the two years following. The Unionists, supported by the popular press, raged that eight should be laid down at once. Two members of the Cabinet, Lloyd George and Winston Churchill, stood out against the clamour. They pointed to the published German figure of ten for March 1911; four British battleships a year, added to the existing number, would be adequate to meet this. Germany, they argued, was a constitutional country. Battleships could not be built without the financial authorization of the Reichstag. What evidence, they asked, was there that the German admiralty was cheating either the Reichstag or the British experts?

The question could be given a theoretical answer. Germany, it could be alleged, was not a constitutional country in the British sense. The Reichstag would forgive a breach of the rules – as the Prussian parliament had forgiven Bismarck in 1866 – if it brought strategic gain, and of course the German government had no moral obligation towards Great Britain to observe its published programme, whatever it might have towards the Reichstag. But there was also a more practical answer. There was evidence that some of the contracts for the German 1909–10 programme had been given out in the autumn of 1908, and evidence too that material for the projected ships had been collected in advance.

This is the most puzzling part of the story. We do not know to this day why the Germans 'anticipated' their 1909 programme. It may have been to break the ring of contractors or to provide continuity of employment. To suspicious British eyes it looked like an attempt to steal a march. The information came from secret sources. It could not be used publicly. But Fisher saw to it that it did not stay with the Government; it reached, probably in exaggerated form, the leaders of the Opposition and the press. Thus there were two supposed dangers: the theoretical possibility of German 'acceleration', the actual probability of German 'anticipation'. The argument plunged into inextricable confusion – men hinting at the second when they were ostensibly talking of the first.

Asquith handled the crisis with his customary adroitness, apparently doing one thing with the intention later of being forced to do the other. In the debates of March 1909 he stood solid with Lloyd George, Churchill and the bulk of Liberal MPs. There was, he insisted, no danger, no need for panic; the building programme would remain at four battleships.

But he asked also for authorization to lay down four 'contingent' ships later in the year, if this proved necessary. Both parties were satisfied. The Liberals thought that agitation had been defied; the Unionists found that their thunder had been stolen. In July McKenna, first lord of the admiralty, announced that the four contingent ships would be built. He made no reference to German acceleration or anticipation; his new excuse was that German's two allies, Austria-Hungary and Italy, were proposing to build four Dreadnoughts at some time in the future. Everyone knew the real 'contingency': the Liberals had just suffered resounding defeat in a by-election at Croydon.

Only seventy-nine Liberals voted vainly against the contingent ships. Thus the British public got their eight ships and did not wait. But the panic did the Unionists no good. To meet the increased naval bill Lloyd George devised the People's Budget, and soon his Limehouse speech drowned the cry of 'We want eight'. As to the supposed danger period of spring 1911, the Germans did not then have twenty-five battleships or twenty-one or seventeen or thirteen; they had six. A year later they had nine, against the British sixteen. Had they ever planned to have more? The answer might be found in the German naval records which, for some years after the second world war, reposed at Admiralty House and maybe are there still. No curious eye has looked upon them. British admirals guard the secrets of their German colleagues as carefully as they guard their own, or perhaps, considering Fisher's constant leakages, rather better.

24. *The Use of Monarchy*

Tribune. A review of King George V: His Life and Reign, by Harold Nicolson (1952).

Bentham asked of every law, custom and institution : 'What's the use of it?' Harold Nicolson's life of George V is an attempt to answer this question for British monarchy in the twentieth century. He shows what part George V played in the democratic constitution, and he justifies that part with insidious persistence. At the end it is difficult not to feel both that George V was a very good king and that this is a very good life of him.

Such feelings need scrutiny; after the chorus of praise, a little criticism, or even fault-finding, will do no harm. Mr Nicolson writes with all his accustomed charm and ability. He is grave without being pompous, and he does not pretend that George V played more than a minor part, though occasionally a decisive one, in determining the course of events. He has worked conscientiously through the royal archives and includes enough original material to satisfy the historian without tiring the general reader. He strikes the right balance, very difficult to achieve in royal biography, between the personal life of his subject and general history.

But his detachment lessens as he comes to events within his own experience. For instance, he looks at the economic crisis of 1931 with the eyes of a contemporary who has learnt nothing, though he may have forgotten a certain amount. It passes belief that in 1952, after the experience of the New Deal and years of Keynesian economics, anyone can still regard deflation and a cut in unemployment benefit as the right answer to a slump. The members of the Labour Government may have been at sixes and sevens, but at least they recognized the wrong course, though they were vague about the right one. The National Government were obdurate in wrong-doing and wasted the most precious decade of the century.

It would be tolerable if Mr Nicolson treated all politics and politicians with amiable frivolity, but his blind eye is turned in only one direction. George Lansbury, perhaps the best Socialist of the century, is described as 'a man of quick emotions and a slow sense of reality'. The speeches of Sir John Simon during the General Strike, on the other hand, were 'brilliantly constructive' – so constructive indeed that the Tory Government had to change the law in order to catch up with their interpretation of it. Mr Nicolson concludes his account of the General Strike: 'the tragedy was felt to be a common tragedy ... Every section of the community felt sorry for the other sections, as well as for themselves.' By an odd oversight, the wealthier classes did not carry this sorrow so far as to give the miners a living wage.

This may seem remote from the position of George V; in reality it shows the sympathy between the biographer and his subject. Mr Nicolson, too, belongs to the Establishment, though his sophistication almost enables him to conceal it. There was nothing sophisticated about George V. He was simple, direct, an outdoor man without intellectual interests. Mr Nicolson rubs in his Philistinism in matters of taste and perhaps there was no time in our history when the Court counted for so little in the world of literature and art. On the other hand, no king tried harder to do his duty.

Before 1910 the sovereign often took these duties lightly. Victoria buried herself at Balmoral for months at a time, as George IV had done at Brighton. Edward VII gave to politics only the hours he could spare from a garish Society. George V made constitutional monarchy a whole-time occupation. He was always available to his ministers; constantly visiting factories, hospitals and mills; opening new buildings, receiving civic greetings. He visited India and, if he had had his way, would have visited each of his Dominions. He saw, with startling perception, that the Crown had become essentially a symbol, and he showed how this symbol could be personified in a very ordinary man with very ordinary tastes. He was conscientious; he was decent; he was straight. These are high virtues.

His strictly political activities showed the same virtues, and with their help he gave the political position of the Crown a new and simpler definition. Victoria had often intrigued against her prime minister with other Cabinet ministers or even with his political opponents. George V gave each of his prime ministers unstinted support. Though he sometimes discussed questions with the leaders of the Opposition, the prime minister always knew and approved, and the object of these conversations was to make the Opposition more moderate and conciliatory. In 1913 many distinguished men urged George V to dismiss Asquith and force a general election, in order to prevent Home Rule. In 1923 many distinguished men urged him not to appoint Ramsay MacDonald. The king disregarded these suggestions, almost without argument. He took the simple direct course.

In the bitterness of 1931 many people in the Labour movement complained that George V had abused his constitutional position and had himself manufactured the National Government. The charge was baseless. The Labour Government resigned of its own accord. The leaders of the Liberal and Conservative parties, who together had a majority, advised the king to appoint Ramsay MacDonald as head of a National Government, and he took their advice. He was often urged to insist on a dissolution of Parliament or to refuse one as an independent act of the prerogative. Again, he took a simple direct line; he regarded it as the exclusive right of the prime minister of the day to advise on this as on everything else.

Indeed, the reign of George V reduced the independent actions of the king to one: he appoints the prime minister according to his own judgement. Once the prime minister accepts office, the king follows his advice on everything until he resigns. George V arrived at this position by instinct, and did not openly admit it in argument; it was a wise position all the same. If King George's straightforwardness had been realized at once, it would have been unnecessary for Asquith in November 1910 to demand a secret promise that the king would create enough peers to override the House of Lords if the Liberals won the second general election. The king's own 'fair play' could have been relied on.

'Fair play' was the keynote of all his actions. But is fair play enough? After appointing the first Labour Government, he wrote to his mother: 'They have different ideas to ours as they are all Socialists, but they ought to be given a chance and ought to be treated fairly.' No doubt George V was extremely patient and sympathetic with his Labour ministers, but this was easier the less Socialist they were.

The duties of a constitutional king, according to a hard-worn phrase, are 'to advise, to encourage, and to warn'. When George V received his first Labour ministers, he said to them, 'The immediate future of my people is in your hands, gentlemen. They depend upon your prudence and sagacity.' These were good words to have addressed to a Conservative administration; prudence and sagacity are the best that can be expected of it. They are not the right virtues for a government of the Left. Initiative, energy, creative daring – these are the qualities which even a minority Labour Government should have shown. If not, why go to the trouble of having a Labour party at all? Why not leave it to the Conservatives?

It is the inevitable function of a constitutional monarchy

to act as a brake and therefore to slow down the process of political and economic reform. This is held to be a desirable result. Is it? Would it not be better to have the change over and done with? There would surely have been advantages, not only for the Labour party, in settling the nationalization of steel in 1948 instead of letting the industry drag on in uncertainty to the present day.

Or take some incidents of now purely historical interest. In 1911 the influence of the king and of all moderate opinion persuaded the House of Lords to accept the Parliament Act at the last minute and so saved the House with its existing composition. Would it not have been better from every point of view to create the five hundred new peers that were designed? Mr Ensor, no radical witness, says of Asquith's list: 'they were a very strong body, and in proved character, intellect, business, and public activity certainly outweighed the then existing House of Lords, if a score of leaders in the latter were deducted'. As to Home Rule itself, it is difficult to measure the advantages to both Ireland and the Commonwealth if it had become law without the delays of the Parliament Act.

There is something to be said for conservatism (though I can never recollect what); there is much to be said for radical change; the defects of gradual reform are greater than is commonly supposed – and it is gradual reform which the British constitution and monarchy inevitably promote.

Still, fair play in all things. Though George V did his best to steer his Labour ministers away from Socialism, he also tried to moderate extremism on the other side. His standards of decency were often higher than those of his ministers. He disliked the campaign against aliens and conscientious objectors during the first world war; he objected to the violence of The British Gazette (edited by Winston Churchill) during the General Strike; he protested against the Black-and-Tans and against the forcible feeding of suffragettes. With General

Smuts's assistance, he made a notable appeal for conciliation in Ireland, when he opened the first parliament in Belfast. He even complained against some of Lloyd George's nominations for honour. He complained in vain.

This is where fair play breaks down. If a government of the Left had nominated an unbeliever or a divorcee, they would at once have withdrawn the name on the king's objection. A Right government did not scruple to insist on these financial scoundrels, even though it offended opinion in more than one dominion. The explanation is simple. The Right always regards itself as 'the loyal party': therefore it does not need to take any notice of the king's objections. Even when Carson set up a seditious and rebellious organization in 1912, its members pledged themselves 'as loyal subjects of his Gracious Majestic King George V'.

With the best will in the world (and George V had it), a king who sees only wealthy and titled people weighs with two weights and judges with two measures. On 27 July 1912, Bonar Law, leader of the Conservative party, said: 'I can imagine no length of resistance to which Ulster will go, which I shall not be ready to support.' Within two months, Bonar Law was a guest of the king at Balmoral. Suppose (an impossibility indeed) that Ramsay MacDonald had said in April 1926: 'I can imagine no length of resistance to which the miners will go, which I shall not be ready to support.' Would he have been the king's guest before the end of June? If at all, it would have been in prison, not at Balmoral.

George V was franker than his latter-day admirers: 'they have different ideas to ours as they are all Socialists'. The function of constitutional monarchy is to conserve, to put the brake on. When Tories are in power, the brake is not needed, and the King can wish them success without reservation. The best he can hope for from a Socialist Government is that their bark will be worse than their bite – and it usually is. We may reverse George V's judgement and say of the British royal house: 'they have different ideas to ours as none of them is Socialist'. Since more than half the electors of this country now vote Socialist, this is perhaps a misfortune.

George V, much against his personal taste, ensured that if the people of this country wanted a social revolution they could have it without a political unheaval. Still, a Labour Government should bear in mind that when a sovereign exercises his right 'to advise, to encourage, and to warn', his admonitions, however sincere, will not be directed to the victory of Socialism. He has different ideas to ours, and we have different ideas to his.

25. A Patriot for One Ireland

Times Literary Supplement. A review of Roger Casement by Brian Inglis (1973).

Roger Casement, an Irishman, was hanged at Pentonville on 3 August 1916, as a traitor to the king of England. Ellis, the hangman, thought him 'the bravest man it fell to my unhappy lot to execute'. For half a century Casement's body lay in Pentonville jail. In 1953 Churchill told de Valera that it must lie there for ever: the law on the subject was 'specific and binding'. Twelve years later Harold Wilson was more generous. On 23 February 1965 Casement's remains were returned to Ireland. They were given a state funeral at Glasnevin. President de Valera had been ill and was told that he should not attend. He insisted that he must. At least, he was told, he must keep his head covered. De Valera replied: 'Casement deserves better than that.' Uncovered, he delivered the funeral oration.

Indeed Casement deserved better than that – better than the treatment he received during his lifetime and better than that accorded to him after his death. Even biographers sympathetic to Casement have been more interested in the authenticity of his private diaries than in his public achievements or, when they dealt with these, have presented him as an isolated, impractical figure – romantic, perhaps, but futile. At long last Brian Inglis has given Casement his due. This splendid book tells the story of a troubled soul who surmounted his troubles and rose to greatness – great as a noble character and greater still as the man who raised high the flag of Irish freedom and unity.

Mr Inglis brings great advantages to his task. Like Casement, he was brought up a Protestant and a Unionist, loyal to the British Crown. Like Casement, he came to put Ireland first and to mean by Ireland the united island. He understands Casement as no previous biographer has done. For Mr Inglis, Casement matters politically. He has looked through Casement's diaries and, though acknowledging them as genuine, emphasizes their unimportance for the study of Casement's career. Connoisseurs of official secrecy will be fascinated to learn that, while the diaries are now available to scholars, the Home Office files on Casement remain closed for 100 years. This concealment is easy to understand. The diaries were used quite irrelevantly to blacken Casement's character and send him to the gallows. We are still not allowed to know which British minister or civil servant hit on this repulsive idea. However we can make a good guess.

Casement's achievements were unexpected. He did not learn Irish patriotism at his mother's knee. He knew nothing of Wolfe Tone or of his later hero John Mitchel. He was hardly aware that there was an Irish language. He grew up in Ulster, a Protestant and a gentleman, regarding himself as a loyal British subject. He pursued an orthodox career in the British consular service. Here fate first took a hand. When stories reached Europe of the atrocities being committed in the Congo during Leopold's pursuit of Red Rubber, Casement, being the man on the spot, was sent to investigate. Casement discovered, to his own surprise, his hatred of human brutality and oppression. Casement was not alone in the Congo affair. E D Morel conducted the campaign in England and merited an equal tribute of admiration. But it was Casement's patient investigation with its deadly array of facts that made the campaign possible.

Mr Inglis tells the Congo story very much from Casement's side. The work of Leopold in the Congo has been studied in much greater detail by Belgian scholars, sometimes to the point of apology or even justification. Others will be content to echo the words of Cecil Rhodes, no mean judge, who said after meeting Leopold II: 'Satan! I tell you that man is Satan!' At Leopold's orders thousands of natives were tortured or massacred. Vast areas of the country were depopulated. Few worse crimes were witnessed in modern history. It is little excuse that Belgium acquired some grandiose buildings from her share of the profits.

Unlike Morel, Casement was not a good organizer, nor was he at this time a good speaker. He relied more on the Foreign Office than on public opinion. Here he was disappointed. In earlier days British foreign secretaries and the Foreign Office had been themselves champions of human freedom. Palmerston, for instance, wrote more dispatches on the fight against the slave trade than on any other subject and declared that he would leave public life if Parliament cut off the money for the anti-slave trade patrols.

In the twentieth century the Foreign Office went sour. In its eyes Casement was a nuisance, a consul who had exceeded his functions. The British Ambassador to Brussels wrote off the humanitarians as being 'always prone to sentimentalism about slavery and other local customs to which the native populations were attached'. Casement's report was emasculated and for a time withheld from publication. Lord Lansdowne, the foreign secretary, acquiesced. Better things might have been expected from Sir Edward Grey, his Liberal successor, particularly since he later described the Congo campaign as the greatest since Gladstone's against the Bulgarian atrocities. But, as Mr Inglis points out, Grey in his memoirs devoted only a few sentences to this campaign and many chapters to his devious diplomacy. Fitzmaurice, Grey's under-secretary, remarked : 'It is not our interest to be having a row with Belgium also, if perchance we are having a row with Germany.'

Casement did not have Morel's persistence. Also he needed new employment in his life in order to keep going financially. It was the Congo that first turned Casement against the British Government and made him distrust British policy. In a sense the Congo also led Casement to the cause of Irish independence. He returned to Ireland while waiting for a fresh appointment and there realized that the Irish people were in much the same situation as the natives of the Congo – ruled for good or ill by others, not allowed to rule themselves. Casement changed almost overnight from a loyal British subject into a potential rebel. This was more striking than it may seem in the light of later events. We know that Ireland was to become a republic. In the first decade of the present century this view was held only by a few Fenians in the obscure Irish Republican Brotherhood. The Home Rulers who dominated Irish politics regarded themselves as British. Their aim was autonomy, not independence. Casement was the first prominent figure who transformed the dreams of the IRB into a practical creed.

Casement said at the end of his life : 'The best thing was the Congo.' He himself contributed little to the final victory, when Leopold II was discredited and forced to transfer the Congo to Belgium. E D Morel received and deserved the principal credit for this. Mr Inglis might have added that the pursuit of Red Rubber with all its horrors became unnecessary once plantation rubber proved practicable and more profitable.

Casement, however, had a further encounter with the evil he had exposed in the Congo. This time the scandal was on the Putomayo in South America. Once more Casement was the man on the spot. Once more he investigated and produced a damning report. The response of British opinion was less emphatic. The same sort of campaign cannot be conducted twice, much as the Armenian massacre of the 1890s failed to provoke the stir that the Bulgarian atrocities had done twenty years earlier. E D Morel was now denouncing Grey's foreign policies. The British and American governments, though endorsing Casement's reports, were only concerned to hush up the scandal. Casement himself left South America and the British consular service.

The few years before the First World War were decisive for Casement's historical fame and for his own fate. Though knighted in 1911, he had ceased to regard himself as a British subject and had become an unequivocal Irish nationalist. He learnt to speak on the public platform. He counted as a political figure. Casement took up the almost unnoticed movement of Sinn Fein and transformed it into a practical cause. Ireland, he preached, should not seek concessions from Great Britain. She should declare her independence and act on it. Like Arthur Griffith, he pointed to the example of Hungary, with the curious personal link that his own father had saved Kossuth when threatened with extradition from Turkey.

Casement added a further point, not made by any other Irish leader. Irish independence, he believed, should be won in cooperation with Ulster, not against her. He even held that Ulster should lead the movement as she had done in previous centuries. Ulster's claim not to be incorporated in a Home Rule Ireland was exactly the same as Ireland's claim not to be incorporated in the United Kingdom. Casement often declared that he and Carson were fighting for the same cause and should appear on the same platform. It was English politicians, such as F E Smith, exploiting Ireland's difficulties for their own party advantage, whom he wanted to keep out.

Ulster provided a more practical analogy. If Ulster were permitted to buy arms in Germany and to seek German support, as the Unionists did, Ireland was entitled to do the same. As an independent country, Ireland should follow an independent policy. British maritime supremacy was no concern of hers, and the British must learn to live with a neutral Ireland. Casement's policy had its forerunners in the 'Wild Geese' and later the Irish republicans who had sought French aid for Ireland's liberation.

All the same, he made a disastrous error. He thought that the Germans would take up the Irish cause for idealistic reasons, just as Masaryk counted on the support of British idealists for the liberation of the Czechs. There were enough British idealists to make Masaryk's line respectable and not a mere act of treason. There were no such idealists in Germany. When war broke out, Casement went to Germany and tried to recruit an Irish legion. The Germans, who preferred the British Empire to a free Ireland, regarded him as a nuisance. Casement became disillusioned, embittered. When reports reached him of a projected rising in Ireland, he travelled to Ireland in a German submarine in order to give warning that there would be no German aid and that, without it, a rising could not succeed.

This was the supreme irony of Casement's career. He was arrested and condemned to death for seeking to provoke rebellion when in fact he had come in order to ensure that the rising did not take place. Casement's trial makes sorry reading. He, an Irishman, was tried by an English Lord Chief Justice and an English jury. How, he asked the jury, would they like it if they had attempted a rising in England and had then been shipped off to Dublin for trial?

Casement wished to conduct his own case and simply to deny the authority over him of an English court. He was over-ruled. His counsel, Serjeant Sullivan, fought the case on a technicality, based on a statute of Edward III's reign. Naturally he lost. At one moment Sullivan ventured to hint that Casement had only done what F E Smith, the prosecuting Attorney-General, had done before him. When pulled up by Reading, the Lord Chief Justice – pilloried by Kipling as Gehazi – Sullivan broke down and withdrew from the case.

Casement was allowed to speak only after the jury had found him guilty. Mr Inglis does the great service of printing Casement's speech in full. It merits Wilfrid Blunt's verdict : 'the finest document in patriotic literature. Finer than anything in Plutarch or elsewhere in Pagan literature.' It moved Blunt to 'anger and delight that anything so perfect should have come from the mouth of a man of our time condemned to death'. Years later, Nehru described the profound impression that the 'extraordinarily moving and eloquent' statement made on him : 'It seemed to point out exactly how a subject nation should feel.'

Casement was condemned to death. There was an outcry in the United States, though President Wilson, himself of Ulster stock, passed by on the other side. It seemed that the trial would win neutral sympathies for Casement instead of discrediting him. Now was the time to produce the 'black diaries' – private jottings of previous years which showed beyond reasonable doubt that Casement was a practising homosexual. The idea of discrediting Casement by means of the diaries seems to have originated with Ernley Blackwell, legal adviser to the Home Office. It was taken up by many others. Herbert Samuel, then home secretary, wrote : 'Had Casement not been a man of atrocious moral character, the situation would have been even more difficult.' Asquith asked Page, the American ambassador, whether he had heard about the diary. Page replied that he had seen it and had been given photographed copies of some of it. Asquith said : 'Excellent, and you need not be particular about keeping it to yourself.'

What was the relevance of the diaries even if they were genuine? None. No one had ever suspected Casement of homosexuality, and it never affected his policy or public conduct. For that matter, there were two practising homosexuals in the Cabinet which determined to blacken Casement. One of them later committed suicide : the other went into exile in order to escape prosecution. Asquith, however, passed no word of condemnation on either of them. Was it worse to run after boys than to develop senile passions for young girls and to be helpless with drink on the Treasury bench? Such was the state of Asquith, and it is held not to derogate from his conduct of affairs when prime minister. The loathsome story has no interest except as illustrating the desperate measures that an Imperial Government will resort to when cornered.

Casement's death had quite other significance. It created the importance of Sinn Fein. The Easter Rising had been conducted by a few members of the IRB, not by Sinn Fein. Thanks to Casement, Sinn Fein got the credit for it. The independence of Ireland triumphed when Casement was hanged. He represented a second cause. He said in his last speech :

We aimed at winning the Ulster Volunteers to the cause of a United Ireland. We aimed at uniting all Irishmen in a natural and national bond of cohesion based on mutual self-respect. Our hope was a natural one and, if left to ourselves, not hard to accomplish. If external forces of destruction would but leave us alone we were sure that Nature must bring us together.

Here is Casement's message for the present day. There is no Irish problem beyond solution. The problem that has racked Ireland for centuries is the British presence in Ireland. That problem can be solved only by British withdrawal.

26. *Politics in the First World War*

The Raleigh lecture on History, given at the British Academy in 1959 and subsequently published in The Proceedings of the British Academy (1959). Lord Stansgate, who had been a Liberal member of parliament during the first world war, was in the audience at the lecture. He said to me afterwards: 'I had no idea it had been like that.'

In 1920 General Groener, Ludendorff's successor and last quartermaster-general of the Imperial army, wrote of the first world war: 'The German general staff fought against the English parliament.' The phrase is quoted and, to a large extent endorsed, in Der deutsche Reichstag im Welkriege, a substantial volume laid before the Reichstag committee of inquiry into the causes of Germany's defeat by Dr J V Bredt, himself a Democratic deputy. Dr Bredt argues that the Reichstag played an important and occasionally decisive part during the war. If it did not shape German policy, this was its own fault, and that of the parties; the general staff gave way whenever it was faced by a parliamentary majority. Dr Bredt looks sadly over to the enemy side across the Channel where things, he believes, were different. The British House of Commons asserted civilian control; the German Reichstag did not. Hence the Allies won the war; hence the sentence of General Groener with which I began.

The defeated – both Reichstag and general staff – have received much attention from historians. Indeed German politics during the first world war are one of the few fields in recent history which is in danger of being over-worked. What did the British parliament and British politicians do during the first world war? The theme has been strangely neglected.

Metternich's complaint against old Austria has become the guiding principle of English historians: 'administration has taken the place of government'. The machinery of public authority has been studied, from the war Cabinet down to local agricultural committees. Only one writer has presented 'a political history of the war', and even he hesitated over the claim.[1] No word of mine should be taken as criticism of Lord Beaverbrook's splendid volumes. Their brilliant presentation, wealth of material and deep understanding of men's motives, stir the admiration of the professional historian, not his jealousy. But Lord Beaverbrook deals, as he says himself, with the Peaks of Politics, not with the general course of political events. Some of the great questions are passed over lightly, of intent. Thus of Ireland: 'The issue is dead, and it does not possess a spark of life or interest to the reader of today',[2] 'it would be unprofitable to dissect its lifeless body'.[3] Lord Beaverbrook adds in his usual disarming way: 'I am quite prepared to admit that I may be wrong in the small importance I now attach to these Irish stories.'[4] Again, conscription – the question which began the disintegration of the Liberal party – 'was not a burning issue'. 'To trace all the ramifications of [the politicians'] beliefs would be tedious to the last degree.'[5]

1. Lord Beaverbrook would have liked to call Volume One of Politicians and the War (1928) 'a Political History' but was 'only too well aware that the description would be a misnomer.' Volume Two (1932), 'does not profess to be a detailed history of the politics of the war'. In Men and Power 1917–1918 (1956), however, he describes the two earlier volumes as 'an earnest attempt to provide an impartial political history'.

2. Politicians and the War, i, 50.

3. ibid., ii, 64.

4. ibid, ii, 13.

5. ibid, i, 207, 206. But on ii, 44: 'A frank discussion and vote in the Cabinet would have broken the administration to pieces ... We find here the germ of a fundamental difference of view as to the aim of the War and the methods by which it was to be conducted which completely transcended party.'

During the great moments of crisis as described by Lord Beaverbrook, the House of Commons provides noises off; it never occupies the centre of the scene. This, though it may well be a true picture, merits examination. This lecture may be taken as a supplement to Lord Beaverbrook's work, or, in a phrase which he has used in a different connection, 'another version of the same'.

The House of Commons, elected in December 1910, was indeed ill-prepared to direct, or even to influence, the conduct of a great war. The general election had been fought, to the boredom of the electorate, on the question of the House of Lords. Thereafter the House plunged from one passionate party controversy to another. Foreign affairs were rarely discussed : less than in the parliament of 1906–10, and hardly at all after February 1912. In August 1914 all these great causes of controversy were dimmed. The House of Lords had surprisingly reached a lasting settlement, or next door to it, in 1911. Irish Home Rule was pushed aside on the outbreak of war when the Home Rule Act, though placed on the statute book, was suspended for the duration. National Insurance had ceased to be contentious – duchesses had long been licking stamps; and Welsh Disestablishment no longer stirred a flame except in the Welsh and Lord Robert Cecil. Even the long-standing argument between free trade and tariff reform appeared irrelevant when set against the background of national survival. The House was united. All members, a bare half-dozen excepted, recognized the necessity of war in August 1914. The way seemed clear for the House to become a great Council of State.

The appearance of national unity was deceptive. There were still deep cleavages in the party outlooks. The Unionists, by and large, regarded Germany as a dangerous rival, threatening either the Balance of Power or Great Britain's imperial interests – maybe both together. They proposed to fight a hard-headed war by ruthless methods and regarded any 'moral' advantage as a windfall. For the Liberals this 'moral' advantage was essential. Many of them had come to support the war only when Germany invaded Belgium, and even the less radical among them were relieved to escape from a 'realistic' position. Entering the war for altruistic motives, the Liberals wished to conduct it by high-minded means, and they found it harder to abandon their principles than to endure defeat in the field. There would have been raging conflict between the two parties if the profound differences of outlook had been brought into the open. The leaders of both were therefore anxious to keep it under cover. The House heard a general oration from Asquith on 6 August and then adjourned on 10 August. It met for a brief session from 25 August to 17 September, solely to finish with Home Rule, and this caused bitterness enough. Then it met again on 11 November. In the nine months of Liberal rule Asquith gave one war survey, on 1 March 1915 – a survey which did not mention the campaign in France, and no debate followed.[6]

This unspoken Coalition between the front benches was not new. The habit had been growing for some time, and the scenes in the House became increasingly artificial. The leaders met amicably at Round Table conferences at Buckingham Palace, still flushed from the passionate debates over the Parliament Bill or Home Rule. Even their disputes here were to some extent staged. The very men who failed to agree at the Palace negotiated secretly for a full Coalition and were impeded only by their backbenchers. Austen Chamberlain, embarrassed as usual by his own honesty, remarked : 'What a world we live in and how the public would stare if they could look into our minds and our letter bags.'[7] Hilaire Belloc exer-

6. Churchill alone dissented from this policy of silence, and twice attempted to survey the war in broad terms (on 27 November 1914 and 15 February 1915). These attempts obviously embarrassed the House, though they set a pattern for the second world war; few members listened, and none followed Churchill's lead.

7. Charles Petrie, *Austen Chamberlain*, i, 258.

cised his satirical imagination on this theme, but, as often happens, reality outdid the wildest flights of fantasy. There is nothing in Pongo and the Bull to rival the improbable scene in May 1915 when Bonar Law, making a morning call on Lloyd George, was conducted through a side-door to Asquith; whereupon the two men destroyed one Government and made another within a quarter of an hour. The war in fact provided the means of stilling party disputes which the leaders had failed to find for themselves.

There were other, less melodramatic, reasons why the House of Commons was virtually ignored. For one thing, Kitchener, the secretary of state for war, sat in the Lords. Here he surveyed the war, inadequately, about once a month, but he did not allow the under-secretary to follow his example in the House of Commons. It is indeed a minor oddity of the war that, until Lloyd George became prime minister, only the Lords discussed broad questions of strategy; and one member, Lord Milner, openly defied the rules of security – to the bewilderment of the Germans.[8] Generally speaking, the Liberal Government practised individual enterprise in politics as rigidly as in economic affairs. Each minister was left free to conduct his own department, and Asquith, acting as the detached chairman, intervened only when it was necessary to arbitrate between ministers. Here incidentally is the explanation, forgotten in later years, why Grey before the war consulted the Cabinet little – and informed the House still less – on foreign policy. That was his department, and it was his job to run it. So, when the war began, the Cabinet never approved the ultimatum to Germany; this was settled by Grey, perhaps with assistance from Asquith. The Cabinet endorsed the dispatch of the Expeditionary Force to France only after this had begun, and their naming of an assembly point

8. Milner discussed the evacuation from Gallipoli a fortnight before it took place. The Germans concluded that this was a ruse, to cloak preparations for a further landing.

(Amiens instead of Maubeuge) was disregarded by the military authorities. The secrets of naval strategy were locked in Fisher's breast, from which they never emerged.

The prorogation on 17 September had behind it the assumption that the war would be lost or won before the House met again. By 11 November this assumption had been belied. Deadlock set in; a long war was in the offing. But this did not provoke any discussion in the House of Commons. A new factor aided the policy of silence. The first world war produced an excessive enthusiasm for secrecy, or 'security' as it came to be called. There was something to be said for keeping shipping-movements and losses secret, though this was carried rather far when the sinking of the Audacious, which took place on 27 October 1914, was announced only on 13 November 1918. But it seems unlikely that the Germans overlooked the presence of a British army in France. 'Security' operated more against the British public than against the enemy. The authorities, military and political, had no idea how to win the war; therefore they wished to keep silence until, by some miracle as yet unforeseen, the war was won. In theory reports of proceedings in parliament were free from censorship. This meant in practice that nothing could be mentioned in parliament which might infringe the requirements of 'security'. Questions were unofficially censored before they were set down; members were kept quiet by the appeal to patriotism.

The policy of silence might have worked if everyone outside the government could really ignore the war, if 'Business as Usual', in Churchill's phrase, really made sense. Quite the contrary. Where direction was lacking, enthusiasm had to take its place. For nearly a year and a half the army was raised by voluntary recruiting, which provided three out of every four men for the greatest armies ever put into the field by this country. The public had to be kept constantly astir by re-cruiting meetings and, though ministers and members of parliament spoke a good deal, these meetings provided a platform for less official orators. Here Horatio Bottomley made his fame. Recovering from the discredit into which he had recently fallen, he rose before the end of the war to become the tribune of the people, respectfully consulted – not only according to his own account – by the war Cabinet itself.

Silence in high places cleared the way for demagogues. Still more, it cleared the way for the masters of the press. The public wanted news and could find it only in the newspapers. Official statements told nothing, and the alternative means of communication, developed later in the twentieth century, were as yet unknown. Soon too the public wanted leadership, and again only the newspapers provided it. The 'press lords' did not snatch at influence and power; these were thrust on them by the abdication of the politicians. Northcliffe, who controlled half the circulation in London, was the most notorious of these press lords, but he was not alone. Robert Donald, editor of The Daily Chronicle, played almost as great a part. C P Scott and J L Garvin were to join him as kingmakers in the great crisis of 1916.[9] The politicians railed and complained without ever appreciating that the fault lay in themselves. Lloyd George alone realized the true position. Always more at home on the public platform than in the House of Commons and unfettered by traditional rules, he early recognized that public opinion must be satisfied somehow. He commented on 23 June 1916: 'The Press has performed the function which should have been performed by Parliament, and which the French Parliament has performed.'[10] Lloyd George used the press, and the press used Lloyd George. The two grew great together. Lloyd George had never cared much for the society of other politicians. Now he built up a group of advisers drawn almost entirely from the press. The chief of

9. It is often implied that Max Aitken who was even more a kingmaker in December 1916 also owed his power to the press. This is not so. Aitken only became a press lord in the decisive sense later.

10. Riddell, War Diary, p. 151.

these were Riddell, who owned the News of the World; C P
Scott of the Manchester Guardian; and Robertson Nicoll,
editor of The British Weekly, a strong though tardy supporter of the war (like Lloyd George himself),[11] who could
best interpret the feeling of the pro-war Dissenters. The only
politician admitted to these gatherings was Addison, a Radical
doctor from the East End, who had entered Parliament in
1910 and had worked with Lloyd George on National Insurance. Through these men Lloyd George gauged public
opinion more effectively than by sitting regularly in his place
in the House of Commons.

Even so, feeling in parliament stirred under the surface.
The backbench Unionists resented the unofficial coalition of
silence to which Bonar Law had committed them. Early in
1915 some of them set up the Unionist Business Committee
under the nominal leadership of Walter Long (once Bonar
Law's rival) to press – irrelevantly – for Tariffs. They were
drawn instead into complaints against the inadequate supply
of munitions, complaints which were seconded by the former
auxiliaries of the Liberal Government – the Irish Nationalists
and Labour. This was a startling development. The Liberals
and Unionists exactly balanced after the general election of
1910, but Asquith had a stable and substantial majority
thanks to the Irish and Labour. These two held the balance,
but only in appearance; for, while they could certainly put the
Liberals out, it would have been intolerable for them to put
the Unionists in. Hence Asquith could make more demands
on them than they on him, simply by evoking the ghost of a
Unionist administration. Labour slipped back into being Lib-
Lab; and at each stage of the Home Rule crisis, the Irish were
pushed from one concession to another as the price for getting

11. On 1 August 1914 Lloyd George received from Nicoll a letter
opposing entry into the war. He found it in the pocket of his dress-
suit on 7 August and pinned it to Nicoll's pro-war leader of 5 August.
Riddell, War Diary, p. 11.

anything at all. In August 1914 Asquith assumed that the two parties would continue their tame acquiescence, apart of course from the few Labour men who actually opposed the war, and he concerned himself more with the Ulstermen than with the Nationalists once Home Rule was technically on the statute book. This was one aspect, and by no means the least, of the fatal self-confidence which brought Asquith to ruin. He took it for granted that for the Irish and Labour (as for everyone else) he was the indispensable man.

For these two parties it soon ceased to be true. The Irish Nationalists had nothing to gain by supporting Asquith now that Home Rule was laid aside. On the contrary they had good reason to attack the Liberal Government, or rather its outstanding member Kitchener, who had depreciated the surge of Irish loyalty by refusing to authorize an Irish Brigade.[12] With Labour it was the other way round. Far from being slighted, Labour – meaning the Labour movement and not merely the handful of Labour men in the House – was called into the seats of the mighty for the first time. The Treasury agreement of March 1915, and its ancillary agreements, made the trade unions partners in the industrial life of the country. It was hopeless thereafter to regard Labour as a mere auxiliary of the Liberal party. Both Labour and the Irish were feeling their way to independence, though for different reasons. Both wanted the war to be won – Labour because the working people of the country were fighting it, the Irish because of Redmond's belief that a victory for freedom abroad would bring freedom for Ireland also. Neither, however, cared particularly that Asquith should win it, still less Kitchener.

12. The Ulster Volunteers, on the other hand, got official recognition. Hence Carson and the Ulster Unionists supported Kitchener and even Asquith, as later they supported other military leaders. Carson indeed was the vital link between Asquith and the generals, a curious and yet appropriate position.

Both were ready to join the Unionist revolt. On 7 May 1915 the revolt exploded. During a debate on the Defence of the Realm Act, Redmond moved the adjournment of the House – ostensibly against state purchase of the liquor trade, really as a protest against its irrelevance to the shell shortage. The Unionist Business Committee were emboldened to draft an open motion on this subject. Bonar Law tried to head the rebels off. On 13 May, just before the House rose for the Whitsuntide recess, he sent a message to the Committee urging postponement. He thought he had succeeded. But Hewins, the real inspirer of the Committee, was unappeased. Hewins had been a Professor of Economics and, like most academics turned politician, combined high principles and impracticality in equal measure. On 17 May Hewins warned Bonar Law that he would force a debate on munitions when the House resumed. Bonar Law at first acquiesced, then asked Hewins to hold his hand. The next day Hewins learnt that the Liberal Government had resigned and that a Coalition was being formed.

Bonar Law had not feared that the Unionist rebels would fail. He feared that they would succeed. Then, perhaps after a general election, 'there would have been a Conservative government which would have had to introduce conscription after terrible controversy'.[13] The Liberals would have become 'an ordinary party opposition with effects most disastrous to the country'.[14] Ostensibly the crisis was provoked by Fisher's resignation as first sea lord on 15 May, not by the threat of Unionist revolt. This was a stroke of luck for Bonar Law, enabling him to cloak the real danger, but the warning from Hewins gave the decisive push which sent him on his dramatic visit to Lloyd George. The first Coalition was indeed made by parliamentary pressure, but it was created to thwart

13. Bonar Law in the House of Commons, 4 April 1917; Hansard, 5th series, xcii, 1392.

14. So Bonar Law told Redmond: D. Gwynn, Redmond, p. 467.

this pressure, not to satisfy it. The only good result of the crisis was the Ministry of Munitions with Lloyd George at its head. Otherwise the party leaders were more in control than ever. Even the semblance of a front Opposition bench vanished. The discontented Unionists were unable to appeal to public opinion; they were denied a conflict and a general election which, according to Bonar Law himself, they would have won; Liberal ministers kept the key posts; so did Kitchener, the worst offender even in the eyes of his Liberal colleagues; the Unionist recruits got the crumbs. The manoeuvre was completed, the new government formed, before parliament reassembled. The backbench Liberals were equally dismayed. Their Government – the last Liberal Government in British history as it turned out – was gone without a word of explanation. Belatedly Asquith called the Liberals together and appeased them with twenty minutes of emotional explanation. 'Some of the members were moved to tears as was the Prime Minister himself.'[15]

The Liberals did well to weep. Despite Asquith's rigging of appointments, the Liberals were now taken prisoner in their turn by 'national unity'. Previously Bonar Law had kept the Unionists quiet so as not to embarrass the government; henceforward the Liberals had to acquiesce in unwelcome policies so as to maintain the Coalition. Thus in May 1916 Bonar Law wrote to Asquith : 'I believe that it is easier for you to obtain the consent of your party to general compulsion than for me to obtain the consent of my party to its not being applied.'[16] Asquith did not understand the great issues which the conduct of the war provoked. Though resolved on victory, he supposed that the only contribution statesmen could make was to keep out of the way, while free enterprise supplied the arms with which generals would win the battles.

15. Addison, *Four and a Half Years*, i, 79.
16. Bonar Law to Asquith, May 1916; Spender, *Life of Asquith*, ii, 211.

The only dividing line he recognized was the old one between tariff reform and free trade. Hence his overriding concern when making the Coalition was to put free traders at the Exchequer and the Board of Trade. Even here his calculation went wrong. McKenna, chancellor of the exchequer, betrayed his own free trade convictions. With the financial rectitude of a born banker, McKenna introduced in September 1915 the first real war budget – a budget on which incidentally his successor Bonar Law did not improve; and this included, among other revolutionary innovations, the McKenna Duties, ostensibly designed to reduce imports, which were in fact Protection. Lloyd George appropriately threw a note across the Cabinet table to Walter Long on 16 September : 'So the old system *goes* destroyed by its own advocates.'[17] The McKenna Duties produced one of the first divisions of the war. Ten Radicals voted against them on 1 October – a tiny number, yet a sign of the coming disintegration.

The dispute was, in the circumstances of war, a triviality, as the division showed. The great underlying conflict was between freedom and organization. Could the war be conducted by 'Liberal' methods – that is, by voluntary recruiting and *laissez-faire* economics? Or must there be compulsory military service, control of profits, and direction of labour and industry? When the Coalition was being formed, Runciman wrote to McKenna :

If we are honoured with an invitation to come in I feel that we must first know with whom we are asked to associate ... in particular ... if they were told that we had an open mind on compulsory service or taxation.[18]

His question remained unanswered. But it was constantly pushed forward by the march of events. Of its two aspects – conscription and the control of industry – the second was the more urgent. For at least a year ahead voluntary recruiting

17. Hewins, Apologia of an Imperialist, ii, 52.
18. S. McKenna, Reginald McKenna, p. 223.

would in fact provide more men than free enterprise could equip. But economic direction was far more difficult to apply. Not only was it more alarming in theory. It was unwelcome to both Capital and Labour, yet it could not work without their consent. On paper the Government had all it needed with the Act setting up the Ministry of Munitions, or indeed with the Defence of the Realm Act. In practice these powers were ineffective unless industry accepted them. Lloyd George grasped this intuitively when he ended the strike in South Wales by agreeing to the miners' demands instead of by invoking legal sanctions as Runciman, at the Board of Trade, wished to do. It was no doubt illogical that men safely at home should kick against lesser sacrifices than those which they expected from the soldiers and which they would willingly make were they themselves in the trenches; but it was an inescapable fact.

Ministers and members of parliament alike felt that they were contending against H G Wells's 'Invisible Man'. Members demanded the enforcement of penalties and railed against the feebleness of ministers. Ministers could not understand their own helplessness and sought to turn the flank of this baffling problem. One such attempt, strangely enough, was liquor control – restricted hours for the opening of licensed premises. The question had been initiated by Lloyd George in the last days of the Liberal Government when he had proposed state purchase of the liquor trade – the first of his many attempts to find an inspiring cause that would sweep him to national leadership. Lloyd George aimed principally to recapture the allegiance of the Radical Dissenters – once his most solid backers – and to reconcile them no doubt to other, less welcome, war measures; he also hoped to establish his reputation as 'the man of push and go' – to borrow the phrase applied to a more forgotten figure, G W Booth – and so dispel the remaining suspicions against his pre-war Radicalism. State purchase miscarried, and Lloyd George forgot it when he arrived at the Ministry of Munitions. But liquor control had the same dual purpose. Liberals (who in any case liked the idea for its own sake) could argue that working men would be industrious and productive without direction of labour, once they were sober; Unionists of the planning school welcomed liquor control as the prelude to control of everything else. At least some Unionists did. Others, though equally 'planners', opposed it, and not merely from their long-standing connection with 'The Trade'. They suspected, rightly, that it was a red herring, ostentatiously displayed to divert them from more serious quarry.

The Unionists answered by pressing for compulsory military service. No doubt many of them did so from simple impulse. They were after all simple men, and conscription was the obvious sentimental response to the situation, as Sir John Simon – one of its opponents at the time – recognized in later life. But conscription, too, was a red herring. There was little to be said in its favour from a military point of view Sir Auckland Geddes, Director of National Service, said when all was over :

With, perhaps, more knowledge than most of the working of conscription in this country, I hold the fully matured opinion that, on balance, the imposition of military conscription added little if anything to the effective sum of our war efforts.[19]

The immediate effect of conscription was to stop voluntary recruiting, which ceased on 27 January 1916 – the day when the first Military Service Act became law. Thereafter the compulsory system, far from bringing more men into the army, kept them out of it. Men in reserved occupations who were doing vital work could not be prevented from succumbing to patriotic enthusiasm so long as enlistment was voluntary. They stayed at their jobs once conscription went

19. The words have often been quoted. I take them from Simon, *Retrospect*, p. 107.

through. The figures prove it. There had been a great outcry in the autumn of 1915 that 650,000 single men were evading military service. When the Act was passed, it raised 43,000 recruits in its first six months of operation (about half the average number raised in a single month by the voluntary system). Its more important result was to produce 748,587 fresh claims to exemption, most of them valid.[20] This was not at all what the simple-minded enthusiasts for conscription had expected. More clear-sighted Unionists were unperturbed. They were content either way. If compulsion produced millions of fresh soldiers, then their needs would overwhelm the 'free' economic system. Alternatively if it produced only claims for reservation, industrial conscription was being attained by the back-door.

These considerations were appreciated on the Liberal side. The strictest Liberals opposed any hint of conscription, military or industrial. The proposal to set up even a National Register produced the first division of the war on 5 July 1915, when thirty voted in the minority. Sir John Simon resigned from the Government at the end of the year, thus drawing on a stock of moral inflexibility that was not much replenished later, and 105 votes were cast against the Military Service Bill for single men on 5 January 1916 – fifty-odd Liberals when the Irish are deducted. Others, including Pringle – later an assiduous 'wee free' – acquiesced, however, when they were assured that industrial conscription would not follow. McKenna and Runciman took this line inside the Cabinet. On 29 December 1915 they, too, determined to resign, then thought better of it and stayed in the Cabinet to thwart the economic effects of conscription, which they did with marked effect. Runciman especially remained a rigid free trader at the Board of Trade, and his helplessness in face of shipping losses produced on 9 November 1916 what Addison described as 'the most invertebrate and hopeless of any memoranda

20. Military Operations: France and Belgium 1916, i, 152.

presented to the Government during the war by a responsible head of a department on a great issue'.[21] By the autumn of 1916 economic liberalism was played out. The only logical alternatives were to abandon liberalism or to abandon the war. Hence the cry for 'peace by negotiation', first faintly heard in November 1915 and raised even within the Cabinet a year later. But on the whole this cry came only from those who had opposed the war all along. Most Liberals drifted in the wake of Asquith, their leader, trapped like him by the decision of August 1914. They had willed the end, but would not will the means.

This great conflict was not confined to the House of Commons or even to the press. It was voiced also by the demagogues of the recruiting platform. Uninstructed public opinion agreed with the Unionists in clamouring for military conscription. On the other hand it agreed with the Liberals in opposing any sort of economic interference or control. This was shown when Independent candidates first appeared in defiance of the electoral truce. The truce remained unbroken until December 1915, except in the anomalous instance of Merthyr Boroughs, vacant by the death of Keir Hardie, where the 'official' pacifist, nominated by the I L P, was beaten by a pro-war Labour man. The first real breach came at Cleveland on 10 December 1915. Here Bottomley and his Business Government League ran a local publican on the combined ticket of compulsory military service and no liquor control. Bottomley, himself disreputable, attracted only disreputable supporters. Pemberton Billing was a more formidable and more successful campaigner. In January 1916 he almost won Mile End; on 10 March he captured East Hertfordshire from a Unionist. To the usual popular demands for a free liquor trade and universal conscription, he made an addition of his own : 'a strong air policy'. The Zeppelin raids had begun, and Pemberton Billing, voicing the demand for reprisals, be-

21. Addison, Politics from Within, ii, 10.

came the one and only 'Member for Air'. It seems odd that he should defeat a Unionist, but this conformed to the general rule: official Unionists always did worse at by-elections than official Liberals, and for a topsyturvy reason. Unionist voters were contented with the Coalition and therefore supported the official Liberal when they had no nominee of their own. Liberals resented the Coalition and voted for the independent candidate, however eccentric, who received time and again roughly the Liberal poll of 1910.[22] The Liberals felt that they were being dragged further and further away from Liberalism; the Unionists complained only that the process was not going on fast enough. Ultimately the two complaints coincided to cause the crisis of December 1916.

Before this, there was to be a last display of Asquith's virtuosity. Asquith developed over conscription all the tactical hesitations which had bedevilled Home Rule, waiting for events to enforce the solution which he himself could not impose nor even foresee. He had no policy of his own, only a desire to keep the Unionists in without driving the Liberals out. First he postponed decision by the Derby scheme – presenting attestation to the Liberals as a device for evading conscription, to the Unionists as its preliminary. In January

22. Contested by-elections in 1916, with programme of unofficial candidate. *January*: West Newington: Independent against the Liquor Control Board. Mile End: Pemberton Billing (almost successful) against the Liquor Control Board and for air-raid reprisals. *March*: East Hertfordshire: Pemberton Billing, successful. Hyde: Independent against the Liquor Control Board and for conscription. Market Harborough: Independent for conscription. *April*: Wimbledon: Kennedy Jones, 'Do it Now'. *May*: Tewkesbury: Independent for strong War Council. *August*: Berwick: an Independent called Turnbull on whom I have no information. *September*: Mansfield: Turnbull again. *October*: North Ayrshire: 'Peace by Negotiation' candidate. Winchester: Independent was merely described as 'author and journalist'. The disappearance of pro-war Independent candidates after the passing of general conscription is striking. I have not included Irish by-elections, which shed no light on British politics.

1916 he accepted conscription for single men, again appeasing Liberals by a reminder of all the married men who would escape. The demand for general conscription continued to grow, and on 19 April Asquith expected the Government to break up. He devised another elaborate compromise which satisfied neither party, and on 26 April presented this scheme to the House in the first secret session of the war. The secrecy was imposed in order to conceal the party rifts from the public, not to deny knowledge to the enemy. Asquith had a stroke of luck – his last. 26 April was the Tuesday after Easter. On the previous day Dublin had broken into revolt. The House, too, revolted. In a surge of patriotism, it demanded a final, comprehensive measure, and this demand grew even stronger three days later when the news arrived that Kut had surrendered to the Turks. Asquith gave a sigh of relief. He withdrew his compromise, carried universal military service and yet preserved the unity of the government.

This was a triumph of tactics, however undeserved. But it was disastrous for Asquith's prestige. Everyone knew that the solution had been imposed upon him. The House had intervened effectively for the only time in the war; it had dictated to the Government instead of being led. Moreover there was a price to pay. Asquith had escaped an explosion over conscription only by raising the yet darker shadow of Ireland. Now he attempted to retrieve his reputation by 'solving' the Irish question. He crossed dramatically to Dublin. Then, as usual, he shrank from the creative effort that a 'solution' would imply. There was someone eager to take his place. Lloyd George had come near to resignation in protest against the delays over conscription and had been urged to it by Scott and Robertson Nicoll. He had been deterred by a message from the king[23] and perhaps more by his reluctance ever to carry out the threat of resignation. But

23. Riddell, *War Diary*, p. 170.

his advocacy of conscription was known, and he had lost the favour of 'that crowd' – his former Radical supporters. Ireland was the way to regain it and to eclipse Asquith as well. Lloyd George came nearer to solving the Irish question than anyone had ever done; secured agreement, by means however equivocal, between Carson and Redmond. The unity and confidence of the Liberal party seemed restored; that of the Unionists endangered. Bonar Law cared much for Ulster, little for the rest of Ireland. When Hewins complained that the proposed Irish settlement would break the Conservative party, Bonar Law replied pugnaciously: 'Perhaps the Conservative party has to be broken.'[24]

Once more Asquith wasted this great opportunity. The approval of Bonar Law, a mere iron-merchant from Glasgow, meant nothing to him, but he started back in alarm at opposition from Lansdowne, a great Whig aristocrat, though of trifling weight in the Unionist party. The Irish settlement was abruptly jettisoned. The failure did Asquith incalculable harm. It lost him the last scrap of support from the Irish Nationalists. It shook his position inside the Liberal party; for, though Liberals might be in two minds over conscription, most felt strongly about Home Rule. Addison reflected this opinion when he wrote of Asquith: 'His conduct of this business had more to do with determining the attitude of many Liberals, including myself, than any other circumstance.'[25] Asquith used a favourite manoeuvre to cover his retreat. He distracted attention from his failure over Ireland by agreeing, on 20 July, to a committee of inquiry into the campaign in Mesopotamia and threw in, for good measure, an inquiry into the Dardanelles as well. Such inquiries had in the past clearly displayed the power of the House – the inquiry into the Walcheren campaign, for example, in 1809 and, most assertive of all, the inquiry into the conduct of the

24. Hewins, Apologia of an Imperialist, ii, 81.
25. Addison, Politics from Within, i, 260.

Crimean war. These past inquiries had been forced on a reluctant government by the House – the Crimean inquiry brought the Government down. The inquiries of 1916 were offered to the House as substitutes for real action : raking over dead campaigns instead of facing the great undecided question of economic direction. When the House accepted them, this was not a proof of its power, merely a sign that the crisis over conscription was exhausted.

For the moment the life seemed to go out of political controversy. There were no more Independent candidates at by-elections, demanding a more energetic conduct of the war. Few members listened to Winston Churchill on 22 August when he preached the doctrine of full War Socialism : rationing, direction of industry, industrial conscription. Still fewer applauded. Lloyd George, unexpectedly translated to the War Office by the death of Kitchener, forgot Home Rule as he had forgotten state purchase, and now hoped to establish his fame by the simple expedient of winning the war. He said on 22 August : 'We are pressing the enemy back ... We are pushing the enemy on the Somme ... He has lost his tide.' [26] A month later he committed himself to the knock-out blow. He was to make out later that he had done this in order to anticipate Wilson's proposal for a negotiated peace.[27] In fact he championed the knock-out blow because he supposed that, as secretary of state for war, he was himself about to deliver it. He had believed what Robertson and Haig told him. Hence his annoyance with them when their prophecies proved wrong; hence, too, his brisk publicizing of this annoyance – he had to erase the memory of his own confident prophesying. In the autumn of 1916, with failure on the Somme, the inexorable question again raised its head : *laissez-faire* or controls? This time it could not be diverted by the irrelevant controversy over military conscription. Economic liberalism

26. Hansard, 5th series, lxxxv, 2556.
27. Lloyd George, War Memoirs, ii, 851–9.

was on its last legs. Food, shipping, coal, manpower, all clamoured for control. Asquith talked action, did nothing.

The stage was set for a new Unionist revolt, this time against Bonar Law. The occasion seems a triviality, as Lord Beaverbrook and other writers have pointed out: the debate of 8 November over the disposal of enemy property in Nigeria. Yet even this was an appropriate symbol of the difference in outlook between idealistic Liberal and hard-headed Unionist. The Unionist rebels wanted to confine the sale of this enemy property to British subjects; the Government, on Liberal principles, to dispose of it according to free trade rules. Sixty-five Unionists voted against the Government, only seventy-three for it. The moment had almost arrived at which Bonar Law must leave the Government or split the party. He talked of destroying the rebels at a general election, and Beaverbrook takes this threat seriously. It was surely empty, as Bonar Law must have known. The Unionists in the country were ahead of the rebels in parliament. The rogue candidates of the spring had become official Unionist candidates by the autumn. Kennedy Jones, for example, fought Wimbledon in April with the cry, 'Do It Now'. In December he was returned unopposed as official Unionist at Hackney. A general election would not have destroyed the rebels; it would have returned them in greater force. Bonar Law could save the Unionist party, and in particular his own leadership of it, only by destroying the Asquith Government. In this sense, the division of 8 November was the decisive event of the war so far as the British House of Commons was concerned. It set the train to the mine which brought down Asquith and put Lloyd George in his place.

But it was only the beginning. Bonar Law could destroy the Coalition. What would be its successor? Why not a predominantly Liberal Government such as had existed until May 1915? The answer could not be determined by the Unionists. It rested with the Liberals themselves and with their former associates. One striking change, though little perceived at the time, was the gradual estrangement of these satellites. The Irish Nationalists had lost all faith in Asquith after his feebleness over Home Rule in the summer. Moreover, despite their insistence on Irish members remaining at Westminster in full strength, they had unconsciously abandoned the Union and henceforward acted only when Irish interests were affected – especially over the extension of conscription to Ireland. But this was a negative development: eighty supporters lost to Asquith, not found by anyone else. The transformation in regard to Labour was more positive. The Labour movement grew more self-confident with each day of the war. 'Labour' supported Asquith so long as he was there, and even on 1 December Henderson called him 'the indispensable man'. Yet essentially Labour did not care about Asquith as against any other leader. They were only interested in winning the war. In December 1916 the Labour party came of age. The moment can be precisely defined: it was the meeting of Liberal ministers on 4 December which advised Asquith not to cooperate with Lloyd George. Henderson attended the meeting, no doubt regarding himself and being regarded by others as one of Asquith's humbler followers. Then in a flash of blinding truth he declared (much to his own surprise) that Labour would support any prime minister who got on with the war, and a couple of days later he was in the war Cabinet – no longer a Lib-Lab hanger-on, but spokesman of an independent Labour movement.

Still, a Unionist Government, sustained only by Labour votes, would have been a shaky affair and would have brought with it the revival of party strife which Bonar Law dreaded. The position could be changed only by a Liberal split. Lloyd George himself could not provide this. He had powerful elements of the Liberal press on his side – both The Daily Chronicle and The Manchester Guardian; he had other prominent journalists backing him as the saviour of the country –

Burnham, Geoffrey Dawson, Garvin, to say nothing of North-cliffe; he had even the support at this time of the military leaders from Robertson to Henry Wilson. But he had no contact with the Liberal rank and file in the House of Commons. He knew few of them and never tried to extend his personal influence. His political actions were shaped by intuition and the advice of journalists – Riddell or Robertson Nicoll – who claimed to know public opinion. At this moment knowledge of public opinion was not enough. A new Government had to count votes. The counting was done with decisive results by Christopher Addison, the one man in Lloyd George's intimate circle who was also in the House of Commons. Addison had already taken a preliminary sounding during the critical days over conscription earlier in the year. On Monday, 4 December, he began canvassing the Liberal members more systematically. He soon reported that forty-nine Liberals supported Lloyd George unconditionally; by Wednesday, 6 December, he had found 126 who would support Lloyd George if he could form a Government.[28] By this canvass Addison became the real maker of the Lloyd George Government. The Unionist rebels forced Bonar Law into action. Max Aitken brought Lloyd George and Bonar Law together. It was Addison, and the Liberal rebels, who put Lloyd George in the first place.

The Liberal split, which in fact ended the great Liberal party for ever, was more than a split over the conduct of the war. It revealed a deep division within the party which had been long a-growing. The Liberal leaders, associated with Asquith, were 'patricians': Asquith himself, 'last of the Romans', Crewe, Grey, Harcourt, McKenna – men of almost excessive culture and refinement. The supporters of Lloyd George were lower-class in origin, in temperament, in position. As an historian I rely more on feel than on figures, but I

28. These are speculative figures. Lloyd George gives 136 in all as his supporters.

ran over the brief biographies which The Times appended to the successful candidates in the general election of 1918, and these confirmed my impression. Most of the Lloyd George Liberals were businessmen who had founded their own firms or were running a firm still with their family name. The Times says of one what could have been said of nearly all: 'a fine example of the self-made man'. The firms were all in wool or engineering, and no doubt doing well out of the war. None of these Liberals was a banker, merchant or financial magnate. Those who were professional men also belonged to the second eleven: solicitors, not barristers; school teachers, not schoolmasters (a term reserved by The Times for those who taught at public schools). Hardly any had been educated at Oxford or Cambridge.[29] They were nearly all Nonconformists – usually Methodists – often the sons of Nonconformist ministers. Many of them had been keen Land Taxers before the war. In short, they resembled Lloyd George in everything except his genius. Their political ability was low; all they had was impatience with the arrogance and incompetence of the Asquith group. None made a serious mark on public affairs, and Lloyd George found it hard to recruit ministers from among them. Addison was the ablest of them, a proof how second-rate they were.

Still, Addison and these second-rank Liberals made Lloyd George prime minister. Bonar Law recognized Addison's crucial importance when he fired the mine on 28 November by asking: 'One cannot go on like this, Addison, do you think?'[30] Lloyd George had often threatened to resign – over munitions, over Gallipoli, over conscription, over his restricted powers at the War Office. He had always dodged away at

29. Even the rare exceptions to these generalizations had something exceptional about them. Gordon Hewart, though a barrister, began as a journalist and went to the Bar late. H A L Fisher, though a fellow of New College, was vice-chancellor of Sheffield University when invited to join Lloyd George's Government.

30. Addison, *Four and a Half Years*, i, 269.

the last moment. No doubt it was more difficult for him to dodge on 4 December when Asquith turned against him, but the preliminary information coming in from Addison also made it unnecessary. By 6 December Lloyd George had a cast-iron guarantee in his pocket that he alone could be prime minister: the Unionist rebels ruled out Asquith, the Liberal rebels would not have Bonar Law. It must have given him considerable amusement to watch first Asquith and then Bonar Law stubbing their toes on the submerged rock of the backbenchers. For Lloyd George's Government sprang much more directly from parliamentary feeling than Asquith's coalition had done. The first Coalition was made against parliamentary discontent, to silence and thwart it; the second Coalition owed its existence to parliamentary discontent, which dictated to Bonar Law as much as against Asquith. The second Coalition was not a deal between the leaders of the two parties. Rather it was a defeat for all the leaders except Lloyd George, a defeat for the 'Three C's' as much as for the 'Squiffites', a defeat even for Bonar Law despite his tactical change, of course at the last moment. The backbenchers represented a sort of unconscious plebiscite to make Lloyd George dictator for the duration of the war.

Lloyd George himself looked beyond party and parliament. He did not address the Unionist MPs. He never attended a meeting of his own Liberal supporters until after the armistice, and then did not know what to say to them. His only speech, on becoming prime minister, was to 'Labour' – that is, to a joint meeting of the Labour MPs and the national executive. Ramsay MacDonald surmised that Lloyd George planned to become leader of the Labour party. A shrewd guess, but not shrewd enough. Lloyd George planned to become leader of 'the people', and Labour was merely one instrument to this end. His disregard of party came out clearly when he chose the war Cabinet. When the Government was being formed, Addison and Carson allotted the jobs under Bonar Law's eye – the one speaking for the Coalition Liberals, the other for the Unionists. Yet neither was included in the war Cabinet. Instead Lloyd George put in men of no party weight : Milner and, later, Smuts. Even Curzon counted for little with the Unionists in the House of Commons. Only Labour, the smallest party of the Coalition in numbers, had a more or less official representative in the War Cabinet, Arthur Henderson. Again, Lloyd George made no attempt to build up a Coalition Liberal organization. Addison repeatedly complained about this.[31] He supposed that Lloyd George could not devise a party programme. This was true, but it was still truer that Lloyd George would not even try : he wanted neither a programme nor organized backing. He preferred to keep the Coalition Liberals as individuals with no leaders except himself. He soon humiliated Addison and divorced him from the Coalition Liberals.[32] Their other spokesmen on joint committees with the Unionists, such as the committee on Home Rule, were Gordon Hewart and H A L Fisher, both singularly unrepresentative.

Lloyd George made no secret of his intentions when he first addressed the House as prime minister of 19 December 1916. Parliamentary government, as it had been known for the last century or so, ceased to exist. A war Cabinet without departmental or party ties would run all the affairs of the country; businessmen would head the important ministries instead of politicians; and there would be 'a franker and fuller recognition of the partnership of Labour' – meaning that

31. He records these complaints in his diary on 12 April, 15 October, 21 November, 28 December 1917. In the end Lloyd George paid a penalty. He had few candidates ready for the general election of December 1918 and so was taken captive by the Unionists.

32. In June 1917 Lloyd George made out (quite falsely) that he had had to intervene in the engineers' strike and clear up the mess made by Addison, as minister of munitions. Once Addison was safely shunted to the ministry of reconstruction, Lloyd George put the blame for the misrepresentation on his press-officer.

Lloyd George would address the TUC, not the House of Commons when he wished to speak to 'the people'. Lloyd George carried out his threats. He rarely appeared in the House of Commons, leaving its leadership to Bonar Law – the first commoner prime minister to separate the two functions. The war Cabinet submitted its annual reports for 1917 and 1918 direct to the nation without even inviting debate in the House of Commons. At least one of the leading ministers, Sir Joseph Maclay, never became a member of the House. And in January 1918 Lloyd George defined British war aims in a speech to trade union leaders, not to the House of Commons. The House was not browbeaten into impotence. It acquiesced. The backbenchers had confidence that Lloyd George would win the war and, having this confidence, insisted that he be left alone.

Lloyd George had another asset, perhaps an even greater one : the Opposition. Its existence was something new : there had been no Opposition since May 1915. Asquith made out that his function was independent support for the Government as Bonar Law's had been in the first nine months of the war. But there was an essential difference. Bonar Law sustained the Liberal Government against his own rank and file; Asquith hoped to destroy the Lloyd George Government so far as he hoped for anything. What difference of principle divided the Opposition from the Government? The great issue of *laissez-faire* or controls was settled – dictated by events as much as by policy; soon not even Runciman was denouncing convoys or rationing. The obvious course was to support Peace by Negotiation, since Lloyd George's was preeminently a war Government. But Asquith never touched it, despite repeated alarms that he would do so. On the contrary, Lloyd George was pinned to relentless prosecution of the war for fear that Asquith would re-emerge as the war leader if he weakened. Peace by Negotiation certainly looked up in the course of 1917. It was carried to a division more than once; it was stimulated later in the year by the Lansdowne letter; it produced candidates at three by-elections, all of whom did badly.[33] None of the support came from the 'official' Opposition. They were even more hostile to it in the House than the Government benches and, in their anxiety not to be tarred with Peace by Negotiation, failed even to formulate war aims, abandoning this opening first to Labour and then to Lloyd George himself.

An Opposition in wartime might have been expected to claim that it could run the war better than the existing Government. This claim was so grotesque in view of what had gone before that Asquith never dared to make it. In his usual fashion, he drifted, waiting for an issue to turn up; and what turned up was defence of the generals against interference by politicians. There was no principle behind this: no man had more cause than Asquith to resent the interference of generals in politics. His support of them sprang from lethargy, that fatal reluctance to lead which had brought him down. He had ruined himself as prime minister by sheltering behind Kitchener. 'If it had not been for Kitchener, Asquith might have gone right through the war',[34] according to Bonar Law. Equally he ruined his Liberal followers by backing Robertson and Haig. The best chance of discrediting the Government came with the wasted victory at Cambrai – the only victory in the war for which the church bells were rung. But Asquith and his followers were saddled with their devotion to Haig and made nothing of it. The outcry in parliament came from a strange coalition of Kennedy Jones, the 'Do It Now' Unionist, Joseph King, advocate of Peace by Negotiation, and David Davies, a former associate of Lloyd George's. They were told that Haig had made an inquiry and that Smuts was making a further inquiry for the war Cabinet. The result of these inquiries was never published, and this

33. Rossendale, 13 February; Stockton on Tees, 30 March; South Aberdeen, 3 April 1917.

34. Riddell, War Diary, p. 234.

was perhaps as well. For they reached the complacent, though not surprising, conclusion that 'no one down to and including the corps commanders was to blame'; the fault lay with the regimental officers and the other ranks.[35] It was a conclusion worthy of Asquith himself.

The Liberal Opposition indeed stood only for the principle that Asquith was divinely appointed to go on being prime minister for ever. This principle was enough to scare even the most discontented back on to the side of Lloyd George. Asquith often seemed to be on the point of splitting the Unionists, as Lloyd George had split the Liberals. Each time the Unionists cowered into silence at the question – Asquith or Lloyd George as prime minister? For instance, many Unionists resented the apparent predominance of press lords in Lloyd George's administration. Austen Chamberlain voiced this resentment with the backing of the Unionist War Committee. To his dismay he was applauded by the Opposition Liberals and at once repudiated their support. 'They and I do not act from the same motives or pursue the same objects. I have tried from the first ... to support the Government of the day in carrying the War to a successful conclusion. When these hon. Gentlemen can say the same, and not before, shall I desire their cheers or their approval.'[36] The applause indeed so horrified Austen Chamberlain that not only did he drop his attack; within a month he joined the war Cabinet and accepted the press lords as his colleagues.

The same story was repeated even more dramatically during the series of disputes between Lloyd George and the generals during the spring of 1918. The danger seemed menacing. Asquith espoused the cause of the generals; it was backed even more emphatically by Carson and the Die Hard Tories. Yet essentially the danger was unreal. The Die Hards would not dethrone Lloyd George, if this meant restoring

35. Military Operations: France and Belgium 1917, iii, 296.
36. 11 March 1918; Hansard, 5th series, civ, 77.

Asquith. On the eve of the Maurice debate, which was expected to destroy Lloyd George, Carson attended the Unionist War Committee, and reported sadly : 'Their hate of Asquith overrides all other considerations, and they will not back him tomorrow.'[37] So it proved. Even Carson voted for the Government. Only Asquith and 97 Liberals went into the Opposition lobby.[38] The division was indeed an historic occasion – the only time in the war when the official Opposition promoted a vote against the Government. But it was merely a political manoeuvre, not a parliamentary revolt. Far from reasserting the authority of parliament, it made Lloyd George secure as he had never been before.

Asquith's leadership of the Opposition sustained Lloyd George in the country even more than in the House. Opposition was renewed at by-elections in the autumn of 1917 after the military failures of that year, but it was opposition demanding more vigorous measures, both military and economic, not the overthrow of Lloyd George. Ben Tillett, the only rogue candidate to repeat Pemberton Billing's success and get in, had an Asquithite as his 'official' rival at North Salford on 2 November. Tillett adroitly combined Labour and Die Hard extremism. His programme : vigorous prosecution of the war; better pay for soldiers and sailors; more direct Government control of the necessaries of life; anti-profiteering of food; and air-raid reprisals on a large scale. There was no grist here for Asquith's mill. Again the famous 'Black Book' which symbolized popular loss of faith in the governing classes contained the names of Mr and Mrs Asquith, so far as a non-existent Book can be said to contain anything; it did not contain the name of Lloyd George. Incidentally, Darling, the judge who conducted the case, though he could hardly believe in the Black Book (since this was said to contain his own

37. Repington, The First World War, ii, 298.
38. The total vote against the Government was 106. The others were Irish Nationalists and anti-war Labour.

name also) obviously thought that there was something in
Pemberton Billing's allegations – striking evidence of the
widespread contemporary hysteria. Pemberton Billing's last
fling was to demand the internment of all enemy aliens. This
nearly brought victory to his candidate at Clapham on 21
June 1918; it also produced a monster petition with a million
and a half signatures, backed by the lord mayor of London.
The proposal was even more abhorrent to Asquith and his
followers than to Lloyd George.[39]

Asquith could not reverse Lloyd George's feat and split the
Unionists. Could he rival his other accomplishments? Could
he win back Labour? Or reunite the Liberals? Labour ought
to have given him a chance. The Labour leaders had no great
trust in Lloyd George and no affection at all for the profiteers
round him. Moreover in the summer of 1917 Henderson left
the war Cabinet over the affair of the Stockholm conference.
This did not revive his allegiance to Asquith. He had seen
too much of Asquith as head of a Cabinet; besides the Liberal
Opposition gave him no support when he was in trouble.

39. Contested by-elections during the Lloyd George Coalition. 1917.
February: Rossendale: Peace by Negotiation. *March*: Stockton on
Tees: Peace by Negotiation. *April*: South Aberdeen: one Independent
Nationalist; one Peace by Negotiation. *June*: Liverpool (Abercromby
division): candidate backed by 'Discharged Soldiers' Federation'
against the son of the secretary of state for war. *July*: South Mon-
mouthshire: Prohibitionist. West Dundee: Prohibitionist. *October*:
East Islington: town clerk of Hertford, a 'Vigilante', backed by Pemberton Billing; a 'National' candidate backed by Page-Croft. *November*: North Salford: Ben Tillett – successful.

1918. *February*: Prestwich: Cooperative candidate. *April*: Keigh-
ley: Peace by Negotiation. A woman candidate was also nominated
but her papers were declared invalid. *May*: South Hereford:
Farmers' Union. Wansbeck: Labour candidate, almost successful.
June: Gravesend: one Independent Coalition; one Independent (pro-
war) Labour. Clapham: Vigilante, backed by Pemberton Billing –
'intern the lot'. *July*: East Finsbury: Vigilante, backed by Pemberton
Billing, 'intern the lot'; Liquor Trade Independent – 'boycott German
shipping'.

Instead Henderson resolved to make Labour the second party in the state. Stockholm set in train a development which ultimately ruined all Liberals, the supporters of Lloyd George and Asquith alike. Between July 1917 and the end of the war Henderson created the modern Labour party. Labour continued to support the war and the Labour ministers other than Henderson remained in office. At the same time Henderson formulated Labour's own foreign policy, with Mac-Donald's assistance, and so secured the future backing of the idealists. More important still, he enlisted Sidney Webb to transform the programme and organization of the party so as to make it national instead of a sectional interest. The Labour party was standing on its own feet even before the war ended. At Wansbeck on 29 May 1918 a Labour candidate, with the backing of the National party, almost defeated the Coalition nominee. The writing was on the wall. Labour had staked its claim to the front Opposition bench, and soon Asquith would be pushed off it.

The only remaining expedient for Asquith was to reunite the Liberal party. This was Lloyd George's most vulnerable spot. He could not remain prime minister if he lost his Liberal supporters, and the threat was the graver because it did not necessarily imply the return of Asquith. The Unionists might achieve the dream of forming their own war Government. Yet Lloyd George remained cut off from the Coalition Liberals, as he had been before Addison stamped them out of the ground. They had no party organization in the country and little even in the House. The Coalition Liberal Whips were always vague who the whip should go to, and even in the general election of 1918 the only definition of a Coalition Liberal was negative: a Liberal who had been against a negotiated peace. Where party discipline was lacking, 'influence' had to take its place. Hence the sale of honours which Lloyd George conducted on an unprecedented scale. Of course Lloyd George, having to build up a fund in two years where the traditional parties had had half a century, was keen to sell, and the Coalition Liberals, having no social position and much easily won money, were eager to buy. But such transactions were the only way in which Lloyd George could hold his followers together.

Still 'influence' was not enough. The Coalition Liberals could not altogether forget their Radical and Nonconformist origins. Even 'George's bloody knights' of Northcliffe's deadly phrase might respond to a clear Liberal call. Lloyd George rushed into this battle whenever challenged, quite contrary to his ordinary disregard of parliament. Where Asquith had told critics to wait and see, Lloyd George never waited, and as a result his critics never saw. Asquith could not recover Liberal allegiance as the alternative war leader. But someone else might. The gravest threat came from Churchill, excluded from Lloyd George's Government on Unionist insistence and now sitting with the Liberals on the front Opposition bench. On 10 May 1917 Lloyd George held a secret session, apparently to prepare the way for direction of labour and food control. He made an effective speech, but it was Churchill who dominated the House. Lloyd George did not waste a moment. He caught Churchill behind the Speaker's chair while the debate was still in progress and, says Churchill, 'assured me of his determination to have me at his side. From that day, although holding no office, I became to a large extent his colleague'.[40] Two months later Churchill became minister of munitions. The Unionists protested, from Bonar Law downwards; but they could do nothing, short of going over to Asquith. It was safer to offend them than to run the risk that the Liberals might reunite. The operation had the additional satisfaction for Lloyd George of sending Addison from munitions to the impressive obscurity of reconstruction : another potential rival out of the way.

The same preoccupation with Liberal feeling was shown

40. Churchill, World Crisis, 1916–1918, i, 255.

when Lloyd George made one of his rare appearances in the
House to defend the shortlived ban on sending the Nation
abroad. This ban, though indefensible, seems a trivial matter
to have brought the prime minister down to the House at a
critical moment of the war. But the Nation was a revered
Liberal paper, despite its advocacy of a negotiated peace;
revered especially by the former Radicals who now supported
Lloyd George. In this case Lloyd George evaded danger by
retreating in a cloud of words. The conscientious objectors
showed his other method. Sympathy might have been expected from one who had been virtually a conscientious
objector in a previous war. On the contrary, once Lloyd
George abandoned principle, no one else was allowed to keep
it, and he carried his Radical supporters with him simply by
imitating Bottomley or Pemberton Billing: 'I will make the
path of these men a very hard one.' Bonar Law showed more
sympathy to the conscientious objectors, and it was left to
Lord Hugh Cecil to divide the House against their disfran-
chisement – losing only by 171 to 209. The minority included
a number of those usually counted as Coalition Liberals.

Ireland was Lloyd George's real worry rather than the
generals or even the Germans. For one thing he owed his
position largely to the belief of many Liberals that he would
have solved the Irish question, had Asquith not let him down,
and he was therefore almost driven into another attempt at
solution now that he was in supreme command. But what he
has written about his handling of Haig and Robertson applies
also to his Irish policy: 'I never believed in costly frontal
attacks, either in war or in politics, if there were a way
round.' [41] The way round in regard to Ireland was to invite the
Irish to find a solution for themselves, and the Convention of
1917 took the Irish question out of British politics while it
lasted. Even when the Convention failed, the blame could be
laid on the Irish, not on Lloyd George. The rise of Sinn Fein,

41. Lloyd George, War Memoirs, iv, 2274.

too, played into his hands. The Nationalists, discredited by Sinn Fein victories at by-elections, virtually seceded from the House and so finally parted from Asquith. Lloyd George could denounce Sinn Fein as subversive : 'They are organizing for separation, for secession, and for Sovereign independence. ... Under no conditions can this country possibly permit anything of that kind.'[42] This absolved him from blaming Ulster in any way, which would have offended the Unionists, while the Coalition Liberals abandoned the Irish cause in outraged patriotism.

The Irish question raised a final complication in the spring of 1918. The German offensive which began on 21 March marked a moment of supreme crisis. It provoked a cry for something dramatic even though irrelevant. As in 1916, the dramatic act was conscription – this time the raising of the age to fifty. The Unionists threw in the demand that conscription be extended to Ireland. Perhaps they did this to embarrass their Liberal associates. More probably it was merely another illustration of the general rule in British history that even the most reasonable men take leave of their senses as soon as they touch the Irish question. At any rate the proposal offered Asquith positively his last opportunity : he could rally the Liberals, and even the Nationalists, against Irish conscription and for Home Rule. But this was the very moment when Asquith was hoping to champion the military leaders (who also, of course, favoured Irish conscription) with Carson as his ally; hence he remained silent. Lloyd George worked out an ingenious compromise by which the Irish should get Home Rule and conscription together. In fact, they got neither, and Lloyd George covered the muddle by detecting a German plot in Ireland – one of those farfetched stories which a British Government produces when all else fails. In June 1918 this story served to tide things over

42. 23 October 1917; Hansard, 5th series, xcviii, 790.

until the end of the war. The Irish question never threatened to lead the Coalition Liberals back to Asquith.

The House in fact disliked discussion of great issues. It stirred uneasily when anyone, even Lloyd George himself, attempted to survey the general course of the war. It was aggressively intolerant when anti-war members raised the question of peace terms, or strayed otherwise into foreign policy. For instance, when Joseph King tried to discuss British policy towards Bolshevik Russia, Lord Robert Cecil espied strangers and secured a secret session with general approval. There was nothing secret in the topic; the House simply did not want to discuss it or indeed anything else connected with the war. This is not to say that members were idle or indifferent to public affairs. Away from high policy, they showed considerable competence and devotion. They worked hard on electoral reform, virtually without guidance from the Government, and made Great Britain a genuine democracy for the first time: universal manhood suffrage, and limited women's suffrage into the bargain. They helped Fisher to revolutionize secondary education. But they would have nothing to do with the great questions of the war. They believed, rightly as it turned out, that the Opposition would be slaughtered at a general election. More important, the supporters of the Coalition were determined not to reveal their own internal differences. The unavowed compact of the front benches with which the war started became an equally unavowed compact of the back benches before the end. The backbenchers had no idea how Lloyd George would win the war; they often disapproved of his policy when they understood it. But they clung firmly to the belief that he was not one of the 'Old Gang' under whom they had groaned for the first two years of the war. This was Lloyd George's decisive asset, though also his final liability. He was enough of a 'rogue' to eclipse wilder demagogues like Pemberton Billing and Horatio Bottomley. But, not being one of the 'Old Gang', he was expendable. When the war was over, he was expended.

27. *Lloyd George: Rise and Fall*

The Leslie Stephen lecture for 1961, give in the Senate
House of Cambridge university.

On 7 December 1916 Lloyd George had a busy day. In the evening he returned to his room at the War Office with his devoted adherent, Dr Christopher Addison. The building was empty. A solitary messenger produced a cold chicken – what strange things they kept at the War Office; warmed up some soup and a bit of fish; Lloyd George unearthed a bottle of champagne. This scratch supper celebrated the triumph of 'the people'. It was Lloyd George's first meal as prime minister. Years afterwards he wrote: 'There had never before been a "ranker" raised to the premiership – certainly not one except Disraeli who had not passed through the Staff College of the old Universities'.[1] Like many of Lloyd George's best remarks, this is not strictly accurate. The Duke of Wellington did not go to a university. The rule has often been broken since. With Lloyd George's successors, the old universities have scored a draw – four all. Yet essentially Lloyd George's remark was true. No other premier has been a 'ranker' to the same extent. Even Ramsay MacDonald took on the colour of his surroundings despite his origins – perhaps too much so. Lloyd George remained the great 'rogue' of British political life in more senses than one.

Lloyd George was not marked out only by having escaped the staff college of the old universities. He was an exception among British prime ministers in almost every way – in

1. Lloyd George, War Memoirs, i, 621.

nationality, in economic origin, in religion, in profession. He was Welsh; he was born in a poor family; he was a Nonconformist; he was a solicitor until politics absorbed him. He was the only prime minister with a native tongue other than English – perhaps I should say as well as English; the only one with a sense of national oppression or at any rate inequality. He was much poorer at the start than any future prime minister except Ramsay MacDonald, and, unlike MacDonald, he did not marry a rich wife. He was the only practising Nonconformist to become prime minister other than Neville Chamberlain,[2] though his religious outlook does not seem to have been orthodox – it was a sort of pantheism of the people, combined with pleasure in the singing of Baptist hymns. He was the only solicitor to become prime minister, and this, though it seems less significant, had its influence also. Solicitors are, by definition, the 'ORs' of the legal profession. Barristers like the ringing phrase and the drama of open dispute. Solicitors prefer to settle behind the scenes.

How did this ranker attain supreme power? And how, having succeeded, did he come to lose it? These are questions of endless fascination, whether considered in terms of the individual man or as an exercise in political history. The first question – how he got there – has been much discussed. Indeed there are few political episodes which have been canvassed in greater detail. But even the incomparable dissection by Lord Beaverbrook, which will be read as long as men are interested in political tactics, leaves much unsaid. The accounts of this affair start off, as it were, with the great topic settled: Lloyd George is clearly the man who will win the war. They deal with the mechanics of how he got to the top when his reputation was made; they do not explain how so

2. Asquith, though of Nonconformist origin, had ceased to have any open Nonconformist allegiance by the time he became prime minister. The other non-Anglican prime ministers, of whom there have been several, were Scottish Presbyterians and therefore conformists in their own country.

many people reached agreement on this reputation, or exactly what it rested on. The second question has been more casually treated. Lloyd George himself was perhaps bewildered that he had fallen, others bewildered that they had ever put him into a position from which to fall. Who, having fallen out of love, can explain why he was ever in, let alone how he got out of it again? These are my two themes – the rise to power, and the fall from it; two different aspects of the same baffling personality.

Lloyd George was a politician from first to last and nothing else, though he sometimes made claim to distinction as a journalist, an author and – perhaps with more justification – a nursery-gardener. He did not come late into national politics with his reputation already established elsewhere, as some other outsiders have done – Joseph Chamberlain for example. He became a member of parliament at the age of twenty-seven and achieved a record for uninterrupted representation of the same constituency which no other prime minister can equal or nearly approach. He lived only for politics. He talked politics in his leisure hours – either the politics of the moment or political reminiscence. Political history was his only serious reading. He found diversion in cheap thrillers. His favourite bedtime author was Ridgwell Cullum. He had no taste in art or music, no knowledge of contemporary literature, no interest in the affairs of the mind outside the political world. I doubt whether he understood economic principles, though he was quick to turn them to advantage.

Though Lloyd George spent his life among politicians and in parliament, he cared little for either of them. He was never intimate with established politicians of the ordinary kind, and he did not frequent the recognized social centres. His associates were men outside the conventional pattern like himself: Churchill, the grandson of a duke, who crossed the floor to become a Radical; Rufus Isaacs, son of a fruit merchant who rose to be an earl, lord chief justice, and viceroy of India; F E Smith – the smith of his own fortunes – who invented a youth of extreme poverty for himself and perhaps came to believe in it. Even with them Lloyd George was reserved. Only Churchill called him 'David'; for all others he was 'LG'. He stood out against the growing use of Christian names: 'I am not very active in that way. I don't believe in being too familiar with people.'[3] Similarly, he took little trouble to sound parliamentary feeling outside the debating chamber. He rarely appeared in the smoking room. He knew few members by sight and, before becoming prime minister in 1916, had to entrust Christopher Addison with the task of discovering which Liberal members would support him. He relinquished the leadership of the House to Bonar Law with relief and thereafter never made a speech as prime minister without complaining that the House was distracting him from his real work. In later years, after his fall from power, he held court in his private room and did not welcome stray visitors.

Coming into the British system from outside, he had no respect for its traditions or accepted formalities. As prime minister, he failed to sustain the elaborate shadow-play which treats the monarch as something more than a figure-head. He promised peerages without first securing royal approval. He appointed ministers and then informed the king by telephone. He detested titles. This, no doubt, is why he distributed them so lavishly. If others were fools enough to buy, he was willing to sell. It gave added zest to his campaign against landowners that the greatest of them were dukes, and he would have derived less pleasure from humiliating Curzon, if Curzon had not been a marquis (of Lloyd George's creation) and for ever parading pride of birth. Most of all, he distrusted the permanent officials. Sometimes he overrode them. He is said to have been the only minister of modern times who could defeat the

3. Riddell, *Intimate Diary*, p. 287.

obstinacy even of Treasury officials. Usually, however, he preferred to circumvent them. He carried his private secretaries with him from one department to another, much as a French politician does, culminating, when he was prime minister, in the creation of a duplicate civil service dependent on himself, the 'Garden Suburb'.[4] After the war, Philip Kerr, one of this 'suburb', was more influential in foreign affairs than Lord Curzon, the foreign secretary, just as J T Davies, Lloyd George's principal private secretary, was a more important figure than the permanent head of the civil service.

Lloyd George never hesitated to go behind the backs of his established advisers, listening to amateur advice and then forming his opinion with little regard to the official papers. He consulted junior officers back from France, including his own son, for arguments to use against Haig, the commander-in-chief, and Robertson, chief of the imperial general staff. He got Lieutenant Commander Kenworthy to brief him against the Lords of the Admiralty. Kenworthy was smuggled into No. 10 Downing Street late at night by Northcliffe through the garden door. The most striking instance of Lloyd George's unconventional methods is the origin of the National Health service – that revolutionary contribution to modern life. One can imagine how it would have begun in the ordinary way: a royal commission, long papers from experts, an accumulation of facts and figures. Lloyd George merely sent

4. Lloyd George introduced two other French innovations into British political life. Until 1915 British ministers were secretaries, first lords, presidents of boards. The first avowed minister was the minister of munitions, Lloyd George himself; he soon created others. Again, British ministers with nothing to do were given a sinecure. They were not ministers without portfolio – strictly speaking, no British minister has a portfolio, he has seals or a royal warrant. The first minister without portfolio, Lansdowne, was appointed in 1915 on Lloyd George's suggestion, and the list was soon full of them. Perhaps Lloyd George's casual attitude to his private finances was also learnt from France, or perhaps it was natural to a Welshman.

W J Braithwaite, a junior official in the treasury, to find how Bismarck's system of insurance worked in Germany. Braithwaite toured Germany and then travelled overnight to the south of France. On 3 January 1911 he caught up with Lloyd George at Nice. Lloyd George, accompanied by some friends, took him to the pier; set out chairs not too near the band; ordered drinks; and said : 'Now tell us all about it.' Braithwaite discoursed for four hours. When he had finished, the Welfare State had been born. A symbol of Lloyd George indeed – the pier at Nice, the band, the hastily improvised explanation and then the gigantic results. It gives added point to the story that there is no pier at Nice; perhaps there was one then.

Lloyd George rarely showed loyalty to those who broke ranks to work with him. J T Davies was rewarded by being made a director of the Suez Canal Company. Others were less fortunate. Braithwaite created the National Health system almost single handed under Lloyd George's inspiration. As soon as it was made, Lloyd George deposited him in the obscurity of a special commissioner of income tax. They met again only once, twenty years later. Lloyd George said : 'Hello, Braithwaite, what have you been doing all this time?' Braithwaite replied : 'My duty I hope, sir, where I was sent to do it.' Politicians who worked with Lloyd George were treated in the same way. Christopher Addison had a large share in making Lloyd George prime minister. Some years later, when Addison's lavish expenditure on housing – incurred on Lloyd George's prompting – aroused Unionist hostility, Lloyd George jettisoned him without warning and apologized to the House that loyalty to an old friend had led him to keep an incompetent minister in office. For Lloyd George no ties were sacred. Churchill stood solidly by Lloyd George during the Marconi scandal in 1913. Lloyd George did not repay the debt when Churchill ran into trouble over the expedition to the Dardanelles. He said, quite untruly:

'Churchill is the man who brought Turkey into the war against us', and let the Unionists drive Churchill from office. Lloyd George was fond of saying: 'There is no friendship at the top.' It was certainly true in his case.

Lloyd George did not rely on individuals, however eminent. He recognized no intermediaries between himself and 'the people'. His relations with the House of Commons were a mixture of uneasy mastery and distrust. His set pieces in parliament were not remarkable. His long speech introducing the People's Budget of 1909 was poorly delivered, and one listener surmised that Lloyd George himself did not understand what he was saying. It was different when he was answering criticism or silencing opposition by last-minute concessions. He met objections to the National Health scheme so skilfully, and with such moderation, that in the end most Unionists voted for it. As prime minister, he never allowed his opponents to get the issue clear and always raised some unexpected red herring which left them baffled. So, when accused of weakness towards Germany during the peace negotiations of 1919, he rode off with an irrelevant attack on Lord Northcliffe which delighted even his strongest critics. His greatest triumph came in the Maurice debate of May 1918. Asquith, who launched it, was universally described as the greatest parliamentarian, and he had a good case, but no novice was more catastrophically out-manoeuvred. Lloyd George summed up the debate afterwards: 'They have gone away saying – we have caught the little beggar out speaking the truth for once.' Whether he was speaking the truth on that occasion, no one has been able to decide from that day to this.

For Lloyd George, parliament was less important than the public meeting. He said: 'My platform is the country.' This was the time when all political leaders did a great deal of public speaking. The period opened in the 1880s, after Gladstone's Midlothian campaigns; it tailed off in the 1930s, perhaps because interest in politics declined, perhaps because of the radio. Lloyd George came just at the top of the wave. His style was all his own. Other statesmen spoke in formal terms, carefully prepared. Churchill, for instance, learnt his early speeches, word for word, by heart and read his later ones. Lloyd George spoke with his audience, not to them, and snapped up phrases as they were thrown at him. 'Ninepence for fourpence' was the result of one such interruption; making Germany pay to the uttermost farthing, the less happy result of another. Most public speakers seemed to be the contemporaries of Henry Irving or Beerbohm Tree. Lloyd George gave a music-hall turn, worthy of Harry Lauder or George Robey, the prime minister of mirth, and the great days of the music hall, roughly from 1900 to 1930, corresponded exactly with his. In 1923 Lloyd George was persuaded to use a microphone for the first time, and he accepted it ever afterwards. I suspect that it ruined his public style, as it certainly ruined the music hall.

Speechmaking was not Lloyd George's only instrument for projecting himself on the country, perhaps not even the most important. No public man has made more use of the press. This was not new. Palmerston wrote leaders for The Globe and The Morning Chronicle, often reproducing the very words of his dispatches and rewarding the proprietor of the latter with a baronetcy. Salisbury wrote in The Standard, and made his ghost, Alfred Austin, Poet Laureate. Even Sir Edward Grey briefed J A Spender of The Westminster Gazette. Lloyd George approached the press in a different way. He was never forthcoming to reporters. On the contrary he was the first prime minister who employed a press secretary to keep them at bay and even then often complained of their misrepresentations. Lloyd George went for the man at the top – the editor and, still more, the proprietor. Why bother to make a case when the proprietor could make it more decisively simply by issuing an order? The most famous example came in 1918.

Lloyd George, angered that The Daily Chronicle had enlisted his critic, Frederick Maurice, as military correspondent, got a group of Coalition Liberals to buy the paper and turned out the editor, Robert Donald, at twenty-four hours' notice.[5] This was not his first exercise in financial influence. As early as 1900 he persuaded George Cadbury to buy The Daily News and to turn it overnight from a pro-war to a pro-Boer paper. Usually he used less direct means. Common sympathy with the Boers established a deep intimacy between Lloyd George and C P Scott, owner-editor of The Manchester Guardian, an intimacy not really broken even when Scott was denouncing the behaviour of the Black and Tans in Ireland. Scott remained faithful even unto death : almost his last act was to swing The Manchester Guardian against the National Government and behind Lloyd George during the financial crisis of 1931. Even more important for Lloyd George was his friendship with Sir William Robertson Nicoll, editor of The British Weekly, a man now forgotten, but wielding decisive power in his time. It is hardly too much to say that Robertson Nicoll was the man who first, by supporting Lloyd George, raised him up, and then, by withdrawing his support, cast him down.

Newspaper proprietors in the stricter sense were flattered by Lloyd George and often ennobled by him : Riddell, owner of The News of the World, the first divorced person to be made a peer; Rothermere; Beaverbrook. Lloyd George had a curious on-and-off relationship with Northcliffe, the greatest of them all, intimate at one moment, hostile at the next. The two men had much in common, despite their conflicts, both sprung from the people, both impatient with conventional politicians. There was in both the same mixture of impulsiveness and calculation, though Northcliffe was the less calcu-

5. This manipulation of 'public opinion' proved useful to Lloyd George in another way. He put some of his private political fund into The Daily Chronicle and sold out in 1926 at a fourfold profit.

lating of the two. When once asked to cooperate with North-cliffe, Lloyd George replied: 'I would as soon go for a walk round Walton Heath with a grasshopper.' A good analogy; but who more like a grasshopper than Lloyd George himself? Lloyd George did not court the newspaper proprietors merely as the makers of public opinion. He genuinely believed that they understood this opinion and could interpret it. How else had they achieved their enormous circulations? Hence he canvassed their advice before taking decisive action. He supposed also that they possessed executive ability of the highest order. When he filled his administration with 'press lords', this was not only to 'buy' them; he thought that the work would be done better by them than by anyone else, and it often was. Then, by an odd twist, he discovered the same abilities in himself. After all, if the inarticulate Northcliffe and the ponderous Rothermere had journalistic genius, how much more must Lloyd George have it too. I doubt if this were the case. Though he was highly paid by American papers after he ceased to be prime minister, this was rather for his name than for the quality of his contributions. But Lloyd George believed himself suited to a great journalistic post. In 1922 it was seriously proposed that a group of wealthy friends should buy The Times, then being hawked around after Northcliffe's death, and set him up as editor. Lloyd George was ready, eager to resign the premiership for this purpose. No doubt he had other reasons for wishing to be rid of office. Nevertheless the affair is striking testimony that Lloyd George rated the world of journalism highly, perhaps even more highly than the world of politics. Editors of The Times have often believed that they were more important than prime ministers. Lloyd George was the only prime minister who apparently agreed with them.

Parliament, platform, press, one element needs to be fitted into place, maybe the key place: politics. Though Lloyd George was never a good party man, indifferent to many party doctrines and regardless of party discipline, he was first returned as a Liberal, and managed to call himself a Liberal of some sort or another throughout his political life. The peculiar circumstances of the Liberal party gave him his opportunity and later snatched it away again.

Few writers have noticed how peculiar these circumstances were. Historians of recent times assume, perhaps rightly, that the two-party system is a permanent feature of British politics, and they go on to assume, with less justification, that the swing of the pendulum follows inevitably from this. Hence they find nothing surprising in the Liberal victory of 1906. On the contrary, it was against all the rules. When Lloyd George entered parliament in 1890, the Liberal party seemed clearly on the way out: sustained by Gladstone's great name and then doomed to decline and disintegration. So it happened: defeat in 1895, and thereafter disruption into warring factions. This is not surprising. Historic liberalism was a *bourgeois* cause, inspired by the advance of *laissez-faire* capitalism and successful in the days of limited suffrage. It lost drive as individual enterprise diminished and it offered little which could attract a mass electorate. This was the common pattern all over Europe. The National Liberal party in Germany, the Liberal party in Austria, the French opportunists, the moderate Italian Liberals who followed Cavour, all saw their greatness disappear. Old-fashioned British liberalism really ended in 1874, as Gladstone recognized by resigning from the leadership. The party was revived only by the freak controversies first over the Eastern Question and then over Home Rule. But Home Rule could not keep it going permanently, particularly when most Liberals were not interested in it.

How, then, did British liberalism come to have its greatest success in the early twentieth century, when – on any rational calculation – it should have been dead? The answer is to be found in economic developments which also went against the rules. Individualistic capitalism had a second innings, a sort of deathbed repentance. It is rather like the Solent which, owing to the bottleneck in the Channel between Cherbourg and St Catherine's Point, has four tides a day. You are just resigning yourself to a desolate stretch of sand or pebble when the tide comes flooding in again. So it was with British economy and for a paradoxical reason. The terms of trade, which in the later nineteenth century had been moving in favour of Great Britain, at the end of the century turned against her. As all Europe and much of the United States became industrialized, the cost of raw materials went up, so did the price of food-stuffs which everyone was importing. There was increased social discontent in Great Britain, as real wages declined – a social discontent which Lloyd George did much to exploit; there was increased hostility to the 'stomach taxes' which Tariff Reform involved. There was something else : a renewed demand for the products of the old British staples – coal, ship-building, textiles; staples which had been losing their pre-eminence. Suddenly, with the increased prosperity of pro-ducers of raw materials outside Europe, they boomed again. All three surpassed their previous records, and British exports, thanks mainly due to the old staples, reached their all-time peak in 1913.

Instead of undertaking a new industrial revolution, Great Britain could prosper again in the old centres of industry in the old way. This unexpected revival brought with it a second edition of new men, self-reliant, self-made, impatiently Radi-cal, far removed from the intellectual refinement of the established Liberal leaders. They were more assertive than their predecessors of fifty years before, unawed by the prestige of the conventional system. Cobden, for instance, despaired of ever attaining real power. His lesser successors had no such doubts. Here is a significant indication. Like their predeces-sors, the new men were mostly Dissenters, at any rate in upbringing, though – like Lloyd George – most of them did not take their religious allegiance at all precisely. They were Dissenters with a difference. The nineteenth-century Dissenters called themselves Nonconformists – recognition that they were a tolerated minority. Early in the twentieth century they changed their official description and became the Free Churches – assertion of equality, perhaps even of superior virtue. The Dissenters swarmed into the parliament of 1906. As Halévy pointed out long ago, that parliament had more non-Anglicans in it than any since the time of Oliver Cromwell. Barebones had come again.

These new men were the making of Lloyd George. The very things which distinguished him from other Liberal leaders brought him close to the self-made businessmen. He had no university education; nor had they. He was of poor origin; so were they. Above all, he was an avowed Free Churchman, and this became the symbol of his unique position. This first picked him out from the Liberal backbenchers and made him a national figure. It started with the Boer war. The Boers were regarded, rather perversely, as champions of the small man against the encroachments of the City and monopoly finance. Moreover they were Free Churchmen, or something like it. There would have been much less pro-Boer enthusiasm in Great Britain if the Boers had been Roman Catholics. It was an added advantage to Lloyd George that most Liberal leaders supported the Boer war almost as heartily as Unionist ministers did. Still, this was a passing phase. What really made Lloyd George's standing was the controversy over the Education Bill of 1902. Here again many Liberal leaders – influenced by the Fabians and friendly to Morant, its author – favoured the Bill. Lloyd George fought it almost alone. When the political argument shifted from Education to Free Trade, he lost his pre-eminence. He never cared much for Free Trade or understood the topics in dispute. Others took up the running. Asquith, always strongest in negation, eclipsed him. Nevertheless, thanks to the earlier conflicts Lloyd

George had forced his way to the front and established his claim to high office.

Lloyd George was the outstanding 'new' Radical in the Liberal Government of 1905. Office gave him the opportunity to show his great executive capacity – his unrivalled ability for getting things done. The things he did were all his own, things not envisaged by ordinary liberalism or by the party programme. Everyone knows the rather synthetic passions which he aroused over the People's Budget of 1909. Yet curiously he was the least involved in the subsequent controversy over the House of Lords. He knew instinctively that the people – his sort of people – were not deeply stirred by the constitutional intricacies which fascinated Liberal lawyers. His judgement was correct. The two general elections of 1910, and particularly the second, produced more excitement among candidates and less among the electors than perhaps any others of modern times. Lloyd George showed his real opinion of the affair by quietly devising the National Health scheme, and carrying it, when the constitutional storm was blowing its hardest. Indeed, he proposed to settle all the burning issues between the parties – dead issues in his opinion – by agreement. He tried quite sincerely to promote a Coalition Government; less sincerely perhaps even at the price of his own withdrawal. What he really wanted was 'a government of businessmen' – a revealing phrase – in other words of Radical backbenchers.

Lloyd George had something else in common with the new men. His financial position was improving like theirs. The private finances of public men are rarely touched on by their biographers. Still, it is pretty clear that most public men have been the poorer for their life of service, particularly when they held office. Lloyd George was in debt when he became president of the Board of Trade in 1905; his position was very different when he ceased to be prime minister in 1922. He was the first prime minister since Walpole to leave office markedly richer than he entered it. This is not all mystery. Wealthy admirers entertained and endowed him. Riddell gave him a house at Walton Heath – burnt by suffragettes during the building – which he later sold at a good price; Andrew Carnegie bequeathed him an annuity of £2,000 in remote applause for his democratic achievements. But most of his success defies inquiry. Though Lloyd George became well-off, he did not acquire a country-house near London until after the war. Disliking life in London, he went off, whenever he could, to a luxury hotel at Brighton or the south of France, with an accompanying flock of civil servants and political adherents, all presumably paid for by the Treasury. It did not occur to him that he was cutting himself off from 'the people' by living in this way. 'The people' whom he knew, the Free Church Radicals, lived in exactly the same way.

Besides, he remained closer to the people than any other Liberal minister including John Burns. Lloyd George was the link between the Liberal Government and Labour on its trade-union side. Trade unions have now become an accepted, indeed an essential, part of the social order. It is hard to think back to a time, only fifty years ago, when unions were not recognized in many leading industries, when workingmen were held to be 'not like us', and when it could be solemnly affirmed that miners would keep coal in the bath if they were given bathrooms. Labour was asserting its independence in the early twentieth century, and the Liberal Government were repeatedly drawn into trade disputes. Their mediation was still embarrassed and aloof. A minister thought he had done well if he got masters and men – another revealing phrase – into the same room. Lloyd George interpreted mediation differently. He was out to conciliate the men, and he extracted concessions from the employers by any means that occurred to him. It is tempting to surmise that he made his Mansion House speech of 21 July 1911, stirring up the Agadir crisis, so as to frighten the railway companies with the spectre of war into settling the great railway strike much in favour of the unions some three weeks later. At any rate, in the years before the war, Lloyd George was the favourite and most successful industrial mediator among ministers. He always got a settlement which enhanced his reputation at the same time.

The outbreak of war advanced Lloyd George's position in three ways. He was essential as the spokesman of the Radical Free Churches; he could display, still more, his great executive powers; he was the only minister who could handle Labour. The decision to go to war revolved round him. There would no doubt have been a majority for war in any case: the Unionists and the moderate Liberals would have supported it. But it seemed until the last moment that there might be also bitter opposition and opposition of the most dangerous kind, opposition on grounds of morality. It is a common opinion nowadays, and was a common opinion then, that wars are opposed for motives of class, that is by the working-class movement. Experience is quite other: opposition to war is effective and decisive only when sustained by moral principle, though it may be that the working class is more moral than others. This was true in regard to the Boer war; it was true over the Suez affair; even, I think, true over the proposed war of intervention against Soviet Russia in 1920. That war was prevented because it was wicked, not because Soviet Russia was 'the workers' state'. So, too, in August 1914, the Free Churches, not the Labour movement, held the key position. When Lloyd George, sustained by Robertson Nicoll, came down on the side of war, he determined that there would be national unity, though, in a longer perspective, the two men sealed the death warrant of the Free Churches as a great moral force. His action mattered not only in August 1914; he was the principal guarantor of national unity as long as the war lasted, in a position – though he did not appreciate this for some time – to dictate his own terms.

The war also gave Lloyd George the opportunity to run things in the way he liked to run them. He could improvise; he could disregard precedent. Any other man would have quailed at starting a ministry of munitions from scratch. Lloyd George rejoiced that, when he entered the requisitioned hotel allotted to the new ministry, it contained a table, two chairs, many mirrors – and no civil servants. Alone among Liberal ministers, he appreciated that the war could not be conducted on the basis of *laissez-faire*. Perhaps he did not altogether deserve his reputation as the man who got things done. But at least he tried to get them done, which was more than could be said for anyone else in high office.

The third, and perhaps most important, asset came to Lloyd George unforeseen and by accident. It had hardly occurred to him that he would be the chief conciliator of Labour. Indeed it did not occur to him, or to anyone else, that in wartime the conciliation of Labour would be even more urgent than the raising of recruits. Until August 1914 the British people played a negative part in public life. Their only duties were to pay their taxes and not to cause trouble for the governing class. Suddenly their position changed. It was not enough to keep them quiet; they had to cooperate actively. Lloyd George was the chief instrument in industrial mobilization, thanks to his previous successes with the trade unions, and this even before he became minister of munitions. On 27 March 1915 he met the leaders of the engineering unions at the Treasury : they agreed to drop restrictive practices for the duration and received in return some rather vague promise of industrial partnership. This was a date of historic importance : the moment when the trade unions ceased to be merely instruments of resistance and stepped, however half-heartedly, into a share of control. It was the most significant event in the history of British trade unions, and hence of the British working class, since the repeal of the Combination Acts, and it was all Lloyd George's doing. He has left a vivid account of the scene – the union leaders leaning casually against a chair which Queen Anne was reputed to have used when she attended the Treasury Board, and A J Balfour, appropriate representative of the governing class, regarding them with tolerant surprise. Lloyd George writes : 'His ideas of government were inherited from the days when Queen Anne sat on that throne... This scene was fundamentally different. He saw those stalwart artisans leaning against and sitting on the steps of the throne of the dead queen, and on equal terms negotiating conditions with the Government of the day... Queen Anne was indeed dead. I felt that his detached and enquiring mind was bewildered by this sudden revelation of a new power and that he must take time to assimilate the experience.'[6] Lloyd George went further along the same path after he became minister of munitions. Though, strictly speaking, engineering alone was his concern, he acted as the unofficial minister for industry, called in whenever there were difficulties in the coalfields or the shipyards, and overriding the dogmatic follies of the minister technically responsible – Runciman, president of the Board of Trade. In this work of conciliation, Lloyd George established a partnership with Arthur Henderson – nominally president of the Board of Education, actually the representative of 'Labour' in the Coalition Government. Henderson always preferred to play second fiddle, and he transferred to Lloyd George the support which he had previously given to MacDonald. The two men tackled industrial unrest together – not always successfully, but better than anyone else did.

Here then were Lloyd George's unique assets, assets which grew in strength as the war proceeded. Moreover the circumstances of the war made it easier for him to exploit these assets. Not only did 'the people' count for more; their voice became unexpectedly more effective. The Asquith coalition was a pact between the two front benches, a pact to avoid

6. Lloyd George, *War Memoirs*, i, 177.

dispute and to keep things quiet. The press had to provide the criticism which was silenced in parliament, and practically all the press was on Lloyd George's side. It is often held that this was due to his personal intrigues. He is supposed to have 'nobbled' the press lords. I doubt whether anyone could 'nobble' Northcliffe. I am sure that no one could 'nobble' C P Scott, J L Garvin, Robert Donald or Geoffrey Dawson. All these men passionately wanted Lloyd George as prime minister, and their united support is the most powerful evidence that he was the right man for the job. There was another factor. The backbenchers, both Unionist and Liberal, were increasingly restive at the silence which had been imposed upon them. They threatened to revolt, and this revolt brought Lloyd George to supreme power. In the crisis of December 1916, he had three kingmakers, none of them from the front bench. Max Aitken brought over Bonar Law, a backbencher in spirit, even though he was Unionist leader; Christopher Addison mobilized the backbench Radicals; Arthur Henderson delivered the solid backing of Labour, to his own surprise. There was one striking gap : the party Whips played no part at all. They were the instrument which broke in Asquith's hands.

Lloyd George was given two tasks as prime minister : a more energetic conduct of the war and a closer partnership with the people. It was because Lloyd George enjoyed the confidence of 'the people' that the Unionist leaders came over to him, even though the revolt had been directed originally as much against them as against the frontbench Liberals. The Unionists had always been readier to make their peace with 'democracy' from the time of Disraeli onwards. The Liberals feared it and Asquith tried to fight the revolt entirely within the closed circle of the governing class. The Liberal leaders had a curious belief in their divine right to rule. Bewildered by their defeat, they grasped at the myth that Lloyd George had intrigued himself to the top and, by dint of repeating it, got others to believe it too. In reality, Asquith fought to retain power as much as Lloyd George fought to gain it, and his later complaints resemble those of an ageing heavyweight who has been knocked out by a younger, more agile, opponent. Nevertheless, Lloyd George paid a bitter price for victory. In Churchill's words, he had seized power, and the governing class never forgave him. Even the Unionist leaders who went with him meant to discard him once the emergency was over.

Lloyd George also suffered, in the long run, from the backing which the press gave him. Members of parliament like to regard themselves as the sole voice of the people and see in the press a rival power, illegitimate and irresponsible. The House of Commons has never forgiven its defeat at the hands of John Wilkes, and there is no more joyful scene there than when some editor appears at the bar for public rebuke. If members of parliament had their way, press, radio and television would not exist, or at any rate would be silent on political questions. Press support for a politician is the kiss of death, though of course most members canvass for it behind the scenes. Lloyd George obviously preferred press lords to politicians – preferred them not only as companions, but as ministers. He treated the House with increasing casualness. His war Cabinet was composed virtually without regard to parliamentary need; one member of it, Smuts, served for eighteen months without ever having any connection with either House – a unique case; the first full statement of war aims was made to a trade-union conference, not to the House of Commons. Lloyd George often trembled for his position. He was really in no danger so long as he had 'the people' on his side. Every stroke which he delivered against established authority – against admirals, field marshals and conventional politicians – strengthened him, though he often hesitated before delivering it.

The fatal mine against Lloyd George exploded almost unnoticed, particularly by Lloyd George himself. This was his breach with Arthur Henderson. Lloyd George had been quicker than any other politician to grasp the importance of the Labour movement, but he only grasped the half of it. He regarded it as an interest just like the Free Church interest which had originally raised him up – a pressure-group with limited sectional objectives. He never understood the political side of the movement. Keir Hardie seemed to him a fine Radical pro-Boer; Ramsay MacDonald a somewhat wordy Fabian who would one day become a Liberal minister. It is fair to say that most Labour leaders also did not understand the political importance of their movement until it happened. Keir Hardie hawked the Labour leadership around to Morley, Dilke and Lloyd George himself; MacDonald was not indifferent to Liberal offers. Nevertheless, the Labour movement made no sense without its political content. Lloyd George never appreciated that the Labour leaders whom he praised, condescendingly, as simple working-men of sterling character were also long-standing members of the ILP or the SDF, though not all of them remained faithful to their origin. When Lloyd George put Henderson in the war Cabinet, he supposed that he was enlisting a useful agent for managing the trade unions, and Henderson modestly accepted this slighting estimate.

Nevertheless, Henderson had a special position. Lloyd George's Government was composed otherwise of individuals, except for Bonar Law – men who had to depend on their personal weight and achievement. Henderson was the voice of Labour and therefore, when conflict arose, acted with an independence such as none other of Lloyd George's ministers dared to show. The question at issue was whether British Labour should attend the conference at Stockholm, to discuss possible peace terms with other Socialist parties. Henderson answered this question according to his own judgement and the outlook of the Labour party, not according to the decisions of the war Cabinet. He was kept on the mat and driven to resign. Lloyd George attached little importance to the incident. He put another Labour man, George Barnes, into the war Cabinet and thought that by doing so he had automatically made Barnes Labour leader, much as the king automatically made a politician leader of his party by appointing him prime minister. Nothing of the kind. Labour did not take its leader by nomination from Lloyd George, and Barnes was civilly dead so far as Labour was concerned from the moment he entered the war Cabinet. Labour continued to support the war; Labour ministers, other than Henderson, remained in office. This no doubt gave Lloyd George the illusion that nothing important had happened. He was wrong. August 1917 marked the real parting of the ways between Lloyd George and 'the people'. Labour then gave notice to quit, a notice, like so many others, deferred for the duration.

Lloyd George was secure while the war lasted. He supposed that he was even more secure when the war ended. He had fulfilled his bargain : he had won the war. The general election of December 1918 turned on the simple question whether Lloyd George should go on as prime minister. No issues of policy were at stake, despite later beliefs to the contrary. The election was a plebiscite which Lloyd George won. The Unionist and Liberal parties as such had no significance. Most electors merely wanted Lloyd George as prime minister, and, though they could express this wish only by voting for candidates who accepted the 'coupon', this was a vote against party, not a vote for Coalition Unionists or Liberals. Yet this moment of triumph saw also the appearance of a decisive threat against Lloyd George's position. He aimed, whether consciously or not, at becoming sole voice of the people by destroying the existing parties and reducing politics to a collection of individuals. The Labour party provided a new representation of the people and, as well, resurrected the two-party system just when Lloyd George had got rid of it.

This was Arthur Henderson's delayed revenge for his humiliation the year before – not that so nice a man ever thought in terms of revenge. Lloyd George's Coalition was reduced from all the nation to two-thirds (a third being a generous estimate for the Liberal party). There was never at any time a hope that he could pull Labour back. Thanks to Henderson it had become fully independent: independent in its programme; independent in its constituency organizations; independent in its finance, which came from the political levy of the trade unions and not, as with the other parties, from the sale of honours.

Lloyd George was not alone in failing to read the writing on the wall. Hardly anyone did so. The defeated Asquithians thought that they would soon be back in first place on the front Opposition Bench. They were still strong in privy councillors, though weak in voters. The parliamentary Labour party was unimpressive. Its real leaders lost their seats at the general election, and it was difficult to grasp that a party of the people could be led almost as well from outside the House as from within it, though Lloyd George himself had played country against parliament. Henderson, with his usual abnegation, found the predestined leader of the Labour party in Ramsay MacDonald. He, not Lloyd George, became the symbol, adequate or not, for the triumph of democracy. It is fascinating to watch how Lloyd George missed the meaning of all this. He actually wanted to see 200 Labour members of parliament so that he could balance more adroitly between the contending 'interests'. But where was the base from which he could operate? During the war the 'interests' could sink their differences in a common will to win; after the war this uniting principle disappeared. Lloyd George made repeated attempts to found a Centre party. This was possible only if it included representatives from both extremes. There would be none from Labour. Therefore the Centre party could only be another name for the Conservatives, and they preferred their own. Even the Coalition Liberals recognized this and refused to be swallowed up, clinging to the rags of their Radical origin – Free Trade and the Free Churches. Lloyd George's Centre party remained a one-man band.

Lloyd George had still one asset, achievement, and he worked it to the full. His balance sheet of success after the war was remarkable, perhaps more so than during the war itself. It is possible to debate how much he contributed to victory. Lloyd George himself said that the war was won not by him, but 'by the man in the steel helmet'. What he did after the war was all his own doing. Peace with Germany. Lloyd George alone, against Clemenceau and Wilson, secured a moderate territorial settlement, which did not deprive Germany of any 'ethnic' territory; he alone arranged reparations in such a way that they could be settled in agreement with Germany as soon as the Germans wanted to agree at all. Peace with Soviet Russia. Lloyd George secured this not only against his French allies, but against the majority of his own Cabinet including particularly Churchill. Peace with the trade unions. Lloyd George circumvented the challenges from the railwaymen and the miners until they ceased to be dangerous. Peace with Ireland. Lloyd George performed the miracle which had defied every British statesman for over a century, or perhaps for five centuries – the younger Pitt, Gladstone, Asquith, to go no further back: he settled the Irish question for good and all. There was hardly a problem where he did not leave success behind him. The inter-war years lived on his legacy and exhausted it.

Yet it was all dust and ashes. Each success lowered his reputation instead of adding to it. What went wrong? What turned Lloyd George from the most admired into the most hated and distrusted figure in British politics? It was partly his method. He defined this method in classic words: 'I was never in favour of costly frontal attacks, either in war or politics, if there were a way round.' He was the leader of a predominantly Right-wing coalition, yet his instincts were all to the Left. He did not browbeat his followers. Instead he led them with much blowing of trumpets in one direction until the moment when they discovered that he had brought them to an exactly opposite conclusion. Conciliation of Germany was prepared under a smoke-screen of 'Hang the Kaiser' and 'Make Germany Pay'. The Soviet leaders were Bolshevik untouchables until the day when Lloyd George signed a trade agreement with them. The trade-union leaders were a challenge to civilization at one moment and were being offered whisky and cigars at the next. Ireland was the supreme example. Lloyd George's successful peace was preceded by the Black and Tans, one of the most atrocious episodes in British history. The Unionists were told that Lloyd George had murder by the throat and then found themselves called upon to surrender everything which they had defended for nearly forty years. Men do not like being cheated even for the most admirable cause.

Success ruined Lloyd George in another way. Confident in his own powers, he would tolerate no rival near the throne. During the war he had colleagues of equal, or almost equal, stature – Bonar Law, Milner, Balfour. He had formidable antagonists – admirals and field-marshals. He was the little man asserting the cause of the people against great odds. After the war he reigned supreme. He had no colleagues, only subordinates; men who, however distinguished, had pinned their fate to his and had no resources with which to oppose him. He established with them 'the relation of master and servant', which Churchill acknowledged even years later, when he was chancellor of the exchequer and Lloyd George a mere private member. Though Lloyd George reluctantly restored the full Cabinet in place of the small war Cabinet, he then disregarded it and settled policy on his own behind the scenes.

There was another terrible flaw in his position: the sale

of honours. Lloyd George could plead that Governments had notoriously been selling honours for the last forty years and, less directly, long before. He ran the system too hard. Not only did he sell more honours with less excuse. Lacking a party, he sold them for his own account, as the existence of the Lloyd George fund still testifies. It was one thing for him to maintain a personal dictatorship, based only on his individual gifts. The Lloyd George fund raised the threat that he would turn his disregard of party into a permanent system. Moreover, politics had to become more respectable with the advance of democracy. Corruption was an accepted necessity in the old days of a closed political nation. Appearances had to be kept up now that 'the people' had a voice in government. The integrity of Labour finance was itself a standing reproach to the older parties. Most of all, the supply of buyers was running out. It was easy to be delicate about the sale of honours when few wanted to buy them. Those who had bought honours in the past wished to elevate their position by ensuring that no one did it again, and those who still aspired to honours wished to avoid paying for them.

Some of the forces which had brought Lloyd George to power moved away from him; others lost their strength. Independent Labour removed one prop. The retreat of the businessmen from public life removed another. Some of Lloyd George's business ministers, among them the most successful, returned to their firms when the war was over; others were itching to go. Besides, Lloyd George had one great failure to set against his many successes: he could not stave off the decline of the old Liberal staples which had long been threatening. He came to power on a wave of industrial expansion which drowned financial scruples. After the war, 'the penguins of the City' enforced deflation and unemployment. The self-made businessmen who had prospered along with Lloyd George were now ruined. The Coalition Liberals vanished as abruptly as they had appeared. At the end Lloyd

George was forced back on his origins. In 1922 he was hastily mobilizing the Free Churches as his last line of defence. They were no longer a decisive element in British politics now that education had ceased to be a sectarian question. He who had once seemed the man of the future was by 1922 curiously old-fashioned. He looked, and spoke, like a Victorian. His public speeches, though still effective, sounded like echoes from the past. His audiences often took his point before he made it. His support in the press also dwindled. The press lords moved from him. He quarrelled with Northcliffe in 1918; with Riddell in 1922. Beaverbrook backed away when Bonar Law left the Government. There remained only his private organ, The Daily Chronicle.

The fall of Lloyd George was provoked by his attempt to resist the Turkish advance on Constantinople – an attempt incidentally which, like most of his enterprises, was largely successful. This was the occasion, not the cause. He was brought down, as he had been raised up, by a revolt of the backbenchers. The Conservative meeting which ended the Coalition was actually summoned by the leaders in order to break this incipient revolt, and the rebels thought, until the last minute, that they would be defeated. It is curious how Lloyd George repeated, in every detail, the mistakes which had destroyed Asquith. He, too, came to believe that he was 'the indispensable man', safe from all storms. He, too, came to count solely on 'the talents' at the top and disregarded the other ranks of politics – the very men in the trenches who had made him prime minister.

There was an odd outcome. The revolt of the backbenchers in 1916, which raised Lloyd George to power, destroyed the party system; their revolt of 1922, which flung him out, restored it. The rebels of 1922 acted in the name of Conservative independence. But essentially what drove them to act in this way was Labour's independence, asserted in 1918. Once Labour became a distinct party, it could be answered only by another party, not by an individual however brilliant. Lloyd George's fall dates back to the day when he kept Arthur Henderson waiting on the mat. The rise of the Labour party, which seemed to disrupt the pattern of politics, paradoxically restored the two party-system in a new form. Class became the determining factor in party allegiance, and there was no place for Lloyd George, the man who bounced from one class to another.

Lloyd George had triumphed when men wanted a national leader, who would save the country by opportunist means without regard for party principles or party ties. It is not surprising that Lenin admired him and dedicated a book to him; for Lenin, too, became great as the opportunist saviour of his country, jettisoning party doctrines of a far more rigid kind – and jettisoning party comrades also. Crisis had been Lloyd George's opportunity. Men disliked the atmosphere of crisis after the turmoil of the Great War. Even when there was a crisis, as with the General Strike, the strikers solemnly played football against the police to demonstrate that nothing unusual was happening. Lloyd George had one more chance. In 1931 a financial crisis threatened, real and inescapable – or so men thought then; nowadays a chancellor of the exchequer who was faced only with the deficit of 1931 would think he was in luck's way. Ramsay MacDonald, himself at sea, invited Lloyd George to join the Labour Government as leader of the House and in control of the Treasury. The cuckoo seemed once more on the point of entering the nest. Lloyd George could be again the saviour of his country, inaugurating a British New Deal. At the decisive moment he was temporarily knocked out of public life by a serious operation. MacDonald and Baldwin, the two men who had destroyed him, were left to face the financial crisis as best they could. Lloyd George remained a lone voice, with no political supporters except members of his family, pathetically trying to revive the Free Church interest at great cost to his private fund. By the time of the second world war Lloyd George was too old and perhaps too jealous of others. He cast himself, if at all, in the part of a British Pétain. The former Radical was now the lamenter of past days, resentful that the great National Government was composed on the basis of parties, instead of disregarding them. This final protest came appropriately from him. Lloyd George's success marked the last triumph of individual enterprise. His fall showed that the days of individual enterprise were over. Combines ruled, in politics as in everything else. Nowadays even historians work in teams.

28. *Spam on a Gold Plate*

New Statesman. A review of King George VI, His Life and Reign, by John W Wheeler-Bennett (1958).

No one who lived through the Blitz of 1940 is likely to forget it: a terrible ordeal, but also a triumph of dogged courage. While women and children were evacuated by the thousand, everyone who had worked in London, from Cabinet minister to factory hand, stayed there and got on with his job. Among them was George VI. The king and queen, though sleeping at Windsor, commuted to London each day and endured repeated bombing at Buckingham Palace. Yet there was a difference between the king and his subjects. They had essential work to do in London; he attended at Buckingham Palace solely to be bombed. He could have gone through his 'boxes' just as well at Windsor or contributed more usefully to the war effort by turning shells on his lathe in the basement. This was the king's duty as he saw it: to share the sufferings of his people.

Mrs Roosevelt, dining at Buckingham Palace in 1942, was given a meal 'which would have shocked the King's grandfather'. It was served on gold plate, and 'spam on a gold plate' would be a good motto for the reign. Another example. In 1947 George VI was in South Africa when the fuel crisis struck Britain. He wrote to Queen Mary:

I am very worried over the extra privations which all of you at home are having to put up with in that ghastly cold weather with no light or fuel. In many ways I wish I was with you having borne so many trials with them.

Yet all the king could have done in England was to consume precious fuel.

Worry is the predominant note in the admirable, if somewhat courtly, biography which Sir John Wheeler-Bennett has written. Before the Abdication of Edward VIII:

It is all so worrying and I feel we all live in a life of conjecture.

During the Munich crisis:

It is all so worrying this awful waiting for the worst to happen.

In the early days of 1940:

I am very worried over the general situation, as everything we do or try to do appears to be wrong, and gets us nowhere.

Only in June 1940 was there a cheerful note:

Personally I feel happier now that we have no allies to be polite to and to pamper.

This cheerfulness did not last. At the end of February 1942:

I cannot help feeling depressed at the future outlook. Anything can happen, and it will be wonderful if we can be lucky anywhere.

At the end of 1942, after Alamein and the landings in North Africa:

Outwardly one has to be optimistic about the future in 1943, but inwardly I am depressed at the present prospect.

Nor did victory improve matters for long. The king wrote in January 1947:

I have asked Mr. Attlee three times now if he is not worried over the domestic situation in this country. But he won't tell me he is when I feel he is. I know I am worried.

A few days later to Queen Mary:

I do wish one could see a glimmer of a bright spot anywhere in world affairs. Never in the whole history of mankind have things looked gloomier than they do now, and one feels so powerless to do anything to help.

Finally to Attlee in December 1950:

I have been very worried lately over affairs in general.

George VI worried himself to death for the sake of his people; truly a sacrificial king, led as a lamb to the slaughter. Life imitates art, and George VI's reign reflected unconsciously the doctrines of Frazer's Golden Bough. No king has had a greater sense of duty or followed its promptings more strictly. This book inspires admiration for its subject, but also regret. The British were not aboriginal savages despite the attempt of sociologists to treat them as such. They did not really want one man to die for the people. Though they were grateful for the king's sacrifices they would also have appreciated a king who had fun, and in the long run Edward VIII's waywardness may do as much for the monarchy as George VI's high principles. George VI had been trained to respect the throne, not to occupy it, and no man can change his character in mid-life. There is sincere indignation in the note of his first meeting with the Duke of Windsor after the Abdication:

He seems very well, and not a bit worried as to the effects he left on people's minds as to his behaviour in 1936. He has forgotten all about it.

George did not forget. Though he scotched Sir John Reith's proposal to introduce the former king as Mr E Windsor, he denied the title of Royal Highness to the duchess and effectively prevented the return of the Windsors to England. George VI sustained the magic of monarchy.

Monarchy is also a practical affair, involved in the day-to-day workings of politics. Sir John Wheeler-Bennett provides much new information on this subject, some of a disturbing nature. The most important political act of a British sovereign is the choice of prime minister. It has been the last prerogative which he exercises without 'advice'. George VI did his best to let this prerogative lapse. It was on Churchill's advice, superfluous as it may seem, that he sent for Attlee after the general election of 1945. During the war, he worried over the possibility of Churchill's being killed on one of his trips abroad and asked the prime minister to nominate his successor. Churchill 'formally tended advice' that the king should send for Anthony Eden. This satisfied George VI but not for long. Soon he worried again : what should he do if both Churchill and Eden were killed? Once more Churchill 'tendered advice'.

There can be no doubt that it is the Prime Minister's duty to advise Your Majesty to send for Sir John Anderson.

This surprising suggestion disturbs even Sir John Wheeler-Bennett's complacency.

One change of prime minister involved a real decision by the king. What should happen after the House of Commons turned against Chamberlain in the early days of May 1940? Here was a rare moment for the king to voice the wishes of his people. On the contrary, George VI supported Chamberlain and sought to keep him in office.

It is most unfair on Chamberlain to be treated like this after all his good work. The Conservative rebels like Duff Cooper ought to be ashamed of themselves for deserting him at this moment.

The king offered to tell the Labour party 'that I hoped that they would realize that they must pull their weight and join the Natl Govt' – under Chamberlain's leadership. The resolute negative of Attlee and Greenwood saved the country from this dismal prospect. George then delegated the choice of successor to Chamberlain, and he in turn delegated it to a committee of four – himself, Halifax, Captain Margesson and Churchill; a strange quartet to find the saviour of the country. Even on 10 May the king clung to Chamberlain : 'I was terribly sorry that all this controversy had happened.' Failing Chamberlain, the king wanted Halifax, 'I thought H. was the obvious man, & that his peerage could be placed in abeyance for the time being.' But H. 'was not enthusiastic'.

Then I knew that there was only one person whom I could send for to form a Government who had the confidence of the country, and that was Winston.

Such was the reluctance with which George VI appointed the man who was to be the greatest prime minister in British history. The episode does little credit to constitutional monarchy.

The king strove incessantly to keep up with political affairs. In the well-worn words of Bagehot, quoted again by Mr Wheeler-Bennett, it was his right to be consulted; to encourage; and to warn. Chamberlain did not always trouble to observe the constitutional proprieties. The king first learnt of Eden's resignation in February 1938 from 'the Beaverbrook and Harmsworth press'. Later that year, Chamberlain announced his departure to Berchtesgaden in a casual postscript and forgot altogether to seek permission for his departure to Munich. Nevertheless he received wholehearted encouragement from the king. The Munich settlement had no warmer admirer than George VI. He shared, too, Chamberlain's distrust of Soviet Russia, and recorded of his conversation with Roosevelt in June 1939 : 'He was definitely anti-Russian. I told him so were we.'

The constitutional maxim was slightly changed when Labour took office. Then George VI thought it his right to be consulted; to discourage; and to warn.

I told Attlee that he must give the people here some confidence that the Government was not going to stifle all private enterprise.

Again with Herbert Morrison:

We discussed the whole of the Labour programme. I thought he was going too fast with the new nationalizing legislation.

The king exercised decisive influence in one matter connected with the Labour Government, despite its curious failure to leave a mark on Lord Attlee's memory. Of their first interview, the King recorded:

I asked him whom he would make Foreign Secy. and he suggested Dr. Hugh Dalton. I disagreed with him and said that Foreign Affairs was the most important subject at the moment and I hoped he would make Mr. Bevin take it. He said he would.

A memorandum made by the King's private secretary immediately after Attlee's audience confirms the story:

Mr. Attlee mentioned to the King that he was thinking of appointing Mr. Dalton to be his Foreign Secretary. His Majesty begged him to think carefully about this, and suggested that Mr. Bevin would be a better choice.

Attlee's lapse of memory began at once. When the king told the story to his new foreign secretary, Bevin replied that it 'was news to him'. So the country lost a foreign secretary who disliked the Germans, and a chancellor of the exchequer who knew something of economics.

In a longer perspective George VI's reign will mark the end of Empire. Ireland became a republic and the king asked the Eire minister of external affairs: 'Tell me, Mr MacBride, what does this new legislation of yours make *me* in Ireland, an undesirable alien?' India, too, became a republic, but then accepted the king as Head of the Commonwealth – by a strange twist, as Sir John Wheeler-Bennett observes, adopting De Valera's principle of 'external association' just when Ireland abandoned it. The Crown retained its position, but in an impersonal way. George VI never visited India, and it is difficult to believe that his visit to South Africa retarded republicanism. The coronation stone, or any other inanimate object, would do equally well as the symbol of association. For George VI, of course, these symbols had an importance. During the change in India, his main anxiety was when to abandon the 'I.' in his signature.

Against the record of withdrawal, there was one symbol of advance. George VI rescued the Garter from the prime minister of the day and made it 'non-political & in my gift'. Britain had lived through the most stirring years in her history. Never had so many citizens devoted themselves to public service. Whom would the king, of his independent will, delight to honour? The first list of his nominations contained the obvious warleaders. There followed in 1948: the Duke of Portland, Lord Harlech, the Earl of Scarborough, and Lord Cranworth. In 1951 there was a further batch; the Duke of Wellington, Lord Fortescue, and Lord Allendale. Who were these men? What had they done to deserve any honour, let alone the highest in the land? Did they even exist? They belonged to a world of shadows. In this world monarchy too had its being, and Sir John Wheeler-Bennett's eight hundred pages make it more shadowy still.

29. Unlucky Find

New Statesman. A review of Neville Chamberlain by Iain
Macleod (1961). Chamberlain's system of local government
has now been superseded, alas.

Napoleon used to ask of a man : 'Has he Luck?' Ability, experience, integrity were important; without luck they were
useless. Neville Chamberlain had many great qualities. He
had courage and industry. His intellect was clear and sharp.
No politician this century has had a finer administrative brain
or used this gift better. When he became minister of health
in 1924 he set out his reforming programme in twenty-five
draft bills and carried twenty-one of them in the following
four years. His Local Government Act of 1929, devised almost
wholly by himself, had 115 clauses and twelve schedules. It
shaped the structure of English local government to the
present day. As chancellor of the exchequer, he recast the
fiscal system, again with lasting effect. He commanded for a
time the unquestioning allegiance of the Conservative party
as none other of its leaders had done this century, not even
Bonar Law. In Chamberlain's case, the allegiance was as
strong on the front bench as among the rank and file. Yet it
was all to no avail. The decisive element of luck was lacking.

Neville Chamberlain was without luck from the beginning.
In the period of imperialist expansion, he stumbled on one of
the few products, sisal, which failed to show a profit and after
five years of hard work in the West Indies came out with a
loss of £50,000. In the first world war he was saddled with the
hopeless task of organizing National Service and failed again,
though he was abler than most of those who reaped high

honours. Lloyd George called him 'not one of my lucky finds'. When the Conservative leadership became vacant after the death of Bonar Law, Chamberlain found ahead of him a man of few administrative or creative gifts, easygoing and evasive: Baldwin, constantly threatened by party revolt, yet repeatedly surviving, perhaps by innate political skill, perhaps by the essential quality of luck.

Chamberlain's reforms were dwarfed by other events. Not many cared about local government during the great depression; protective tariffs were less important in the 1930s than quotas and currency management. As prime minister, Chamberlain intended to be the initiator of domestic legislation. Instead he was caught by foreign affairs and then led his country lamenting into war. His fall was a further irony of no luck. The Norwegian campaign was inspired and directed by Winston Churchill. Its failure brought down Chamberlain and put Churchill in his place. Even then Chamberlain could have been in charge of administration at home. He was struck by cancer and died.

Neville Chamberlain has also been without luck after death. He has had to carry the sole blame for the failure of British foreign policy, despite protests from his more honest colleagues such as Hoare. By now one would imagine that Chamberlain conducted appeasement single-handed against an almost unanimous Conservative and an entirely unanimous Labour party. In 1946 Dr (now Sir Keith) Feiling published an authorized biography. This was soundly based on the material then available: Chamberlain's letters to his sisters and his rather dry diary. There was a full and carefully drawn picture of Chamberlain's life in its various aspects, though Dr Feiling did not claim to be a specialist on the period. The book attracted less notice than it deserved. Maybe Englishmen were stunned by recent events or did not wish to disrupt the new national unity against Russia by arguments about the past.

Still, Chamberlain's life was a subject which had been covered. Apart from writing a polemical tract, a new biographer would need to strike a fresh hoard of private material (or be able to prove that Dr Feiling had suppressed really important evidence). Alternatively, the new writer would use the material published since 1946 from the official records of the Foreign Office and the Cabinet; he might even get permission to see records not yet published, as some others have done. Even without new information, he might provide a new perspective and show wisdom after the event. But once more: no luck. It is excessive even in Chamberlain's run of bad luck that a biographer claiming to vindicate him should neither vindicate him in any serious sense nor offer new information of importance.

Even an author who has been in the Cabinet and, like so many figures now forgotten, a future prime minister has a duty to his readers; in this case a duty to explain why they should read a second biography when a first, satisfactory, biography exists. This duty is not performed. The earlier biography is not mentioned, though the name of Sir Keith Feiling appears occasionally in the text. There is no hint that the diaries and private letters have been examined before and have already yielded practically everything. The most interesting quotations all appear in Feiling's book; indeed for the period when Chamberlain was prime minister there are many more of them. When Mr Macleod has a new scrap to offer, this is produced with exaggerated emphasis. Thus a memorandum of 25 February 1931 from the Director of the Conservative Central Office, stating the dissatisfaction of the party with Baldwin as leader, is described as 'never before published'. Correct, but the gist is accurately summarized by Feiling.

Again Mr Macleod prints in full from Chamberlain's diary the story of the events which led to Eden's resignation as foreign secretary in February 1938 and asserts that this 'makes clear much that has hitherto been conjectural and contradicts much that has hitherto been accepted'. In fact, Feiling printed five extracts from the account in Chamberlain's diary, which made the story clear, though passing over some details. Feiling's book is superior on nearly every point.

A few omissions are rectified. Feiling concentrated on Chamberlain and left out some episodes which might embarrass others, particularly when they were fellows of All Souls. It is, for instance, odd that Sir John Simon, then a Liberal, should have drafted the Conservative vote of censure on the first Labour Government over the Campbell case, when the Liberals were only asking for a committee of inquiry. Again, during the outcry over the Hoare–Laval plan, some members of the Cabinet, including Chamberlain, felt that, since they had in fact endorsed the plan, they should not make a scapegoat of Hoare. One member of the Cabinet however insisted that 'unless Sam went, the whole moral force of the Government would be gone'. Hoare went. In 1940, when Chamberlain proposed to move Hore-Belisha from the War Office to the Ministry of Information, a Cabinet minister objected that 'it would have a bad effect on the neutrals both because H.B. was a Jew and because his methods would let down British prestige'. As Mr Macleod says, 'to all intents and purposes Hore-Belisha's career was broken'. On both occasions, the Cabinet minister concerned was Lord Halifax. Such new information, though welcome, does not justify a book. Many writers have the experience at some time of taking up a subject which seems rewarding, only to discover that it has been adequately treated already. It is usual in such cases to abandon the subject with regret.

We might at least have expected that the passage of time would bring a more detached judgement, if not a more effective defence. In this, too, we are disappointed. There is little here which was not said better by Chamberlain at the time. Mr Macleod does not much explore public opinion. He has a good quotation from the Labour spokesman at the time of the German reoccupation of the Rhineland.

It is only right to say bluntly and frankly that public opinion in this country would not support, and certainly the Labour party would not support, the taking of military sanctions or even economic sanctions against Germany at this time.

The speaker was Dr Hugh Dalton. Generally Mr Macleod is content to reiterate two points. First that 'Hitler was insatiable, war inevitable, and appeasement therefore a forlorn hope'; second, that Chamberlain, knowing the weakness of British armaments, was concerned only to buy time. Both points have become the current orthodoxy, so much so that any attempt to question them, or even to examine them dispassionately, is met not with argument, but with cries of abusive rage. Of course Hitler was bent, as other German statesmen had been, on making Germany again the dominant Power in Europe, and this undoubtedly made some war probable, if not inevitable, at some time. This is far different from saying that the war which started in September 1939 was inevitable, a war in which Great Britain found herself fighting Germany without any effective ally. Once Germany recovered from her defeat in the first world war, the only choice was between her domination over eastern Europe and Russia's, and the only clearheaded opponents of appeasement were those who preferred Russia to Germany. Most of those who condemn appeasement are even more indignant at the consequence of its failure, a consequence which was, in their own favourite word, 'inevitable' – the eclipse of the British Empire by Russia and America.

Chamberlain perceived some of this, though he did not perceive all of it. He certainly appreciated the weakness of British arms and indeed exaggerated it. He supposed, as the experts did, that bombing was a decisive weapon and that more bombing was the only answer to it. Mr Macleod waves aside the suggestion that Hitler was 'bluffing' in 1938. At this time, the Germans had forty divisions, only one armoured; the Czechs alone had thirty-six, four armoured. Hitler placed two divisions on his western frontier against eighty-two French divisions and planned to send two more later. What was this if not bluff? It is too simple to say that Chamberlain merely aimed to buy time. He did this, but also hoped, and even believed, that appeasement might succeed.

Men, particularly statesmen, do not always think with precise and rigorous logic. Yet Chamberlain was not muddled or an appeaser by nature. On the contrary, he was more hard-headed than most of his contemporaries; he liked to get things settled one way or the other. At the beginning of the Abyssinian crisis, he was the Cabinet minister most insistent for oil sanctions, though he was also the first to demand the ending of sanctions when they had obviously failed. Again, during the Abdication crisis, Chamberlain wished to present Edward VIII with formal Cabinet advice to the king that he should end his association with Mrs Simpson, together with a warning that the Cabinet would resign if the advice were not taken. It was not that, as a Unitarian, he had religious principles against divorce; but the uncertainty was 'holding up business and employment'.

So, too, in foreign politics. Chamberlain did not have the emotional dislike of 'Versailles' common to most Englishmen at that time. He was merely irritated by the instability of the existing order and regarded revision as an unpleasant necessity. And he was not taken in by Hitler. He found Hitler detestable, but not much more so than most foreigners except musicians. Chamberlain was neither blind nor stupid, least of all was he a coward. On the contrary, his courage was his undoing. He wanted to end uncertainty, to speed things up. In this he succeeded. His policy helped to produce in 1939 the war which everyone else, including Hitler and Mussolini, expected in 1943. His aim was to avert war. He failed; and failure on this scale cannot be excused by a plea of good intentions. Chamberlain is now beyond defence or condemnation. He needs a biographer who will try to understand him. Probably none will be found. Neville Chamberlain is fated to go on being the man of no luck.

30. *Daddy, What Was Winston Churchill?*

New York Times Magazine. Written for the hundredth anniversary of Churchill's birth.

On 24 January 1965 there died Winston Spencer Churchill, Knight of the Garter and, if he had not refused the title, Duke of London. Six days later he was given a state funeral in St Paul's Cathedral, an honour previously reserved for two great men of war – Admiral Lord Nelson, victor at Trafalgar, and the Duke of Wellington, victor at Waterloo. What brought Churchill into this select company? The men of the time had no doubt as to the answer. He was the saviour of his country, the first Englishman to be so hailed since King Alfred the Great.

How does Churchill look now, nine years after his death and 100 years after his birth? The second world war, in which Churchill won his fame, has receded into history. Its memories are fading; the antagonisms that it inspired are almost forgotten. The British Empire that Churchill championed has vanished, and Great Britain is no longer numbered among the World Powers. Was Churchill's policy mistaken and his victory barren? Future historians may give a confident answer. One of the present generation cannot speak with detachment. He sees the consequences of the war but he also remembers the circumstances in which it was fought.

Success and achievement came to Churchill late in the day. If he had died in 1939 at the age of sixty-five, he would now be regarded as an eccentric character, sometimes a radical, sometimes a Tory, and running over with brilliant ideas that were more often wrong than right. In the years before the second world war he reached the height of his unpopularity. He had only two supporters in the House of Commons and was disregarded in the country. He was almost alone in advocating great armaments and steadfast resistance to Nazi Germany. Underneath the surface there was always a current of opinion on his side. It may well be that Hitler never wanted war against Great Britain and was willing to respect the British Empire. But the British people, despite their anxiety to avoid war, would not tolerate a German domination of Europe, even if it had been less barbarous than the Nazis made it. In September 1939 British public opinion forced a reluctant Government into war, and Churchill entered the war Cabinet as a symbol of the national resolve.

Seven months later, when the Germans invaded Norway, Churchill was already directing operations as minister of defence. It was on his orders that a weak, ill-armed expeditionary force was sent to Norway and that the British attempted a strategy beyond their strength. Nevertheless when the House of Commons revolted against the Chamberlain Government, it turned to Churchill. Though he had made mistakes, they were mistakes of action, not of caution. On 10 May 1940 Churchill became prime minister and thus attained supreme power. He held this position, virtually unchallenged, throughout the war.

June 1940 was the moment of decision for Churchill and for the future of the British Empire. When France was defeated and fell out of the war, it could be plausibly argued, and was argued by some, that Great Britain should accept the compromise peace which Hitler offered and watch with detachment while Germany and Russia tore each other to pieces.

We now know that this policy was advocated in the war Cabinet by Lord Halifax and, more cautiously by Neville Chamberlain. Churchill rejected it. He told his colleagues: 'Of course, whatever happens at Dunkirk, we shall fight on.' His first speech in the House of Commons as prime minister defined all that was to follow:

You ask, What is our aim? I can answer in one word: Victory – victory at all costs, victory in spite of all terror; victory, however long and hard the road may be.

This was a rash promise to make when Great Britain stood alone against a European Continent united under Hitler. But it was what the British people wanted to hear. They did not feel like a defeated people, particularly after the German Air Force had been thwarted in the Battle of Britain. Churchill was their guarantee that somehow total victory would be achieved, and this is what gave Churchill his hold over the British people. He and they had made a pact with death. They would win the war or perish in the attempt.

And something more. Unconditional surrender by Germany and her associates did not have to wait for President Roosevelt at Casablanca. It was already implicit in Churchill's speeches in 1940: 'All, all shall be restored.' This insistence on unconditional surrender has often been condemned. Yet what was the alternative? Presumably to deal with Hitler or some other German government. At whose expense were the British and later the Americans to buy peace for themselves? Was Poland to remain under Germany? Was Czechoslovakia? Perhaps Belgium would have made a suitable bribe? It has been suggested that an offer of generous terms would have led to the overthrow of Hitler. But even the leaders of the so-called resistance in Germany assumed that she would keep some of Hitler's conquests as a reward for getting rid of him. In any case, the German people, apart from a few generals and politicians, remained solidly behind Hitler until the very end of the war. Hitler aimed at total victory. Unconditional surrender was the only possible answer to him, and any idea of negotiated peace is too nonsensical to merit serious discussion.

Churchill was, therefore, never in search of a policy. The policy of defeating Hitler was imposed upon him by events. His sole problem was how to apply this policy, a hard nut to crack in the circumstances of 1940. At home his position was never endangered though he often thought it was. His critics were an impotent handful. Despite grumbles and discontents, Great Britain was never so free from political controversy as during the second world war. National unity was complete particularly after Hitler attacked Soviet Russia and so turned the British Communists into enthusiastic supporters of the war. This unity rested on a partnership between Churchill and the British people. His speeches, a mixture of old-fashioned rhetoric and homespun humour, struck the right note and made him uniquely popular. Even those most harassed by him always ended by asking: 'What should we do without him?' There have been many great British leaders. There has only been one whom everyone recognized as the embodiment of the national will.

Great Britain's task was to survive. As Stalin said later, accurately summing up the record of the war, 'Great Britain provided time; the United States provided money and Soviet Russia provided blood.' Churchill recognized this in his cooler moments and always worked to call in the New World to redress the balance of the Old. But he was not content to wait. As minister of defence he was a war lord, directing strategy, and he often talked as if Great Britain might overthrow Hitler all on her own. This was a fantasy, though it was what the British people wanted, and Churchill often attempted too much with limited resources. The strategical decisions that he took when Great Britain stood alone continued to shape the war even when the United States had joined in.

The first of these decisions was for the bombing of Germany. Churchill wrote in July 1940 : 'There is one thing that will bring Hitler down, and that is an absolutely devastating, exterminating attack by very heavy bombers from this country upon the Nazi homeland... Without this I do not see a way through.' This strategy was applied. German towns were laid waste. Over half a million Germans were killed. Yet all the time German war production went up and German morale also. Much of British and later American production was devoted to heavy bombers, and the strategic bombing offensive did more harm to Allied than to German economy. Yet, once started, it could not be stopped, a striking illustration of the rule that in wartime it is better to do the wrong thing than to do nothing. In the end Churchill grew ashamed of what he had initiated and turned against Sir Arthur Harris, the chief of Bomber Command. But he could not shake off the responsibility for indiscriminate bombing and all the decline in morality which that implied.

The second legacy which Churchill passed on to Anglo-American strategy was an obsession with the Mediterranean and the Middle East. Here again there was nothing else Great Britain could do in the circumstances of 1940. She had a fleet in the Mediterranean and an army in Egypt. She could win battles against the Italians, which gave the British people a sensation of victory. But it was a side issue. Hitler never had offensive plans in the Middle East, though perhaps he should have had. Italy was a burden to Hitler, not an asset, and later became a burden to the Allies. Vast demands were made on shipping and military resources for a campaign that never engaged more than a handful of German divisions. The back door into Europe about which Churchill had dreamed even in the first world war remained firmly closed against the Allies. Yet when America entered the war, the Mediterranean front alone was active. President Roosevelt wanted some immediate stroke to influence the Congressional elections –

though in fact it came too late to do so – and the American forces, therefore, followed where Churchill had led. This persistent commitment to the Mediterranean postponed any landing in Northern France for two years and so helped to prolong the war.

Churchill's third decision was negative and, therefore, less obvious, though perhaps even more fateful. With the British Army engaged in Egypt and the Royal Navy engaged in both the Mediterranean and the Atlantic, Great Britain had no forces to spare for the Far East. Churchill had to gamble that Japan would not go to war. This gamble rested on a fundamental misjudgement. Churchill always exaggerated the strength and the prestige of the British Empire. With his mind rooted in the past, he did not appreciate that its strength had crumbled and that the Japanese were not impressed by a prestige that existed only in name. Even when Churchill grew alarmed, he imagined that the Japanese would be overawed by what he called 'the vague menace' of two capital ships. The battleship Prince of Wales and the battle cruiser Repulse were sent to the Far East. The aircraft carrier allotted to their support scraped her keel in Jamaica and never joined them. Thus defenceless against air attack, the two great ships were sunk by Japanese torpedo-bombers on the third day of the Far Eastern war. So much for the vague menace. Moreover, the defences of Singapore were neglected by Churchill as much as by his predecessors. When Singapore fell, Great Britain's empire in the Far East fell with it and was never to be effectively restored.

Churchill's achievements in the eighteen months between the fall of France and Pearl Harbor were outstanding. His strategy was not always successful, and some of the mistakes, particularly at Singapore, were his personal responsibility. But he worked closely with the Chiefs of Staff and, despite many wranglings, never overruled them, as Hitler did with his generals and as President Roosevelt often did later with

General Marshall. Churchill was also the driving force, even if less directly, in home affairs. All the great decisions stemmed from him, and some of the lesser ones also. At the height of the war, for instance, he concerned himself with the question of whether the transport of cut flowers from Cornwall to London should be permitted.

Churchill went through the charade of consulting the war Cabinet. He recognized one member of it as a formidable figure: Ernest Bevin, trade union leader and minister of labour. Thanks to Bevin, the industrial workers remained loyal, cooperative and productive, and Churchill was the first to acknowledge Bevin's achievement. All the other Ministers were Churchill's agents and subordinates however politely this was disguised. When criticisms were voiced in the House of Commons, it was always Churchill who answered them and secured a parliamentary majority.

From the first Churchill was also his own foreign minister with Anthony Eden as his loyal associate. It was Churchill who conducted the harrowing negotiations with the French Government when the German armies were overrunning France, and thereafter it was Churchill who handled General de Gaulle. Though Churchill often complained that his cross was the Cross of Lorraine (de Gaulle's symbol) he never doubted that de Gaulle would be the saviour of France at some time in the future, and it was solely thanks to Churchill that de Gaulle subsequently attained greatness.

Churchill's hopes for victory were based on the prospect of American aid – at first economic and ultimately military. When the American fleet was attacked at Pearl Harbor, he exclaimed: 'So we have won after all.' He even felt that his work was done and is said to have contemplated retirement. He soon thought better of this. He had now a new task: to cement what he called The Grand Alliance and to assert Great Britain's claim to a place in it. Anglo-American partnership was closer than any alliance in modern history. There was a combined Chiefs of Staffs' committee, directing a common strategy, and Supreme Commanders over Anglo-American forces. Without any formal agreement, this alliance rested on the personal intimacy between Churchill and President Roosevelt.

Yet it is hard not to feel that Churchill misunderstood the spirit of American policy. Certainly Roosevelt was whole-heartedly engaged in the war. He was not equally engaged in preserving the British Empire or even in preserving Great Britain as a great power. Lend-Lease enabled Great Britain to keep going, but the Americans drove a hard bargain. The American financial authorities stripped Great Britain of her gold reserves and her overseas investments before they would institute Lend-Lease. As a condition of Lend-Lease, British exports were restricted, American officials supervised and checked all British foreign trade and American exporters moved ruthlessly into overseas markets that had hitherto been British. Moreover, a postwar abolition of imperial pre-ference and controlled exchanges was dictated to the British. As an independent financial centre, London ceased to exist. There was here a sharp contrast with Canada, whose mutual aid was given without strings or conditions. Keynes said truly : 'We threw good housekeeping to the winds. But we saved ourselves and helped to save the world.' Great Britain was just as essential to the United States as the United States to Great Britain. Churchill accepted without demur the stern terms of Lend-Lease. He gave to the Americans all the British scientific secrets and asked for nothing in return.

Churchill received from President Roosevelt a formal promise that Great Britain, having revealed how to make a controlled nuclear explosion, should share equally in all further nuclear discoveries. The promise was subsequently evaded by President Roosevelt and was altogether repudiated by President Truman. Churchill counted on 'the special relationship' and put his trust in American generosity. The trust was misplaced.

Churchill's relations with Soviet Russia were inevitably more remote and took longer to ripen into intimacy. When Hitler invaded Russia, her defeat was expected within a few months. The German generals told Hitler the defeat of Russia would be easier than that of France. Sir Stafford Cripps, the British Ambassador, gave the Russians a month. Sir John Dill, Chief of the Imperial General Staff, said six weeks. American intelligence told the President: We can count on a minimum of one month and a maximum of three. Even Stalin believed on the outbreak of war that Russia was facing disaster and exclaimed: 'Everything that Lenin worked for has been destroyed forever.' Naturally Churchill hailed Soviet Russia as an ally, but it did not occur to him that any great decision of principle was involved. Russia was fighting Germany and so giving the British a breathing space. Her victory seemed so remote as not to be a matter of speculation. The British and Americans sent Russia what aid they could, but geographic obstacles prevented them from sending much. The situation changed when the Russians halted the German armies outside Moscow in December 1941, and still more when they defeated the Germans at Stalingrad in the autumn and winter of 1942. It gradually became clear that Russia was not merely going to survive. She was going to win. Once Germany was defeated, Soviet Russia would emerge as the only Great Power on the Continent of Europe.

In theory the British and Americans were faced with a vital question: Should they allow Soviet Russia to step into this great position? In practice, the question was never considered, least of all by Churchill. Great Britain and the United States were at war with Germany and welcomed any power that aided them. As Churchill said: 'If Hitler invaded Hell I should make at least a friendly reference to the Devil in the

House of Commons.' Roosevelt in his usual way evaded the problem by postponing any discussion of the postwar world until the war was over. Or maybe he assumed, too easily, that American power would then be overwhelming. Churchill was more direct. He tried to establish relations of personal intimacy with Stalin, the Soviet dictator. He tried to secure some limitations on Russian power while the war was on. In the first task he largely succeeded, certainly more than any other man could have done; with Churchill, Stalin became a human being. The second task was one impossible to accomplish. In concrete terms, how could Poland, Russia's essential concern, be both friendly to Russia and a democratic country? The answer was that it could not be done, and the Polish Government was as great an obstacle to this as the Russian.

As the war proceeded, the magnitude of Soviet Russia's coming victory became ever clearer and with it Churchill's anxiety to limit it. In October 1944 he seemed to have succeeded. He went to Moscow and proposed to Stalin a division of Europe into spheres of interest. This proposal later came in for much condemnation and was regretted by Churchill himself. Yet in fact it provided the answer. Certainly it handed over Eastern Europe to the Russians. But equally it handed over Western Europe to the British and Americans.

Soviet forces have remained in Eastern Europe to the present day. Similarly, British and American forces have remained in Western Europe. Each party has justified or excused itself by pleading an invitation from the Government concerned. The Russians were constantly asked to compromise. The Anglo-Americans would have been awkwardly placed if the Russians had responded and offered to abandon, say, the secret police and the labour camps on condition the Anglo-Saxon powers abandoned private property in land and the means of production.

As it was, the British were able to suppress the resistance forces in Greece by armed force, the only such action by any

Allied power in the course of the war. In Italy, Togliatti, the Communist leader, returned from Moscow with orders to cooperate with the Allied authorities. And the Italian resistance, composed of 150,000 fighters, surrendered their arms uncomplainingly. Thorez, the French Communist leader, accepted de Gaulle's authority and helped to preserve the French state. Even in Eastern Europe, Communist Governments were a consequence of the cold war, not its cause. In the Far East, Stalin aided the recovery of China by Chiang Kai-shek, and the subsequent victory of Mao Tse-tung was highly unwelcome to him.

With the war drawing to a close Churchill became increasingly anxious. As is well known, he urged Eisenhower to abandon his strategy of a broad advance and to march on Berlin ahead of the Russians. Eisenhower rejected this prompting and has sometimes been criticized for doing so. But what was the purpose in the Americans incurring 300,000 casualties for the sake of Berlin when the Russians were eager to do so? Churchill's immediate apprehensions were exaggerated and misplaced. The Russians had no intention of penetrating further into Germany. Their momentum was exhausted; their losses in men and material were beyond all counting. At the moment of unconditional surrender by the Germans, it was Anglo-American forces, not Russian, that were often a hundred miles beyond the agreed zonal boundaries. On the other hand it was a fantasy to suppose that the Anglo-Saxon powers could suddenly switch sides and oppose the Russians with the aid of the defeated German armies.

The end of the war brought an anticlimax in Churchill's career. Though the British people supported him wholeheartedly as the wartime leader, they had bitter memories of Tory rule during the nineteen thirties and now put their faith in the Labour party. Churchill was cast down, but not for long. His speech at Fulton, Mo., in 1946 proclaimed the coming of the cold war. Yet a few years later, with his physical powers failing, he clung to office as prime minister in the belief that he was the only man who could win over Stalin's successors to a policy of peace and reconciliation. It must be said that Churchill's mind was not constructive. Despite his radical outbursts, he was essentially conservative. He wanted to preserve Great Britain and the British Empire as he remembered them from his romantic youth. He understood nothing of the social and political forces that were changing the world. Fundamentally, his outlook was sombre. He did not share the contemporary belief in universal betterment nor did he await the coming of some secular Heaven on Earth.

Late in life, Churchill pronounced a gloomy verdict on his career. He remarked that the final verdict of history would take account not only of the victories achieved under his direction, but also of the political results which flowed from them, and he added : 'Judged by this standard, I am not sure that I shall be held to have done very well.' Churchill did himself an injustice. The results were not his doing; the victories were. The results were foreshadowed when the British people resolved on war with Hitler. From this moment it followed inexorably that, unless Hitler won, Soviet Russia would establish her domination over Eastern Europe and become a world power.

Was the price worth paying? The men of the time had no doubt that it was. When we consider the barbarities of Nazi rule – the tyranny, the gas chambers, the mass exterminations – we must agree that Hitlerism had to be destroyed whatever the cost. No one can contemplate the present state of things without acknowledging that people everywhere are happier, freer and more prosperous than they would have been if Nazi Germany and Japan had won, and this applies even to the countries under Communist control. Future generations may dismiss the second world war as 'just another war'. Those who experienced it know that it was a war justified in its aims and successful in accomplishing them.

Churchill defined his policy once and for all when he said: 'Victory at all costs.' The British people agreed with him. How right they were.

31. Manchester

Encounter. A contribution to a series on The World's Cities. I wrote this description of Manchester just on twenty years ago. Since then much has changed. The city is now clean and the people have brightened up also. The Midland Hotel has emerged a glossy red. Victoria Park has lost its toll gates and most of its wealthy inhabitants. The Royal Cotton Exchange has closed. A repertory company now treads the boards once crowded with cotton merchants. The John Rylands Library has been absorbed by the University. The Manchester Guardian has moved to London and dropped Manchester from its title. Though it still has a Manchester office, this is no longer housed in the historic building where C P Scott, W P Crozier and A P Wadsworth edited the paper. Manchester has become an agreeable provincial town. It is no longer one of the world's great cities.

When I recall the great cities of Europe, I see myself first of all clambering in and out of a motor coach on a conducted tour. Some of them later became places to live in, to belong to, but they began as sights. Not so Manchester. There are no conducted tours, no waiting coaches in Albert Square or touting guides in Piccadilly. Yet Manchester is as distinctive in its way as Athens or Peking. It is the symbol of a civilization which was, until recently, an ambition of mankind, though now little more than an historical curiosity. Manchester is the only English city that can look London in the face, not merely as a regional capital, but as a rival version of how men should live in a community. I do not know how Piccadilly, Manchester, got its name. Maybe it was a gesture of piety, but I prefer to think of it as an act of defiance or even contempt, a joke at the expense of Piccadilly Circus. There is no satisfactory English word for what Manchester represents. If 'Burgher' were genuinely acclimatized, instead of being restricted to Carlisle and Calais, that would do. Manchester is the last and greatest of the Hanseatic towns – a civilization created by traders without assistance from monarchs or territorial aristocracy.

Manchester is, however, older and – in some ways – nicer than *das Manchestertum*. It was not represented in the unreformed Parliament and was incorporated only in 1838. Hence we think of it casually as a new town, a mushroom growth of the industrial revolution. This is not so. It was an historical accident that Manchester remained a private manor instead of becoming a borough. Even in the Middle Ages it was a bigger town than many places which had two representatives in Parliament, and by the eighteenth century it was already the commercial centre of Lancashire. Indeed Manchester is older still. It had a Roman foundation, though not worth lingering on. The fragment of wall in a goods yard at the bottom of Deansgate ranks as the least interesting Roman remain in England, which is setting a high standard. The market town of pre-industrial times, however, survived almost intact until Hitler's war. The collegiate church, Cheetham's hospital, the old grammar school and the market place stood unchanged, as they had been before the steam engine was thought of. You could still recapture the Manchester of de Quincey or imagine the scene at the market cross when Prince Charlie passed through on the road to Derby. Still, this too is antiquarianism. It would be perverse to visit Manchester solely to discover what it was like before the Burghers took over.

The most revealing spot in Manchester is not the historic centre or even the Royal Exchange, but Victoria Park. This is still a private estate, with toll gates and keepers in uniform. Gothic palaces jostle each other; gardeners dust the soot from the leaves of the trees; and the ghosts of merchant princes walk in the twilight. These were the men who gave Manchester its historical character. We think of them in retrospect as Radicals, and so they were in lack of respect for traditional authority or in their ruthless destruction of whatever stood in their way. But they were far from a belief in economic equality or even in democracy, if we mean by that putting the needs of the majority first. They had succeeded by their own energy, and they supposed that the duty of society was discharged if it gave others the chance to do the same. It did not worry them that, while the rich man was in his mansion, the poor man at the gates of Victoria Park lived in a slum. The road to success lay open for those who wished to take it. Like the men of the Renaissance they exalted the individual. They lacked one Renaissance characteristic. Of all dominant classes, they were the least equipped with aesthetic taste. Perhaps Money is less beautiful than Intrigue or Wickedness – the Renaissance routes to power – or perhaps it is so beautiful in itself as to destroy the need for beauty elsewhere. At any rate, the result is the same: Manchester is irredeemably ugly. There is no spot to which you could lead a blindfold stranger and say happily: 'Now open your eyes.' Norman Douglas had a theory that English people walked with their eyes on the ground so as to avoid the excrement of dogs on the pavement. The explanation in Manchester is simpler: they avert their eyes from the ugliness of their surroundings.

The great days of Manchester certainly came at a bad time from an architectural point of view, but Manchester comes off badly even by its own standards. It has nothing to compare with St Pancras Station or Keble College. The town hall and the older part of the university are in a rigid Gothic which looks as though it had been bought by the square yard. The remarkable feature of the Midland Hotel is the colour of its brick, not its design. More recent buildings keep the same quality of grandiose tastelessness. It would of course be useless for the Central Library to challenge the pre-eminence of the new Bodleian as the most hideous library in existence, but it would win an honourable mention. Apart from being out of tune with its surroundings, it is remarkable for presenting an exact model of an iced wedding-cake on a gigantic scale. One expects members of the library committee to emerge on high at any moment and cut it into slices. There is also a striking civic building which now fills the gap between the library and the town hall. This tones down their irreconcilable contrast by being itself in a style alleged to be Dutch domestic of the seventeenth century.

The ugliness is not only on the outside of the buildings. Some of the great mansions are comfortable within, though not many; none is pleasing. This character too has been maintained to the present. The professors of the University are accommodated in bare cells with prison furniture, while their common-room attains the impersonal comfort of a modern waiting-room at a Continental station. The Midland Hotel once had a Palm Court of unique Oriental style – I remember a Frenchwoman who used to escape from Manchester merely by sitting there. Now it has vanished, and the Midland has an ordinary cosmopolitan interior like the new House of Commons. The City Art Gallery has a lot of expensive pictures but few good ones: even the pre-Raphaelites seem to have lost colour. The people, too, are remarkably unattractive in appearance. When I was a lecturer at Manchester, I used to peer along the serried rows of note-takers in the hope of finding a pretty girl. The only one I ever spotted turned out to be an Italian visitor. No doubt Puritanism makes the women dress so badly. The stunted growth of men and women alike is said to be due either to their Danish ancestors who settled in the Mersey valley or to the long hours spent by more recent forebears in the cotton factories. I doubt both explanations. Men adapt themselves to their surroundings, as Americans for instance develop crinkly hair and thick lips, and the people of Manchester are anxious to show that they are devoted to the Business of life, not its Art. Manchester is also very dirty – the soot continuously dropping from home fires which are more thickly concentrated than anywhere else in the world. The climate rounds off the gloom – not remarkably rainy as is often alleged, but persistently moist which is even more depressing. There are times when it seems merely wrongheaded to call Manchester the centre of a civilization.

But it is. Manchester has everything except good looks or had until recently. Though the Burghers have gone, their independent spirit remains. Manchester is the only place in England which escapes our characteristic vice of snobbery. Manchester cares no more for the Royal Family and the landed gentry than Venice did for the Pope and the Italian aristocracy. When patrons are wanted for a charity or a club, they are found among the few remaining rich, and these are without titles. The only exception is the Earl of Derby, who has a special position as the decorative leader of Lancashire. There are few royal statues in Manchester – only the Prince Consort in Albert Square and Queen Victoria in Piccadilly. The others are local dignitaries or Liberal statesmen. Many of the Burghers were German in origin and, having shaken off subservience to their own authorities, felt no awe of any other. They sent their sons to Rugby, not to Eton; and this produced highmindedness, not snobbery. Achievement is what matters in Manchester, not a historic name or a cultivated accent. It is an added advantage, of course, that Manchester is in Lancashire and can have its own way of speaking without anyone worrying about it. Manchester is not the best type of Lancashire accent – you have to go to Bury or

Rochdale for that, but it is a great improvement on the flat talk of Liverpool.

Manchester could not have been so independent without a region behind it, though I suspect that Manchester has shaped Lancashire much more than the other way round. Of course Lancashire is quite a place – with the best country in the world to my mind, and the nicest people. Cultivated Englishmen who never go further than Stratford-on-Avon or perhaps Lichfield regard all 'the North' as one in character and scenery – hard, bleak, rugged. Yorkshiremen are hard all right – living in stone houses and sharpened by the east wind. But the Pennines are a truer frontier than the Trent or the Mersey, and Lancashire people are the very opposite from those in Yorkshire. This is the land of the south-west wind, bringing an atmosphere that is always blurred and usually gentle. The men are independent without being aggressive: tolerant, affectionate, sentimental – almost mawkish. Balzac describes Lancashire as 'the county where women die of love'. I think this very unlikely. I have always assumed, though with little firsthand experience, that Lancashire women are as brisk and businesslike in love-making as in everything else. The men provide the romantic atmosphere. It delights them to imagine that the women die of love. In reality a Lancashire woman would merely reply : 'Come on, lad. Let's get it over !'

The men of Lancashire are great tale-tellers. The last great writer in the vernacular, T Thompson (a bookbinder from Bury), combined the sentimental and the humorous into works of high art, but I've heard many a story almost as good in a public-house corner. Northern people in every country like to think of themselves as more honest and straightforward than those further south. They may be honest in Lancashire; they are certainly not straightforward. They are one and all 'romancers'. I don't think that my father ever gave my mother a strictly accurate account of his doings in all their many years of married life, even if he had only been out of the house for half an hour. A fictitious narrative was more interesting to him and, he hoped, to her. But also he was like a man with a lisp: things were bound to come out reshaped however truthful he meant to be. In much the same way the inhabitants romanticize Manchester and themselves. Their softheartedness runs over in the most unlikely places. Harry Pollitt, former Communist leader, revealed his Manchester origin when, kidnapped by Fascists, he spent the weekend playing solo whist with his captors. Left to themselves, the people of Lancashire would have gone on believing in witches and clinging to a hazy Jacobitism as they did in the eighteenth century. It was the 'foreigners' of Manchester – Germans, Greeks, Armenians and Jews – who prodded them into zestful life; also romantic in their way, but without the easygoing Lancashire spirit.

Manchester is truly a frontier-town, as Professor Toynbee thinks every successful capital should be. It is squeezed into the south-eastern corner of Lancashire right up against the Pennines. The frontier with Yorkshire, which I have mentioned already, is the sharpest. As a boy, I always felt that the dark tunnel at Victoria Station which took me to school at York was the beginning of an alien world, and I am still surprised not to see Customs officials on the platform as they are at Salzburg. But Manchester also straddles between Lancashire and Cheshire. The Mersey is no true dividing line. South Manchester is an extension of the Cheshire Plain. The real break comes exactly down the middle of St Ann's Square. There can be no doubt as you move north from there that you are in real Lancashire country. The division is economic as well as geographical. There are no mills in Cheshire though there used to be – except some that remain in Stockport which is a sort of Lancastrian colony. For that matter, commerce has carried the day in Manchester itself. The mills have all been pushed further north. There are engineering works and industries of every variety, but no mills. All the same, cotton still dominates the city as it did when Manchester was first called Cottonopolis. The Royal Exchange occupies the most central position in the city – a position which its appearance does nothing to deserve. The most characteristic sight in Manchester until just the other day was the great horse-drawn dray, slowly carrying bales of cotton to the warehouses. Like all traders, the merchants of Manchester have time to spare or at any rate to chaffer, and they sit for hours at a time in underground cafés playing dominoes. A thorough grounding in advanced dominoes was, I think, the only useful instruction I received from my father.

Cotton is a nice industry to spring from and to live among. The making and selling of cotton is one of the few human activities which is wholly beneficent. It never did anyone harm and it has done mankind much good. Every piece of cotton cloth is going to make someone warmer or cleaner or more comfortable. You don't have to conquer people in order to turn them into your customers, and you suffer no imperialist craving to control your own raw materials. The cotton trade conspires with the climate to make the inhabitants of Manchester a kindly people, inclined perhaps to rather simple solutions, but gentle and sensible. It is no doubt foolish to believe that cotton cloth contains the secret of human happiness, but it is at any rate less foolish than to believe it of motor-cars or machine-guns. Even the local vice of gambling in cotton futures seems somehow a less speculative proposition than running after stocks and shares, though many members of Lancashire families have discovered that this is a mistaken view. Cotton itself has turned out a chancy affair ever since the first world war, and Manchester has lost something of its special character as cotton lost its pre-eminence. But enough remains, much as we still regard Oxford as an academic town though comparatively few of its inhabitants now make a living from learned pursuits.

Manchester grew great as a centre of business and its other distinctions have come, as it were, by accident. It would be silly to pretend anything else. If you think that buying and selling is a wicked affair in the way many people do when they are comfortably off – as Marx did once Engels was rich enough to provide for him – then Manchester will not win forgiveness by its other activities. Once admit that a civilization can be founded on commerce, and everything takes on an acceptable pattern. Manchester society wanted solid worth. The houses were well built, the women plump, the food substantial. There has never been much in the nature of public show in Manchester – no idiocy of a Lord Mayor's banquet, for instance. Private hospitality on the other hand was lavish. The great houses gave dinner-parties to twenty or thirty guests as a normal routine. I used to go to one such house where, only twenty years ago, each male guest received on arrival a card with the name of the lady whom he was to take into dinner; we went in formal procession arm-in-arm. On the other hand that detestable rigmarole of the men sitting over the port was no more than a utilitarian survival; it broke up as the flush of the lavatory died away. There was no nostalgia, as there is in gentry-circles, for the common rooms of Oxford. The women counted for as much as the men – particularly of course the woman who had a fortune of her own.

A society based on money has the great merit of freedom from class. The only difference between the very rich in Manchester and the moderately well-off, or between the moderately well-off and the skilled artisan, was in the amount they spent. All lived on the same pattern, though not on the same scale. The professors of the University and the leading figures on The Manchester Guardian also gave grand dinner-parties to a rather smaller company. Samuel Alexander had eight or ten to dinner every week almost until his death – among the most agreeable evenings I ever spent. The thought of Samuel Alexander makes me feel that I have been unfair to Manchester civilization – stressed too much its devotion to money and business. Alexander, too, was a representative figure – also a foreigner (in his case an Australian Jew) who could never have penetrated ordinary English society, but became fully at home in Manchester. How much at home could be seen at the Hallé Concerts on a Thursday evening, when he sat among the very rich in the front row and read The Manchester Guardian, with much rustling of leaves during the pieces that did not interest him. These were frequent.

The Hallé Concerts were the highest expression of Manchester civilization. Most of the audience were regular subscribers who occupied the same seats year after year. When they changed, it was to move up in the price-list – not in the social scale – until they arrived with the Burghers in the front rows. But the whole audience was a single community, with personal acquaintanceship running from the front rows to the standing room at the back. The orchestra belonged to this community also. Its members greeted their friends in the Hall, and the conductor himself gave a little bow of recognition to the more distinguished citizens. For after all, this was the one genuinely permanent orchestra in England, with the only permanent conductor. In the Free Trade Hall on a Thursday evening, I had no reason to regret my season ticket to the Vienna Philharmonic. Under Richter, the orchestra, I suspect, had been heavily Germanic, and there was still too much Brahms for my taste. But Harty gave us also the new and the unusual to an extent greater than we get now from the Third Programme of the BBC. In other ways the Hallé Concerts were agreeably old-fashioned. The society was technically 'owned' by the £100 guarantors until, in the thirties, economic need forced a democratic revolution and admitted an inferior class – with inferior rights – of those who could only guarantee £10. The programmes gave the precise duration of each piece in the margin, and one waited eagerly to see whether the conductor would break his previous record. Patrons were also informed when carriages should be ordered, while the announcement of a Special Concert Train from Central Station consoled the less opulent.

The Free Trade Hall itself had a special claim to fame, though not from its architecture. It stood on St Peter's Fields, where the battle of Peterloo began the break-up of the old order in England. Its name announced the greatest victory against that order. Other great halls in England are called after a royal patron or some figure of traditional religion. Only the Free Trade Hall is dedicated, like the United States of America, to a proposition – one as noble and beneficent as any ever made. Richard Cobden formulated it in the words: 'As little intercourse as possible between Governments; as much intercourse as possible between the peoples of the world.' It was difficult to sit in the Free Trade Hall, and still more difficult to speak from its platform (as I once did), without recalling its political significance. The men of Manchester had brought down the nobility and gentry of England in a bloodless, but decisive, Crécy. The Free Trade Hall was the symbol of their triumph.

Manchester looked at southern England in Cobden's spirit. It cared little for what was going on 'down there'. London was not expected to provide either ideas or material direction. Manchester had its own daily newspaper of international reputation and, for that matter, its own Sunday journals of somewhat different character. It had too in The Clarion the best Socialist paper ever produced in this country. It had its own banks and, as well, a branch of the Bank of England. It had its own University – not a 'civic' or 'provincial' Redbrick, but a rival version to Oxford and Cambridge or what a national University should be. Its founder revolted against the monopoly of the Church of England. The only conditions he insisted on were that there should be no chapel and no denominational tests, even for the professors of theology. His trustees added the condition of no discrimination between the sexes. The University followed the models in Scotland and Germany, not of the Anglican institutions further south. The example had its drawbacks. The professors reigned over a crowd of helot-lecturers. But I never knew anyone at Manchester who owed his place to good manners, high-born connections, education at an expensive public school, or the right accent, and anyone who has ever heard Great Tom sound his hundred-and-one strokes will admit that this was quite an achievement. Fifty years ago or so, when Rutherford, Tout, Alexander, and George Unwin were in their prime, Manchester University had no rival in intellectual distinction.

With all these advantages, Manchester had good reason to be self-sufficient, though not self-satisfied. Nor was it parochial except in the sense that its parish was the world. The great men of Manchester had family connections with Germany and the Near East. They shipped cotton cloth to India and China and often spent some years there as representatives of their firms. They owned mills in Russia, Austria and South America. The Ship Canal completed the picture when it made Manchester a world port. Only one part of the world was unknown to them : England south of the Trent. Why should they ever want to go there? They had a wonderful sea coast on their doorstep – Blackpool for the masses, Southport always more genteel. The Lake District was only eighty miles away; North Wales even nearer. They could slip off for an afternoon to Old Trafford or spend an agreeable summer's day in the Peak District. Every Sunday in the thirties saw a mass exodus from London Road Station to Kinder Scout, but the struggle which won a right-of-way over Jacob's Ladder was fought as long ago as 1894. For Manchester men England ended at Buxton or at Matlock. My grandfather, I think, never went further south in his life except once on his way to France. My father had been in Egypt and India; he knew Russia and most countries in Western Europe. He spent exactly three days in London and hated them. This was not plain dislike of a city, for he worked in one. He felt that London was the enemy; it represented everything he disapproved of and which he supposed, perhaps wrongly, that Manchester had defeated.

Was my father right, or has Manchester now been defeated in its turn? What remains of the Burghers and their civilization? I went back recently after an absence of nearly twenty years and looked with full consciousness at the things I had previously taken for granted. To start with looks. Manchester is quite as ugly as people say. In fact it has got uglier. I don't much mind the nineteenth-century squalor, though it is only fit for a museum, but the recent buildings are worse. Parts of Manchester are now as bad as Queen Street, Oxford, which has few rivals in England. What is more depressing, this is not Manchester ugliness; it is the architecture of Mr Everyman, and I begin to regret the ugliness that was peculiar to Manchester. Character is fading in other ways. My former impression of Manchester was of double-decker trams in blocks half a mile long, stationary like patient elephants. Now they are gone, and the buses make Manchester look like anywhere else. Their disappearance has one advantage. All the streets have the opulent width of a capital city.

I could produce much more in the way of nostalgia. The professional entertainer is disappearing from the public houses. There are 'concerts' on licensed premises now only once a week, and even these are few and far between. The oyster bars are being smartened up in the modern way. Jolly red-faced women no longer consume stout and oysters with uproarious laughter. Instead there is an air of elegant fatigue, and prices have gone up correspondingly. One house of the old style survives in the Shambles, where the rich food is slapped down on bare boards and no one worries about his appearance. The decline of the tripe shop is sadder still. You have to search hard now for a plate of tripe and onions in a back room, where you used to find it on every corner. Lancashire cheese, almost the county's finest possession, is now made in factories and has lost much of its flavour. Manchester never got the best of it, but I doubt whether perfect cheese can be found even in the Fylde. Yet there must still be rich eating in Manchester. The food shops in the remaining fragment of the Market Place display a richness and variety unknown in southern England. The University remains the dishonourable exception that it always was. The food in its refectory would close a factory the same afternoon if it were served in a workers' canteen.

In other ways the University is changing its character. It is much richer than it was. New buildings are going up all the time; the staff is larger and better paid. But it has given up the struggle against Oxford and Cambridge which its founder enjoined on it. Instead it seeks to imitate them and, as an imitation, naturally slips into the second rank. The strongest feature of Manchester University originally was its close link with the local community. Most of its students used to live at home. Now it is perversely aspiring towards halls of residence, which will echo our ancient and deplorable colleges. Our enlightened educational policy also works, unexpectedly, to the detriment of the newer universities. Before the war, poverty kept many first-class students from Oxford and Cambridge, even when they won scholarships. Now the means test operates only against the professional classes who would not send their children to Manchester in any case, and the intellectual level is going down. No one, I think, could claim

for Manchester University the pre-eminence that it enjoyed
fifty years ago.

Shortage of money has hit the John Rylands Library, which
is probably the greatest private library in England. It is still
an incomparable place to work in, with no other readers to
disturb your peace. The absence of readers, by the way, is
fortunate, for the architect, in the usual perverse way of his
profession, forgot to provide for them. They have to be
accommodated in nooks and crannies, some, one suspects,
reserved for readers long dead. What the library now lacks is
money to buy books, and no new benefactor is likely to
present himself. Already there is a touch of the Sleeping
Beauty as you mount the Gothic staircase. Some venture-
some visitor of the future will find librarian, staff, books
and a single reader plunged in sleep for a hundred years.
By then the building may be all that is left of historic Manchester.

The streets outside have a bustle and prosperity, astonish-
ing to one who remembers the depression twenty years ago.
But it is the sort of bustle and prosperity that might be anywhere. The local speech is dying; it will have gone within a
generation. 'Regionalism' means only that some radio and
television programmes and the northern editions of some
papers are produced in Manchester as a matter of convenience.
They are no different from what is produced elsewhere. The
Manchester Guardian itself has ceased to represent Manchester except in name. Everyone says rightly that it has
never been better. It is the only newspaper produced outside
London to be included in every national survey along with
such lesser organs as The Daily Express and The Times. But
it is now a national paper pure and simple. Fifty years ago,
the City Council was reported in more detail than the House
of Commons; Montague and Monkhouse wrote at great
length on the local theatre; Langford at even greater on the
Hallé Concerts. James Bone sat alone in the London office and

wrote the London Letter unaided. Now all is changed. The London office provides most of the paper. It has a political correspondent, a parliamentary correspondent, a scientific correspondent, a diplomatic correspondent and a London editor with a large staff of reporters. Only the leaders are written in Manchester, and even this is being sapped – at least two leader-writers are now stationed in London. A P Wadsworth often edited the paper from the London office – a thing which never happened in C P Scott's time. When Scott visited London to expostulate with Sir Edward Grey or Lloyd George, it was as the leader of Manchester liberalism, not as the editor of a national paper. Now the editor plays little part in local politics.

The Manchester Guardian now speaks for the enlightened everywhere, not for Manchester. When it went against public opinion during the Boer war, it lost circulation generally. During the recent crisis over Suez, it lost readers in Manchester and gained about twice as many from other parts of the country. I look forward to the announcement: 'Practically nobody in Manchester reads The Guardian.' The moment of divorce is fast approaching: sooner or later (and I would guess sooner) The Manchester Guardian will be printed in London. British Railways can carry no more of the London edition, and the paper, which has trebled its circulation in recent years, is missing thousands of readers only because it cannot reach them in time. When this great change comes, the citizens of Manchester will lose their last advantage, one which they have done little to deserve: they will no longer be the only ones to read a Guardian at breakfast with real news – new news – on the front page. They ceased to be able to read local news long ago.

The readers of the Manchester Guardian have no particular wish to be told what is going on in Manchester. What is more, very little is going on to tell them about. The local theatre began to decline when Miss Horniman withdrew her support during the first world war. Now it is dead except for an occasional piece being tried out before its London run – and even then Manchester is lucky if it can get in ahead of Blackpool. Nobody makes great political speeches at the Free Trade Hall. Only the Hallé Concerts remain in their glory – still the best series in England, still the only genuinely permanent orchestra with its own conductor. The audience is now so large that the concerts have to be given two nights running, though only every fortnight instead of once a week. In these audiences Manchester is still alive. The circle of civilization has indeed widened. The Hallé Orchestra also gives concerts at Belle Vue on a Sunday afternoon among the popular entertainments and the animals.

There is one reservation. The members of the audience no longer think about the Special Concert Train from Central Station, but most of them are going to be carried far from Manchester by bus or car. Like the Russian soldiers in 1917, they have voted with their feet. They have voted against Manchester and run away. This withdrawal has been going on a long time. I once heard the late Sir John Clapham describe how as a boy he lived in the centre of Manchester; when the family went away for a week or so, the domestic servant was locked in the house with a supply of provisions. By the beginning of this century the wealthy had all moved to Withington and Fallowfield; soon after they reached Didsbury and Whalley Range. Now they have evacuated into Cheshire. And not only the wealthy. The City Council has cleared the slum areas of Hulme and Ancoats, and has resettled the inhabitants in Wythenshawe, ten miles off. This is part of Manchester only in name. The writing of doom became clearer still just the other day. The great store of Finnegans, which has been in Deansgate for more than a century, allowed its lease to run out and moved itself bodily to Wilmslow far off in Cheshire. If this goes on, central Manchester will soon offer offices, warehouses and vast stretches

of desolation. You can already stand in the districts cleared
of slums and feel as solitary as in the Sahara; only the rows of
street-lamps remind you that human beings once lived here.
The destruction of German bombing has not been rebuilt.
What was once the Market Place is now a vast car-park,
crammed during the day, deserted at night, with dirty paper
ankle-deep. The effect is like a mouth from which most of the
teeth have been extracted. The Cathedral stands in refur-
bished isolation. It certainly has been restored – in such a
polished manner that, whereas previously the Rylands Library looked like the Cathedral, now the Cathedral looks like
the Rylands Library.

Manchester might keep alive without its centre. The decline of Didsbury and the other suburbs is a graver matter.
The merchant princes have departed. They are playing at
country life in Cheshire or trying to forget Manchester in
Bournemouth and Torquay. There are no more dinner-parties,
no more bustle of social occasions. Some of the great houses
have become private hotels; some are the headquarters of insurance companies or trade unions – an ironical turn of the
wheel. A few have been broken up into flats. For this they are
highly unsuitable. The grand rooms are too big, and the
fortunate flat-dwellers are those who find accommodation in
the attics. Some of these mansions may have found another
use. When I asked my friends what has happened to the
Burgher palaces, I always received the same answer:
'Brothels'. I cannot vouch for this from experience, and suspect another touch of Lancashire romanticism. Manchester
men have always liked to think that their city was great in
vice as in everything else. My father told me that no decent
woman could be in Oxford Street after five o'clock in the
afternoon, indeed that no one could walk down it, so thick
were the whores on the pavement. Oxford Street was never
like that in my day. Now I doubt whether the former palaces
of the Burghers are as disreputable as they are made out to be.

If indeed these mansions deserve their present fame, then Manchester must be the scene of orgies such as the world has not known since the reign of Heliogabalus.

Index

Index

Index